PREACHING the creative GOSPEL CREATIVELY

Francis C. Rossow

Publishing House
St. Louis

Copyright © 1983 Concordia Publishing House
3558 S. Jefferson Avenue, St. Louis, MO 63118
Manufactured in the United States of America

Library of Congress Cataloging in Publication Data
Rossow, Francis C., 1925-
    Preaching the creative Gospel creatively.
    1. Preaching. I. Title.
BV4211.2.R68   1983   251'.01   83-7554
ISBN 0-570-03917-7 (pbk.)

---

1 2 3 4 5 6 7 8 9 10 MAL 92 91 90 89 88 87 86 85 84 83

Contents

Introduction

Introduction

Putting Creativity into Perspective

This book offers four suggestions for added creativity in preaching: (1) a fuller understanding of what literally happened to Jesus on the cross; (2) a greater awareness and use of Biblical metaphors and images of the Gospel; (3) the occasional use of what I call "Gospel-handles"; (4) the periodic use of new approaches and formats in the writing of sermons.

Getting the Most out of This Book

You will derive the most benefit from these suggestions, particularly the third and fourth ones, if you keep in mind two things. First, these suggestions are intended to be supplementary rather than substitutionary, to build on rather than replace what you have already learned from courses in writing and in homiletics. Second, these suggestions will effect creativity in sermons only if they are employed by sanctified preachers, people in whom the Holy Spirit through the Gospel is busy working "both to will and to do of His good pleasure" (Phil. 2:13). Permit me to discuss each of these factors more fully below.

First, the suggestions for creative preaching offered in this book presuppose mastery of the basics of English composition and homiletics. While it is my hope that even a beginning seminary student can benefit from this book, he will do so only if he simultaneously continues to practice all that he has learned in the past about grammar, punctuation, word choice, and word arrangement; and only if he learns the basics of homiletics. It is a truism of writing that only those who are at home with the rules can occasionally go beyond the rules or even break them legitimately and effectively. There can be no extraordinary creativity in our preaching

5

unless we are, first of all, capable of ordinary creativity. As a matter of fact, if a preacher studies his Biblical text thoroughly, determines carefully what it says, and then says what it says in a direct, clear, coherent manner, he will often get credit not only for thoroughness, care, directness, clarity, and coherence but for creativity as well. It is obviously not the purpose of this book to review the basics of English composition and homiletics, but neither is it the purpose of this book to minimize them. Creativity attempted by one who has not learned how to write or by one who neglects his homiletical homework nearly always falls flat or strikes the listener as mere sensationalism. Without the basics, creativity too easily becomes tasteless.

Second, and even more emphatically, the suggestions for creative preaching offered in this book presuppose steady, continuous growth in the preacher's sanctification. To begin with, sanctification generates creativity in the preacher. There is a surprising correlation in the art of preaching between sanctification and creativity, the former being, to a larger degree that most of us are aware, a prerequisite for the latter. It does not follow from this, of course, that the absence of creativity in a preacher signals the absence of sanctification. Such a conclusion would be a classic instance of false obversion or the misuse of opposites, a procedure that in this instance could be tragic as well as illogical. But it does follow that if the preacher is a highly sanctified person, he is more likely to be creative as well.

Creativity will come more easily to him for several reasons. First, faith and virtue are themselves creative processes: they are the unique manufacture of God the Holy Spirit through the Gospel. His work in the human body, His temple, removes the scales from the preacher's eyes; he no longer sees through a glass so darkly as he did before. The insights the Holy Spirit provides, the preacher is able to transmit to others. He understands sin better, for one thing. He sees the corruption in the hearts of his audience more clearly because, thanks to the Holy Spirit, he sees his own corruption more clearly. Effective Law preaching is always intensely personal. This is not to say that the preacher's discussion of sin from the pulpit should be overtly subjective, the "I've done it too, folks; I've been there and back" approach that can so easily become patronizing and condescending, or a kind of exhibitionism—bragging rather than confessing. But it does mean that the preacher's pulpit talk about sin is always honest, always from the perspective of keen awareness of his own specific shortcomings. Given that kind of personal approach, it is legitimate to describe effective Law preaching as a form of confession and the listener's receptivity toward it as a variety of absolution for the speaker. That is, recognizing the accuracy and insightfulness of the preacher's diagnosis of sin, the listeners will give him their rapt attention. They will regard his diagnosis of sin as realistic, on target, rather than stereotyped and predictable. They will marvel at how much their pastor knows about them and may even be tempted to quip,

"Has he been eavesdropping?" They may say of him (to a lesser degree, of course, and for a different reason) what the woman at the well said of Christ: "Come, see a man, which told me all things that ever I did" (John 4:29).

Even more important than the improvement in the speaker's Law preaching is the improvement in his Gospel preaching that results from the Holy Spirit's activity through the Word upon the character of the speaker. Growing in sanctification, the preacher will present the Gospel more insightfully and provocatively. His preaching will reflect not merely the mastery of one or two safe, traditional formulas acquired during his seminary training but rather the vast and imaginative variety of Gospel formulas that the Scriptures themselves provide.

More specifically, growth in sanctification will have a bearing on the preacher's Sunday-to-Sunday sermon preparation and delivery. To be sure, it will result in increased conscientiousness about these activities. But what I primarily have in mind is the fact that creative preaching is often a byproduct of passion for one's subject and compassion for one's audience. An effective preacher is one who is excited about his material and who is eager to communicate that material to his listeners. I sometimes quip to my students: "Seek ye first your subject and your audience, and creativity will be added unto you." We preach to people, not to bewilder or impress them, but to help and serve them. Hence what follows? We do a thorough study of the text so that we—and our listeners—know what we are talking about. We arrange our materials logically so that people can easily follow them. We labor to choose words wisely and to arrange them rhythmically so that people will enjoy listening to them. We are humble, getting our self out of the way as much as possible. We are courteous and fair, thinking like the listener, looking at things from his point of view, seeing them his way—in short, letting that mind be in us which is also in our listener. The pulpit is no place for show-offs, novices, upstarts, sensationalists, status-mongers. It is an arena for the best in good manners, for the ultimate in courtesy, selflessness, and humility. Without such virtues, preacher creativity easily degenerates into mere pomp and bombast.

Not only does Spirit-manufactured sanctification in the preacher generate creativity, but it also makes that creativity more palatable to his audience. Even the pagan Quintilian conceded that a persuasive orator is a *good* man skilled in speaking (emphasis added). The Bible says it so simply: "speaking the truth in *love*" (Eph. 4:15, emphasis added). No technically creative sermon can cover a multitude of the preacher's sins—and I refer not merely to those sins of the flesh for which a pastor may be defrocked (e.g., fornication, theft, drunkenness) but also to sins of the disposition (arrogance, uncharitableness, poor sportsmanship, snobbishness, dictatorialness). Thank God (and I mean the phrase theologically, not conventionally), He, through Jesus, forgives and covers preacher deficiencies and shortcomings (else who of us could stand?), but it doesn't follow from this grace that we are to make a career of our deficiencies and short-comings. The preacher has to be accepted before his creativity will be accepted. He is his own best creative technique. His sermon style cannot rise above the level of his life-style. Before God can work *through* a man, He must work *in* a man. God is Persons (three of them, in fact); He sent His Son as a Person, the God-Man, to effect our salvation; and He still sends persons (preachers) to get to persons (people). This is why good character is so crucial to the preaching task. While it is true that no one can believe *for* another, it is also true, usually, that no one can believe *without* another; that is, God normally gets to people through people.

Ultimately, the correlation between preacher creativity and preacher character has its roots in the concept of the Word. The Word is both a Person and a message (Jesus and the Biblical Gospel); the Word is the God who speaks and it is what God speaks. This is still God's *modus operandi,* His way of working: message through a man. Preachers are transformers for God's power unto salvation. That is why the transformer needs to be in the peak of condition, in good running order. God's method is not exclusion (God without man); nor is it co-operation (God plus man); rather, it is transformation (God through man). We pastors offer ourselves as ordinary bread and wine "in, with, and under" which God is truly present. Hence, we must never divorce the message from the person or, more specifically, creativity from sanctification. We must not put asunder what God has joined together.

What is Creativity?

Admittedly, the concept of creativity, the whole, is greater than the sum of the words used to define it. To begin with an informal definition, creativity is probably initiated when the writer says, "I have an idea," and rushes for pencil and notebook before that idea escapes him. And creativity has undoubtedly occurred whenever the listener responds with such ex-pressions as "Very interesting!" "Where did you ever get that idea?" "I never heard it put that way before!" "I wish I had thought of that first!" To define it more formally, creativity consists of profound insights stated winsomely. Professor Hayakawa has defined creativity as "the verbalization of a cerebral itch."[1] I like that description because it not only defines creativity—it exem-plifies it. Creativity means giving attractive expression to provocative thoughts, making original statements about original ideas—or, more often in the preacher's case, according original expression to familiar ideas, famil-iar because they are from the Scriptures. Creativity occurs when the preacher puts theological truths into non-theological language, timeless verities into timely words, changeless Biblical substance into changing con-temporary forms. To invert the Biblical metaphor, the preacher puts the old wine of the Gospel into new wineskins. He tells the old, old story, but always in new, new language. Normally we associate creativity with such words as "new," "fresh," "original," "imaginative," "insightful," "provocative," and "breathtaking," adjectives that appropriately describe creative preaching so long as that preaching is simultaneously responsible, loyal to the Scriptures.

One caution: as preachers we create the medium but not the message. The Gospel is God's gift to us; in our preaching we neither add to it nor subtract from it. The Gospel is God's gift, wholly His gift, nothing but His gift. But we do create the package in which God's gift comes to people. We wrap it attractively and tie a ribbon around it so as to whet the viewer's curiosity, to entice him to open the package wondering, "What's in it for me?" What's in it for him is, of course, entirely the gift of God. The magic is in the Word, the Word of God, which alone is God's power to salvation. Yet in His wisdom God has chosen to convey that magic through words. Creative preaching simply harnesses the magic of the Word to the magic of words; it couples the unique and exclusive power of the Gospel to the dynamite of carefully selected words and to the harmonious rhythms of skillfully arranged words. Creative pulpit language has been compared to a lens: it brings to focus the light and heat of God's Word. The power and energy are all God's, but the lens brings that power and energy to bear on specific people.

How Does One Acquire Creativity?

To whom does creativity come? I have already indicated that it is more likely to come to that preacher experiencing steady growth in sanctification, to one, more specifically, whose primary concern is his subject matter and his audience. There seems to be a paradox here: Seek creativity directly and it is likely to elude you; seek other things first—mastery of material and service to people—and creativity is thrown in for good measure. The speaker is "surprised by creativity."

Creativity is more likely to come to that preacher who knows his Bible well, because such knowledge enables him to see relationships between widely scattered Biblical truths. This aspect of creativity will be discussed in greater detail in Chapter Four when I take up the subject of multiple text sermons. For the present let me point out that juxtaposing two or more isolated Bible passages often produces surprisingly creative results. Wedding one Biblical concept to another frequently gives birth to a new and, to sustain the marriage metaphor, legitimate family of Biblical ideas. Once again the preacher, who is always a systematician as well, is joining together in a sermon what God hath put asunder in the Scriptures. Obviously, to perform such creative marriages requires familiarity with God's Word.

Creativity comes not only to the preacher who recognizes relationships between widely scattered portions of the Bible, but also to the preacher who perceives connections between the isolated phenomena of his everyday life. He has his eyes open to what God is accomplishing in his day-to-day existence, and he recognizes the emergence of a pattern in God's various dealings with him. In short, he sees life whole. Among all the drab and colorful numerators of daily living, he sees certain common denominators that he attributes to God's grace. He then integrates what he finds, makes sense out of it, and communicates that sense to others in his writing and speaking. Although the listeners may never verbalize their reactions, they will recognize such a speaker as a keen analyst of human nature and will regard his preaching as "creative."

A capacity for analogy, an ability to discern similarities between ostensibly dissimilar things, a gift for seeing likenesses between what is called the secular and the spiritual, this seems to be another prerequisite for creativity. To see sermons in stones as well as in pericopes, to take a tree or rocket or beetle or lamppost and somehow make it suggestive of some Biblical or moral truth is a mark of a creative preacher. "The kingdom of heaven is like..."—thus began so many of our Lord's parables. Has anything ever surpassed them in creativity?

Discipline hardly sounds like a word compatible with creativity. Yet it is really another climatic condition favorable to the germination and growth of creativity. Too easily we confuse preaching with mere talking, and too quickly we christen survival in the pulpit as success. It is a common homiletical quip that if we wish to pull the trigger on a text Sunday morning we cannot wait until Saturday night to load the gun. Fosdick's familiar dictum, that a preacher must spend one hour of preparation outside the pulpit for every minute of speaking in the pulpit, is not the hyperbole I used to think it was. It is rather, in my experience, understatement. Even the poet Robert Frost admitted that good writing must be "worried into being." Creative preaching, inevitably, is the outcome of hard work and disciplined study habits. There is no other way, no convenient shortcut. This kind of preaching "cometh only by prayer and fasting." What is easy to read or listen to has probably been hard to write. Even though it is a cliché, the statement that genius is nine-tenths discipline contains a high degree of truth. Preachers are made, not born. Delivering sermons, like delivering children, requires labor, hard labor. The analogy of pregnancy, in fact, is a tempting one to pursue. In the process of frequent intellectual intercourse, ideas are conceived. The brain becomes the womb for the development of the idea conceived. One grows great with the idea, becomes big with it, feels increasingly uncomfortable with it. As the week wears on, the labor intensifies. When Sunday morning comes the sermon is "delivered," and then there is joy that another sermon, or child if you will, has been born into the world, not merely the joy of relief but also the joy of creativity, the humble but honest recognition of a job well done.

Reading experience is another prerequisite for creativity—and I refer not merely to the obvious reading of theological books and professional journals but primarily to the reading of belletristic literature (novels, dramas, poems, and short stories). "The study of great literature is the study of life, and the serious novelist will do more to enrich experience, awaken imagination, sharpen observation, and explore character, than any other teacher."[2] No less a person than Dr. Martin Luther has said:

> Without knowledge of literature pure theology cannot at all endure, just as heretofore, when letters have declined and lain prostrate, theology, too, has wretchedly fallen and lain prostrate; nay, I see that there has never been a great revelation of the Word of God unless He has first prepared the way by the rise and prosperity of languages and letters, as though they were John the Baptists.... Certainly it is my desire that there shall be as many poets and rhetoricians as possible, because I see that by these studies, as by no other means, people are wonderfully fitted for the grasping of sacred truth and for handling it skillfully and happily.... Therefore, I beg of you that at my request (if that has any weight) you will urge your young people to be diligent in the study of poetry and rhetoric.[3]

I have discovered this in my own preaching experience. Writers like Camus, Cervantes, Donne, Dostoevsky, Fielding, Greene, Herbert, Marvell, Pope, Shakespeare, Steinbeck, Swift, Tolstoy, Waugh, Wharton, plus many others, are seers of the soul, human beings who have wrestled intensely with the issues of life and death and have reported their findings in attractive, non-sermonic form. An occasional writer (e.g., C. S. Lewis, J. R. R. Tolkien) will even supply the reader with a new perspective on the Gospel.[4] While the novelist can seldom be relied upon to narrate in any great detail the saving Good News, he can be relied upon to make clearer our need of salvation. If infrequently a preacher of the Gospel, the novelist is often an effective preacher of the Law. One writer has compared the belletristic author to a sycamore tree from which we Zacchaeuses can better see the Lord Jesus— of whose saving acts, of course, we are told accurately and adequately only in the sacred Scriptures. It is not only the content of belletristic literature that is conducive to creativity but also its style. Creative writing is caught, not taught. We assimilate creative techniques through our frequent exposure to them; some sort of literary osmosis occurs. Even the most honest of us is an unconscious plagiarist; we involuntarily acquire—and use—the writing techniques of those whom we read. As a man reads, so he writes. One cannot read, for instance, C. S. Lewis' delightfully written works for very long without experiencing a decided improvement in his own writing style. In half-jest I have sometimes told my students that I personally derive more homiletical help from belletristic literature than I do from most homiletics textbooks. So what follows? To continue in the semi-jocular vein: "Sell all that ye have and buy Tolstoy"; "Except ye read Dostoevsky, ye cannot enter into the kingdom of creativity."

Writing experience is another desideratum for creativity. Except for a different source (a text from the Bible) and a different goal (the proclamation of the Gospel for the listener's eternal salvation and his everyday growth in God-pleasing living), sermon writing is no different from any other kind of writing. The more one has tangled with ideas in his past compositions, essays, book reports, term papers, and research papers, the easier it will be for him to write sermons. The most profound thing that happens in even the best-structured, best-taught homiletics course is that a student is compelled to write a lot of sermons that are carefully evaluated. He learns by doing; creativity comes through practice. Mark Twain's three rules for successful writing—write, write, and write—seem to apply to sermon writing as well. Creativity comes to him who writes—and writes, and keeps on writing.

Reluctant as we may be to admit it (unless we happen to possess it to a high degree), intelligence is another prerequisite for creativity. Actually, the trait of intelligence exemplifies grace: it is entirely God's gift to us through our parents and through our environment, and there is little we can do about it except gratefully to acknowledge His kindness and cultivate with His help the gift He has given us. The correlation between intelligence and creativity seems so obvious that there is little point in belaboring it. However, because of the periodic anti-intellectualism that surfaces in contemporary culture, there may be a need to remind ourselves that mental ability is not an impediment to creativity, and that in no case should the virtue of intelligence ever be converted into a fault. In brief, there is nothing to warrant the all too prevalent assumption that a preacher is more likely to be a man of God if he is an ignoramus, that he is more likely to be effective in the pulpit if his character is good while his intelligence is weak.

Almost as obvious a requirement for creativity as intelligence is emotional capacity, here defined as the ability to feel deeply or, in Shakespeare's words, "to see feelingly." Effective verbal communication is always intestinal as well as cranial. What a person feels strongly, he writes and speaks about more interestingly. Because of the advantages of voice inflection and body language, the spoken word is more able than the written word to communicate excitement and sincerity. Nevertheless, these emotions can even surface in the written word insofar as they play a significant role in word choice and word arrangement. Feeling has a way of coursing through the pen onto the page—as the appreciative and discerning reader of good poetry, for example, will readily concede.

Finally, creativity comes to him who thinks creativity important, who has an aversion for mouthing banalities and a compulsion for uttering profundities. Whenever the preacher sits down to write a sermon or enters a pulpit to deliver one, he has an intense desire to be the best possible preacher he can be, not for his own sake but for the sake of the Gospel. This assertion is not meant to contradict the incidental aspect of creativity described in an earlier paragraph—that creativity is a byproduct of love for subject matter and for audience—but it is a way of affirming the truism that one must consider a goal worth achieving if he hopes to achieve it.

Why Creativity, Anyhow?

Some might think that so far I have begged the question, assuming as true the very thing—the need for and desirability of creativity—that first needs to be proved. Granted that creativity is a word that has a lot going for it; its connotations are uniformly excellent. Yet we must not be mesmerized by the word. Creativity has its dangers. To begin with, it can so easily degenerate into sensationalism; the line of demarcation between the two is admittedly always vague and tenuous. Further, there is the ever attendant danger of pride, of self-advancement, of the preacher getting in the way of God, even upstaging Him, impeding the saving power that lies in His Word—and in His Word alone. After all, doesn't St. Paul warn against this very possibility in the opening chapters of 1 Corinthians? He came to the Corinthians, he says, "not with excellency of speech or of wisdom" (1 Cor. 2:1). His preaching "was not with enticing words of man's wisdom, but in demonstration of the Spirit and of power" (1 Cor. 2:4). Christ sent him, he observes, "to preach the gospel: not with wisdom of words, lest the cross of Christ should be made of none effect" (1 Cor. 1:17). He goes on to point out that God saves people not through signs or wisdom but through "the *foolishness* of preaching" (1 Cor. 1:21, emphasis added). Some of us, therefore, can hardly be blamed for regarding creativity as an embroidery upon truth, perhaps even a subversion of it; for suspecting the sincerity of a person who has an excessive fondness for originality; for entertaining the fear that style is somehow incompatible with the foolishness of the cross.

Frankly, these are hard words from the apostle, admitting of no easy solution and intended to give pause to the enthusiast for creativity. Nonetheless, if Paul's words are meant as a blanket condemnation of winsome writing and attractive speaking, then I fear that Paul, more than any other Biblical writer, fails to practice what he preaches in this respect and stands self-condemned. Even an unbelieving reader vibrates to the magic of Paul's literary style. He quotes poetry. He uses rhetorical devices. He puns. He employs balance and antitheses. He is a master at logic. Paul is unquestionably a creative writer. I point this out, not to charge him with inconsistency, but to suggest the possibility that we have misunderstood him or at least overstated the case he is making.

Can I offer the following modification without emasculating Paul's argument? Creativity is allowable, even commendable, so long as it maintains a slave's role, not a master's role, in respect to the Gospel; so long as it serves the Gospel rather than upstages it. Correctly interpreted, the foolishness of preaching consists in its content, not in its style. The preaching of the cross is foolishness because it is the preaching of the *cross*—that we are **13** saved by the Son of God's death via the disgraceful mode of crucifixion; and that we are saved entirely by the action of God through Christ, not because of any merit or activity on our part. This is the *skandalon* of the cross, this is the foolishness of preaching, irrespective of the words in which it is proclaimed. What is foolish is our message, not our manner of communicating that message. The foolishness of preaching does not necessitate foolish preaching. Creativity in our sermon construction and delivery is, therefore, in place so long as it stays in place, below the Gospel rather than above it. Creativity is to function as a channel for the Gospel, not as its replacement.

Sometimes the theological objection to creativity comes from a slightly different perspective. The opposition is directed not so much toward "fancy" words, "words of wisdom," as it is toward the process of preparation itself. The accent is on naturalness, genuineness, spontaneity, "doing your own thing" (what I, in less charitable moments, dub "verbal burping" or "the spontaneous me syndrome"). Preparation is considered contrivance, possibly even symptomatic of a lack of trust in the Holy Spirit. One can forget about—or at least minimize—textual analysis, outlining, writing, and revising, and simply wade into the speaking task when the time for speaking arrives. Forget about yourself and trust in God; just take the plunge, for He and His angels will guide you in all your ways. Says William J. Carl III:

> But one has to admit that the 60's were not the best years for the pulpit. In an attempt to avoid the 'golden throat' era of the 40's and 50's, where preachers had taken up permanent residence on a pedestal (some bucking for a place in a stained glass window), we reacted with . . . vacating the pulpit to wander aimlessly in front of the pews. We ventilated our 'real feelings' from the pulpit to show our people that we could hurt too. Some took revenge with what David Buttrick has called the 'Johnny Carson school of casual cats in the pulpit.'[5]

Where this approach is not motivated by mere laziness but seeks a serious theological base, Luke 12:11-12 is sometimes cited: "Take ye no thought how or what thing ye shall answer, or what ye shall say: For the Holy Ghost shall teach you in the same hour what ye ought to say." What is overlooked in the use of this passage is the context, which has to do with appearance in the courts in times of persecution, not with preaching or normal witnessing opportunities. Perhaps R. E. O. White has provided the best-balanced, least-caricatured rebuttal to this approach to preaching: "There is no ground whatsoever to suppose that there is more of the Spirit's guidance and power in a ministry that is haphazard and unplanned than in one carefully and prayerfully prepared, balanced, and purposeful."[6]

Less theologically prompted than the preceding objections to creativity is what might be termed the objection of the intelligentsia. For this group it is sufficient that the ideas be valid and profound; why stoop to selling them through verbal gimmickry? Their accent is on scholarship, not salesmanship; on content, not form; on what, not how. "How" is a concern appropriate only to fix-it-yourself kinds of people and do-it-yourself types of manuals, but for the intellectual elite, let the word not be found in their vocabulary. A growing number of recent publications (not all of them homiletical) stress the impossibility of sharply severing form from content.[7] While the two concepts are not synonymous, neither are they as far apart from each other as the proverbial east is from the west. Ideas do not have existence apart from the words in which they are garbed. If the words are fuzzy, vague, imprecise, unclear, and ineffective, then the ideas are fuzzy, vague, imprecise, unclear, and ineffective. To a greater degree than we realize, form is content and content is form; message is style and style is message; theology is language and language is theology (as the word "theology" in its root meaning partly implies).

A peculiar corollary to the objection of the intelligentsia just described is a phenomenon that surfaced a decade or two ago, sometimes referred to as linguistic analysis or the semantic movement.[8] This movement was frequently characterized by a marked distrust of the very vehicle of communication itself—words. "What do you mean?" and "Can words mean?" were among the questions asked. Historically the chief obstacle to the preaching of the Gospel has been the foolishness of the cross; today it is more likely to be the foolishness of language. Professor Richard Caemmerer points out that the preacher "must face the situation that preaching is foolishness to many potential listeners of our own time not just because it is supernatural or because it offends innate self-righteousness as in 1 Corinthians 1, but because it is said in words, subjects and predicates."[9] Especially the language of theology has been suspect, sometimes considered ethereal, almost meaningless, prompting many "demythologizers" to strip Christianity of its supernatural language in an effort to make it comprehensible and believeable. Where will all such attempts take us? "To hell!" I am tempted to say in all seriousness—except that one would then have to explain what that concept means!

Actually, the distrust of words is not a uniquely contemporary phenomenon; just the degree of it is. No less an artist in words than Shakespeare himself admitted: "A sentence is but a chev'ril glove to a good wit. How quickly the wrong side may be turned outward!"[10] A couple of centuries later another master of words conceded that "human speech is but a cracked cauldron on which we beat tunes for dancing bears, when all the while we long to melt the stars."[11] Yet neither of these writers, despite their awareness of the limitations of language, abandoned language as a vehicle for communication; in fact, both of them excelled in the use of words. Readers of *Gulliver's Travels* recall with delight Jonathan Swift's incisive satire on the attempt of the Laputans to abolish words. Since they considered words to be at best inaccurate symbols of things, why not substitute the things for the words in the conduct of conversation? As a consequence, people carried on their backs sacks containing a variety of objects and when encountering one another would simply, in lieu of normal conversation, extricate objects from their respective sacks and display them to one another. It was all show and no tell. However, the project fell through, according to Swift, for two reasons: (1) a loquacious person was not equal to carrying the weight of a sack containing the numerous objects he wished to "talk about"; (2) the ladies objected—they preferred the old-fashioned mode of conversation.[12] While, admittedly, the increasing disuse of language in television, the perennial misuse of language by politicians, theologians, and many others, and the ever-present phenomenon of jargon in a wide variety of disciplines partly justify diminished enthusiasm for the gift of language, I cannot help sharing Swift's amusement at efforts to eliminate words as a mode of communication. The ultimate irony always is that it takes words to destroy confidence in words.

Despite all its abuses and limitations, language is still our principal means of communication. I suspect that when we doubt the viability of language as a vehicle for the Good News, our distrust of words is often related to a distrust in God; our attempted abolition of verbal meaning may reflect a prior abolition of God. If language is "double," it may be because man is "double," that is, old man as well as new man, flesh as well as spirit. Language is forked largely because the speaker's tongue is forked. If there is fault, it lies primarily in the speaker, not in speech itself. After all, sin and language have been closely associated ever since the Tower of Babel. The problem is not words *per se*; rather, the problem is big words, dull words, abstract words, vague words, anemic words, slovenly words, pompous words. The only thing that can replace language as a means of communication is better language.

Since at least two of the objections to creativity described above seem to have a doctrinal base, it is appropriate at this point to initiate the defense of creativity on a doctrinal level. The rationale for the responsible use of creative language in preaching lies in the character of the Gospel-event itself. To begin with, one of the names of the Second Person of the Trinity is "the Word." "In the beginning was the Word, and the Word was with God, and the Word was God" (John 1:1). Although the designation "Word" has many deeper meanings, it describes, at the very least, the function of Christ from eternity toward God the Father. Even as I am presently using words to describe, reveal, explain, and make clear, so Christ from the very beginning served the purpose of describing, revealing, explaining, and making clear the Father. Among other things Christ disclosed the Father's holiness and love, His wrath toward our sin, but, even more, His determined love to rescue us from our sin. When the fullness of time came for God to carry out that resolution of the "tension" between His

16

holiness and His love that we call His plan of salvation for us, He turned to His Son, the Word, whose function from eternity was to reveal the Father.

To accomplish this, what did Christ, the Word, do? He became incarnate. He became flesh. He became a man. He was born at Bethlehem and spent approximately 33 years on our earth. One might say that Christ, the Word, became a *concrete* Word. (Prior to Bethlehem Christ had been only a spirit, an *abstract* Word, so to speak.) As any reader or listener knows, concrete words are much more effective than abstract words, more fun to listen to and easier to understand. Likewise Christ, in becoming man also, in becoming a concrete Word, more effectively described, revealed, explained, made clear God's saving plan. One can virtually hear the wonder breaking through the apostle's description of this in John 1:14: "And the Word was made flesh and dwelt among us [can you believe it?] (and we beheld His glory, [imagine that!] the glory as of the only begotten of the Father,) [no less!] full of grace and truth [how about that?]." This drastic change of spirit into flesh, of an abstract Word into a concrete Word, that we celebrate every Christmas suggests a precedent for the creative use of lan-guage; at the very least it recommends the substitution of concrete words for abstract ones in our written and spoken witness to the Gospel, in our efforts to describe, reveal, explain, and make clear God's saving love.

But the divine precedent does not end there. In His continuous determination to communicate God's saving love for us, the Word "became" words. God placed the historical event (Christ's birth, life, death, and resurrection) into an account of that event (the Scriptures), an account intended to be spoken by God's people to God's people till the end of time. In short, God chose language, words, as a vehicle to communicate what His Son, the Word, achieved for us during His earthly ministry. More-over, the words that tell us about the Word who in turn tells us about God are not just "any old words." They are remarkable words, extraordinary words: inspired (and therefore inerrant) to be sure, but also, on a more secular level, simple words, good words, graphic words, understandable words, language at its best, simple without being simplistic, profound with-out being incomprehensible (e.g., the first chapter of John's gospel). My point is that the Holy Scriptures are an extension of the incarnation. What God initiated in a stable at Bethlehem, an all-out effort to communicate His love, He continues in the Bible and in Biblical preaching. The divine beat goes on. The revelatory motif continues. Spirit becomes flesh and "flesh" is transmitted through words. Word-words are inseparable even as Christ's deity and humanity are inseparable; hence, the medium cannot really be divorced from the message (and vice versa).

Since God chose language as a vehicle for His saving plan, it follows that we should not hesitate to use language in our preaching—and, in the divine tradition, language at its very best. We should wield it with the conviction that God knew what He was doing when He selected language.

It is incumbent upon us to harness the magic of the Word (that "power of God unto salvation") to the magic of words. An ancient heresy called Docetism denied Christ's humanity largely because it was deemed improper for God to become man, because such a transformation was beneath the dignity of God. It wasn't so much that God *couldn't* become man but rather that He *wouldn't*. A modern variant of this is the conviction that the Word (Christ) shouldn't come to us through words. The contemporary Docetic heresy seems to be a contempt for language, the view that language is somehow beneath God, that He wouldn't "stoop to conquer" through that particular medium. The practical consequence of this mistaken view is not the avoidance of language (an avenue nearly impossible for even the Docetic purist!), but the transformation of our witnessing language into something lofty, ethereal, and incomprehensible, into some sort of special "Holy Ghost" language, theological jargon, or conventional, stereotyped, "sermonic" language.

Any one of these transformations constitutes a serious impediment to our Christian witnessing. Particularly is this true of "sermonic" language, language teeming with trite, familiar expressions and riddled with clichés (what I sometimes call "The Gospel According to Platitude"). As the familiar homiletical quip has it: "Heresy has slain its thousands but dullness its ten thousands." Or again: "Boredom is the root of all evil." This dire outcome occurs because people's minds are faster than preachers' tongues. When the preacher initiates a cliché, the listener's brain, light years ahead of the preacher's words, completes the predictable thought and wanders off to other things—like shiny cars and shapely blondes. Communicating no doctrine at all—the outcome of trite preaching—is as fatal eventually as preaching false doctrine. In the light of this tragic possibility, it is not an overstatement to describe platitudinous preaching as "a sin against the Holy Ghost" and "taking the name of the Lord, our God, in vain."

This need not be. Language is a gift of God. There is magic in it—as poets, dramatists, and novelists have demonstrated for centuries. Language is dynamite; it is charged, explosive. We ought to tap its power in our Christian witness. It is true that our language needs to be "correct" and "orthodox," but it is just as true that our language needs to be alive, vital, packing vim and vigor, fun to listen to and easy to understand. To interest is the first duty of preaching—not the only or main duty of preaching, but "first" in a chronological sense. Before anything can happen—like salvation or sanctification—the preacher must get people's attention and retain their attention. Good preaching, obviously, is more than creative and interesting, but it is at least that. Creativity is not a goal of preaching, but it is a prerequisite for it.

Admittedly, there is a danger in the opposite direction, the danger of the preacher preempting the role of God, of witnessing as if the salvation and sanctification of his audience depended upon himself rather than upon his Lord. If there is the Charybdis of dullness, there is also the Scylla of pride, and the preacher needs to steer carefully between the two. If there is the danger of being boring, there is also the danger of being sensational. In the words of Harold MacMillan: "The difficulty of speeches is that you are perpetually poised between the cliché and the indiscretion."

Acts 12:21-23 describes the reaction of an audience to a speech made by Herod: "It is the voice of a god, and not of a man." Herod must have welcomed their verdict, for the passage adds that he did not give God the glory. You remember the outcome. (Indeed, how could you forget it?) God punished Herod: he was eaten of worms and died.

Every time a preacher steps into a pulpit, Herod's sin is a hideous possibility. The striking illustration, the humorous anecdote, the clever saying, the quotation from the classics, the current "in" phrase—effective as all these devices can be in furthering the program of God, they can also become opportunities for promoting self. Designed to proclaim God as God, these techniques can end up proclaiming self as god. "It is the voice of a god, and not of a man" could well be the audience reaction the preacher is soliciting in his imaginative and interesting pulpit presentation —with the blasphemous result that what gets preached is not a crucified and risen Savior but a well-read and quick-witted pastor.

While it is true that Herod's sin is always a horrible possibility for the preacher, it would be an over-reaction for him to avoid anything imaginative and interesting. In an effort to avoid the sin of pride, he may commit the sin of dullness. He may shun the striking illustration, the humorous anecdote, the clever saying, the quotation from the classics, the current "in" phrase. Needless to say, Christ does not get preached that way either; in fact, nothing does. We must always remember that normally these creative techniques are not intrinsically bad—or good, for that matter. Whether they are bad or good depends upon whether or not the speaker uses them to the glory of God—and dullness is as little to the glory of God as is showiness.

The curious thing is that a preacher is meant to be "the voice of a god" in a sense. After all, he is God's representative on earth pleading: "Be ye reconciled to God through His crucified and risen Son." The preacher has been given this high honor and equipped for this high office by the very God he represents and through the very Christ he proclaims. But the god he is to be the voice of is the triune God, not the god of self. Like John the Baptist, the preacher today is a voice in the wilderness, preparing the way for the Lord. But also, like John the Baptist, he is not that light; rather, he bears witness to that Light. When people hear him speak, therefore, they are to react, not with "This is the voice of a god," but rather with "This is the voice of *the* God." John the Baptist's motto could well serve as the motto for the preacher of today: "He must increase, but I must decrease" (John 3:30). Whatever the preacher does, then, whether he eats or drinks—or preaches —he ought to do it to the glory of God.

19

No one has resolved the tension more effectively than Richard Caemmerer:

> The preacher is indeed unable to add to the power of the Word of God, and it remains the one means of changing the heart in God's directions. But he is in the business of removing obstacles to its hearing. His constant concern must be to find the approach to the hearer and the ways by which he opens his ears and listens. The Word of God does things in the human heart that no other word can do. But it reaches it through the same channels of hearing and attention that any other word must use.[13]

This is why we dare never serve pure doctrine in an impure container. Consistency for "truth and purity" demands that we pay attention to the attractiveness of our language as well as to the orthodoxy of our doctrine. "A word fitly spoken is like apples of gold in pictures of silver" (Prov. 25:11). In short, responsible creativity is in order.

Chapter One

Creativity Through Fuller Understanding of What Happened to Jesus on the Cross

A fuller understanding of what I call "the literal Gospel," more specifically, a fuller understanding of what happened to Jesus on the cross, is not only itself conducive to creativity in our preaching but is also foundational for the creativity-potential of the suggestions in the next two chapters: a more frequent use of Biblical metaphors and images of the Gospel; and the occasional employment of Gospel-handles. Why and how this is the case will become clear as we proceed.

Definition of "Literal Gospel"

By the phrase "the literal Gospel" I mean those things that Jesus did during His life on earth—or which were done to Him—that contributed directly to accomplishing our eternal salvation. They are actual happenings, historical events, like His incarnation, His birth, His life, His circumcision, His baptism, His temptation in the wilderness, His ministry, His suffering and death, His resurrection, His ascension. All of these were key steps in the working out of our salvation.

The Customary Presentation of the Literal Gospel

Customarily our pulpit presentations of the Gospel include one or more of the literal happenings enumerated above, together with explanation of their significance and application to the specific needs of specific audiences. Obviously which literal event(s) we preach about depends upon the church year: Christ's birth at Christmas time, His baptism on the

21

first Sunday after the Epiphany, His suffering and death especially (but not exclusively) during Lent, His resurrection particularly (but not only) during the Easter cycle, His ascension on the day set aside for it on the church calendar, and His life and its significance primarily during the non-festival part of the church year.

Just as obviously we preach about some of these events more often than others. Only a naive homiletical purist would ever make the mistake of trying to touch base with all of these historical events within the confines of one sermon or to give equal time to each of these Gospel-happenings in the course of his ministry. It is not only natural but also defensible to proclaim certain aspects of the literal Gospel more than others. What preacher doesn't say more about Christ's incarnation than about His circumcision; more about His crucifixion than about His baptism; more about His resurrection than about His temptation in the wilderness? While it is desirable for the Christian preacher in the course of His ministry to cover all of the literal Gospel-events, he inevitably says more about the birth, life, crucifixion, and resurrection of Jesus than about the others. He will naturally say the most about the crucifixion and the resurrection since they are the high spots in any Gospel proclamation.

This is only proper. Apart from the resurrection of Christ, everything else in our Christian religion is meaningless. "If Christ be not risen, then is our preaching vain, and your faith is also vain" (1 Cor. 15:14). As for the prominence of the crucifixion in our preaching, there is ample Biblical precedent. Without intending to equate quality with quantity, I think it appropriate to point out that since the Bible devotes more space to the account of Christ's suffering and death than it does to any other aspect of the literal Gospel, this should be an important consideration for us in our Gospel preaching. Besides, Gospel preaching that accents Christ's crucifixion is psychologically valuable. To begin with, people understand what we preachers are talking about when we say that Christ died. Death is something within the listener's experience—not his firsthand experience (although it will be someday), but his secondhand experience. That is, he has seen death among acquaintances, friends, and relatives, and therefore he knows what death is—whereas a virgin birth or the resurrection of a person dead and buried are not within his experience (and hence less comprehensible). Further, Gospel preaching that accents Christ's death for us, in our place, capitalizes on a given in most human value systems (even non-Christian ones), namely, that people regard dying for another so that he might live as the most a person can do. We even speak of it as "the supreme sacrifice." When the listener hears that Christ's execution was a substitute for his own, he again is in a position to understand—even admire—what it is that Christ did in his behalf.[1]

It is precisely here, however, in our customary preaching of the cross that we often fail to proclaim the *full* literal Gospel. Basically, this chapter is an attempt to answer a deceptively simple question: "What happened to Jesus on the cross?" The question may trigger the impatient answer: "He was executed. What else?" The response "He was executed" is correct, and good as far as it goes—very good, in fact—but it does not go far enough. It does not tell the whole story. Something else happened to Jesus on the cross. It is this "something else" that is the subject of this chapter.

A Word of Caution

Before I deal with this subject, however, a caution is in order. What is about to follow is intended as supplementary to our preaching of the cross, not substitutionary; as complementary, not corrective. What is about to follow I consider essential, highly essential, to our proclamation of the Gospel. But enthusiastic as I am for this specific facet of the literal Gospel, I am not a crusader; there is no intention of "straightening out the church," of condemning the preaching of the past and correcting the preaching of the present. This book is simply an attempt to enhance the creativity of our preaching, and the matter at hand is a key step in that effort. Earlier I spoke of our "usual," "most frequent" mode of preaching Christ's crucifixion. These words were meant not in a derogatory sense, but simply as descriptive of what in fact is the case, be it good or bad; and I, for one, think it good—at least as far as it goes—for the reasons already specified. In respect to our customary presentation of the event on the cross and in respect to the additive to that presentation about to follow, perhaps the Scriptural advice is in order: "These ought ye to have done, and not to leave the other undone" (Matt. 23:23).

Perhaps further caution is in order. In the words of C. S. Lewis:

The central Christian belief is that Christ's death has somehow put us right with God and given us a fresh start. Theories as to how it did this are another matter. A good many different theories have been held as to how it works; what all Christians are agreed on is that it does work. I will tell you what I think it is like. All sensible people know that if you are tired and hungry a meal will do you good. But the modern theory of nourishment—all about the vitamins and proteins—is a different thing. People ate their dinners and felt better long before the theory of vitamins was ever heard of: and if the theory of vitamins is some day abandoned they will go on eating their dinners just the same. Theories about Christ's death are not Christianity: they are explanations about how it works....We are in the same boat here. We believe that the death of Christ is just that point in history at which something absolutely unimaginable from outside shows through into our own world....Indeed, if we found that we could fully understand it, that very fact would show it was not what it professes to be—the inconceivable, the uncreated, the thing from beyond nature, striking down into nature like lightning. You may ask what good will it be to us if we do not under-

23

stand it. But that is easily answered. A man can eat his dinner without understanding exactly how food nourishes him. A man can accept what Christ has done without knowing how it works: indeed, he certainly would not know how it works until he has accepted it.[2]

Let me deduce two caveats from the lengthy passage just cited. First, while it is true that knowledge of the Gospel-event is crucial to faith in that event, still knowledge and faith are not synonymous, nor is there necessarily a one-to-one correspondence between the two such that the degree of faith is always in proportion to the amount of knowledge. Most pastors, I am sure, have had the experience of finding among their congregational members persons whom they would call with little fear of hyperbole "heroes of faith," persons whose faith the pastor envies, and persons "the latchet of whose shoes" he considers himself "not worthy to unloose"— and yet people whose knowledge of the Gospel and whose ability to verbalize that Gospel are nowhere near equal to his own. Chances are it is some surprisingly cheerful old lady eking out the remainder of her days in a nursing home and patiently looking forward to her transfer to heaven, or some minor officer in the congregation unobtrusively and good-naturedly doing what needs to be done, however menial the task. But in either case the pastor recognizes that if not a greater than John the Baptist is here, at least a greater than he himself is here. Such persons fall into the category Lewis has described: people who have experienced the nutrition of food without knowing all the theories of nutrition, about the vitamins and proteins and how food works. Quite simply, as vital to faith as is the description of the full literal Gospel here following, still there are people who have gone to heaven—and will continue to go there—without understanding this particular aspect of the Christian Gospel. Knowledge of this aspect, crucial as it is, should not cause us to feel superior or preach that aspect in a superior manner.

My second caveat is that even though the following description of the full literal Gospel explains more, it does not explain all. In my opinion, it gets to the very core of the meaning of the Gospel-event; at the same time, that event is greater than this—or any other—explanation of it. To repeat the words of Lewis, "If we found that we could fully understand it, that very fact would show it was not what it professes to be—the inconceivable, the uncreated, the thing from beyond nature, striking down into nature like lightning." The Gospel-event is "a many splendored thing," a multifaceted diamond. All we are about to do is appreciate just one more of its many facets.

The Full Literal Gospel

Now back to our question: What happened to Jesus on the cross? He was crucified, of course. He was executed. He suffered, He shed blood, and

He died. And He did all this in our behalf, as our substitute. He suffered the suffering we were supposed to suffer and died the death we were destined to die on account of our sins. As we have already seen, and for the proper reasons already delineated, the Bible and Bible-preachers frequently describe Christ's experience on the cross in these or similar terms, as if death were the only or ultimate or climactic event that occurred on the cross.

But every so often the Scriptures go a bit farther in their explanation of what happened to Jesus on the cross. They demonstrate that God the Father and God the Son, in their intense love for us, even went beyond what we call "the supreme sacrifice." They show that Jesus went to an even greater extreme than that which He once described as the extreme: laying down His life for us (John 15:13). I refer the reader now to a careful study of particularly the following Bible passages: Ps. 22:1-8; Is. 53; Matt. 27:46; 2 Cor. 5:21; Gal. 3:13.

Among the strangest of Jesus' words from the cross is His cry recorded in Matthew 27:46: "My God, My God, why hast Thou forsaken Me?" Jesus accuses His Father of deserting Him in the hour of crisis, of turning His back on Him right when He was most needed; and Jesus reacts with a heart-rending "Why?" In Psalm 22 the language is even more shocking. There Jesus, speaking as God's Righteous One, charges His Father with not listening to His cries for help (v. 2) and of always coming to the rescue of the "fathers" (e.g., Abraham, Jacob, Moses) but, inconsistently, not to His own rescue (vv. 4-5). Jesus delineates His own utter degradation ("I am a worm, and no man," v. 6), and He pictures the bystanders at the cross chortling over the Father's abandonment of His Son (vv. 7-8). Isaiah 53 reminds us that Jesus not only was punished by men but also was "smitten of God" (v. 4), that "it pleased the Lord to bruise Him" (v. 10), and that Jesus was "numbered with the transgressors" (v. 12).

What accounted for this "breakdown in relationships" between God the Father and God the Son? Certainly such a rupture was an exception to the rule. Repeatedly the Father had called Jesus His "beloved Son" in whom He was "well-pleased." Many times during His earthly life Jesus had prayed to His Father, and God had always proved to be "a very present help in trouble." Just the night before, in fact, in Gethsemane Jesus had asked His Father for help, and God had sent an angel to strengthen Him. When the arresting party arrived a few moments later, Jesus was confident that, were He to ask His Father for assistance, 12 legions of angels were available. But now on the cross, at the climax of Jesus' suffering, the angels' orders are "to stand back and fold their wings."[3] God is not listening! He is not helping! What had happened?

Together 2 Corinthians 5:21 and Galatians 3:13 give us the answer.[4] In that interval on the cross the pure and holy Jesus, "who knew no sin," was made sin for us. Innocent as He was and loved of the Father as He was, Jesus, nevertheless, was in that moment teeming with sin—our sins, every last one of them. While from our point of view Jesus was absolutely innocent, from God's point of view He was guilty, guilty because the Father looked at Him and saw our sins, the sins Jesus had voluntarily taken upon Himself. The officiating centurion concluded of Jesus, "Certainly this was a righteous man" (Luke 23:47), and a group of people who had witnessed the execution that day went home beating their breasts (Luke 23:48) as an expression of their conviction that justice had miscarried and that an innocent man had been put to death. Prior to them, others not at all prejudiced in Jesus' favor had acknowledged His innocence. The Judas who had turned Jesus over to the enemy finally admitted that he had betrayed "innocent blood" (Matt. 27:4). Pilate, in his damnable attempt to escape responsibility for the condemnation he had authorized, spoke of Jesus as a "just person" (Matt. 27:24), an assessment with which Pilate's wife agreed (Matt. 27:19). Herod had found Jesus amusing—but innocent. Numerous participants in Jesus' passion-suffering declared Him innocent, but at the cross such was not God's judgment. There, indeed, Jesus was "numbered with the transgressors." Not only was He geographically placed between two criminals and not only was He socially reduced to their level, but also, above all, He was considered by God a transgressor, as the sinner of every sin ever committed or yet to be committed.

So what happened? Our sins on Jesus got in the way between Father and Son. God is not only love—He is also holy. Thus, the Father accorded sin the treatment it deserves: damnation. God loathed what He saw. He shrank back from it. He turned away with repugnance. He abandoned Jesus. He forsook Him. In the words of Galatians 3:13, Jesus "was made a curse for us." "To be accursed of God means to be abandoned by God in terms of His grace, mercy, and love. Physical death is the cessation of biological life: to be abandoned of God is spiritual death, the ultimate experience of the wrath of God...."[5] To put it plainly, Jesus suffered hell. "God loved us so much that He was willing to pay the cost of thrusting His own dear Son into our misery, hell and death and having Him drink that up. That is the way we are saved."[6] Jesus on the cross tasted that "everlasting destruction from the presence of the Lord, and from the glory of His power" described in 2 Thessalonians 1:9. While Jesus was dying on the cross, a phenomenal darkness (Luke 23:44-45) covered the earth, a literal darkness symbolic of the darkness that obtained between Father and Son when the latter was made sin for us and made the curse for sin in our place, and a literal darkness suggestive of the darkness of the kingdom of darkness that Jesus was tasting in that dread hour. It would not be inappropriate to speak of *two* descents by Christ into hell: the literal trip to the camp of the enemy that occurred sometime between Jesus' return to life and His emergence from His tomb, a descent described in 1 Peter 3:19 and summarized by the Apostles' Creed with the simple assertion "He descended into hell"; and a prior descent into hell on the cross that can hardly be called metaphorical by way of distinction since there Jesus was immersed into the very alienation of the damned. The descent into hell that the Creed refers to—and the only one it refers to—is, of course, a step in our Savior's state of exaltation. But the descent into hell that this chapter is describing is a step in our Savior's state of humiliation. In "gangster" terminology He "took the rap for us."

"For us"—that's the point. The damnation that Jesus experienced was *our* damnation, the damnation we deserved for our sins. The hell that Jesus tasted was *our* hell, the hell we had coming for our rejection of God. In this ordeal—as well as in the ordeal of crucifixion—Jesus was our substitute.

Before He died, of course, Jesus and His Father were reconciled. Since Jesus had paid the full penalty for sin, death and hell, since His task was "finished" (John 19:30), He was reinstated into the family of God. "Father, into Thy hands I commend My spirit" were Jesus' last words (Luke 23:46), a description of the state of affairs between Him and the Father powerfully confirmed by Jesus' subsequent resurrection from the grave.

A Plea for Preaching the Full Literal Gospel

It is my plea in this chapter that we also talk about Jesus' suffering of hell for us in our presentation of the literal Gospel. So often in our preaching on the crucifixion, we appropriately point out that Christ was executed for our sins but then inappropriately fail to point out that He was also damned for those sins. We see men mistreating Jesus on Calvary, but we fail to see God forsaking His Son there. We see the blood, but we fail to see the hell. Frankly, I do not often find the fact of Christ's damnation in our behalf surfacing in sermons, theological articles, commentaries, or even dogmatics textbooks. Even when the subject does arise, the writer more often than not merely flirts with the fact or engages in euphemism.

Of the reasons for this omission I am not sure. In some cases, perhaps, it is the outcome of a gap in our theological training; seminary silence on the issue begets corresponding pulpit silence. In more cases it is the result of reticence or even a fear to call a spade a spade, a hell a hell, and a damnation a damnation. Says Dr. Francis Pieper:

> ...the question has been discussed whether or not, in the case of Christ's suffering, we may speak of His having endured the punishment or torments of hell. Bellarmine and other Roman Catholic dogmaticians have expressed dismay at this statement and have gone so far as to declare it an "intolerable wickedness" to ascribe to Christ the suffering of the torments of hell. Also timid Lutherans... have disapproved this statement. But their pretended piety has rightly been pronounced folly; for as surely as the wages of sin is not merely temporal death, but eternal punishment in hell, and as surely as Christ has borne all punishment of all sinners in the world, it is Scriptural to call Christ's suffering an enduring of the torments of hell.[7]

27

It does seem a dreadful thing to say that the Father damned His own Son—unless we simultaneously keep in mind the intense love for us that prompted both Father and Son in this ordeal; and unless we remember that to say God damned Jesus on the cross is not different in kind than to say God executed Jesus on the cross, but only different in degree. Further, how can one say it without offending people? They are not accustomed to such words as "hell" and "damned" coming from either preacher or pulpit, even though, given the right context, both words are legitimate, even good. Besides, can people actually comprehend the concept, even if we do succeed in saying it clearly without being crude, plainly without being offensive? Death, as we have seen, is in the realm of their experience, but damnation is not. People have seen people die, but they have not seen people damned. Thus, to say that Jesus died for us is more comprehensible than to say that He was damned for us.

Whatever the cause of our omission, I hope that the formula of literal Gospel-events we tap in our preaching will include Christ's literal damnation; that our résumé of Christ's saving acts will go something like this: His incarnation, His birth, His life, His circumcision, His baptism, His temptation in the wilderness, His ministry, His suffering, His *damnation*, His death, His resurrection, His ascension. To preach "the full Gospel," "the whole counsel of God," means to preach the Gospel occasionally, if not frequently, in terms of Jesus' damnation and reinstatement as well as in the more customary terms of His birth and life, His death and resurrection.

We can do so in the confidence that doing so is Biblical. Admittedly, the fact of Christ's damnation on the cross is more implied than directly stated in the Scriptures—but then so is the doctrine of the Trinity. Much as we might welcome in either case an explicit passage, in both instances the conclusion is inescapable when isolated Bible passages are brought together, when in the best hermeneutical tradition we interpret Scripture with Scripture, "comparing spiritual things with spiritual" (1 Cor. 2:13). Further, the Biblical words "die" and "death" often refer to hell as well as the grave, spiritual/eternal death as well as bodily death (Gen. 2:17; John 8:51; John 11:25-26; Eph. 2:1; and Rev. 2:10-11 being prime examples).[8] In the light of this fact such familiar passages as "The soul that sinneth, it shall die" (Ezek. 18:20) and "The wages of sin is death" (Rom. 6:23) suddenly take on added meaning. If the penalty for sin is death and hell, and if Christ suffered the penalty for sin, it then follows that Christ suffered death and hell. He tasted death in the fullest sense of the word, bodily *and* spiritual, death with a capital "D." On Him, on the cross, the deaths that we often (and frequently for legitimate reasons) put asunder, were joined together when He cried out, "My God, My God, why hast Thou forsaken Me?" This is not only logical; we can preach with the conviction that it is theological as well.

But preaching the full literal Gospel is not only Biblical. It is creative as well. Creative, literally, in that the verbalization of Christ's damnation is a part of that Gospel-account through which the Holy Spirit "creates" faith in our hearts and good works in our lives. Creative, obviously, because it is *news*—in light of the fact that it so seldom surfaces in contemporary preaching. Creative, psychologically, in that it enhances in the listener's emotional response to the Good News his appreciation of what Christ did for him. ("He not only died for me—He suffered hell for me! Oh, how wonderful!") Creative, finally, because it is foundational for the creative techniques discussed in the next two chapters.

A Model for Preaching the Full Literal Gospel

Before I discuss those subsequent creative techniques, however, there is value in demonstrating how to treat Christ's experience of hell on the cross homiletically. This is especially true since reluctance to preach this aspect of the literal Gospel may stem from insecurity about how to preach it precisely yet inoffensively. How can one present from the pulpit the damnation of Christ without being a sensationalist—when that news, however low-key and responsible the presentation, *is* sensational? Can one preach Christ's suffering of hell in our place creatively yet responsibly? The sermon excerpt below may prove helpful.[9]

> Matthew 26:56—"Then all the disciples forsook Him, and fled."
> Matthew 27:46—"And about the ninth hour Jesus cried with a loud voice, saying…My God, My God, why hast Thou forsaken me?"

Has it ever occurred to you how alone, how completely and utterly alone, Christ was in His passion-suffering? Our two texts focus our attention on His aloneness. The one text shows the disciples deserting Jesus; the other text shows even God the Father deserting Jesus. Together our texts paint this picture:

The God-Man Forsaken by God and Man Alike

In view of the fact that the disciples had been so close to Jesus for a period of three years, had witnessed His power, and had tasted His goodness, it would seem safe to assume that if Jesus were to experience some kind of trouble, the disciples could be counted upon to prove themselves friends in need.

But Jesus didn't assume it. He knew better. He knew human nature; as the Bible puts it, "He knew what was in man." At their last meal together He had shocked the disciples by announcing that one of them was going to betray Him to His enemies. A little later He had shocked the group again by predicting that all of them would desert Him when the time of crisis arrived.

It wasn't too long before things began to happen exactly as the Savior predicted. Jesus had taken Peter, James, and John with Him into the

Garden of Gethsemane, hoping that they would strengthen Him as He thought through the staggering task that lay before Him the following day. And what did Peter, James, and John do? Help Jesus? No! They fell asleep. A little later a band of soldiers invaded the privacy of Jesus' retreat in order to arrest Him, guided by, of all people, Judas, the treasurer of the disciples. He was a quisling, after all, just as Jesus had said. For a moment Peter acted big; he blundered around with his sword and made a general nuisance of himself. But when it became apparent that the Master was going to yield to these ruffians and not summon angels to His aid, Peter and the other disciples folded. They forsook Jesus and fled, we're told, right on schedule. Jesus had known what He was talking about, after all.

This desertion of Jesus by His closest friends is to us one of the most disappointing features of the passion story. Some of Jesus' mistreatment we might have expected. That the clergy of the day should try to frame Jesus, well, we can understand that, considering how often Jesus had stepped on their toes and showed them up for the frauds that they were. That Pontius Pilate should sacrifice an innocent man to political expediency, well, that doesn't shock us too much because we see plenty of this today, and that's the way politics can sometimes get. That the common people who loved Jesus should suddenly turn against Him and cry for His blood, well, that figures, for crowds have always been fickle. That the soldiers should maul Jesus and callously gamble for His clothing while He dies, well, soldiers are often a rough crowd. Even Judas we can understand. He had joined Jesus primarily for money and prestige, and we can accept the fact that 30 pieces of silver might make him a traitor. But that Jesus' most intimate friends should let Him down—that we don't understand. It comes as a blow to us. It must have come as a blow to the Savior, too.

But an even greater blow came the next day at Calvary. Surrounded by enemies, deserted by friends, it was then that Jesus turned to One He knew He could count on, God His Father, who more than once had publicly testified that this was His beloved Son in whom He was well pleased. Jesus had turned to Him many times before when He needed strength, and God had always been a very present help in trouble. Just the night before, in fact, Jesus had prayed to His Father in Gethsemane, and God had sent an angel to strengthen Him. Now, in the hour of His greatest need, Jesus turned to His loving Father once again. And God wasn't there! He was gone! He too had deserted Jesus. "My God, My God, why hast Thou forsaken Me?" Jesus cried out. If we are shocked that Jesus' disciples deserted the Savior, we are even more shocked that God His Father deserted Him. Never was a person more alone in trouble than our Lord; He was forsaken by God and man alike.

In a way it's unfair for me today to connect these two desertions. I have done so, of course, in order to show how completely alone Christ was in His passion suffering. But, really, it's not right. Because these two desertions stemmed from totally different causes. The disciples deserted Jesus because of cowardice, fickleness, disloyalty. But God had no such motive. There is nothing cowardly, fickle, disloyal about Him. If He deserts His Son, we can be sure that He has a good reason for doing so.

But I'm still being unfair. Having made clear that God's motives for deserting Jesus were pure, my words now seem to reflect on Jesus. For if God had a good reason for forsaking Jesus, then it would seem to follow that Jesus must have done something awful to deserve such treatment.

Yet that's not the case either. Jesus had done no wrong. The Scriptures are most emphatic in their claim that Jesus was totally without sin.

No, Jesus had done nothing awful. Nevertheless, there was something awful on Him. He had committed no sin, to be sure. Yet on the cross He was teeming with sin—our sins. Jesus in love had assumed those sins, and God in holiness had damned Him for those sins. He had accorded sin the punishment it deserves, that forsakenness of God which amounts to hell itself. I said before that God had a good reason for doing what He did. That's certainly correct. It was His goodness, in fact, His loathing for sin, that made Him desert Jesus the way He did. Not because Jesus had sinned, no; but because Jesus had our sins, that's why. Not because God didn't love Jesus, no; but because God so loved the world, that's why.

There is, then, a closer connection than we thought between the two desertions described this morning. You might say that the one desertion was responsible for the other. The disciples' forsaking Jesus, well, that was part of the problem of sin. That *was* sin; in fact, sin in the bare. What the disciples did after Jesus' capture in Gethsemane, deserting their Lord, was only another painful "for instance" of what they (and all people since Adam) had been doing all their lives, deserting God, ignoring Him, leaving Him out of their planning and thinking and living and going their own sweet way. As you might expect, there are consequences to such conduct. If people desert God, God must desert people. The only way He could avoid this "divine necessity" (if we dare call it that) was to place our sins on His own dear Son and desert Him in our place. That's exactly what God did, so great was His love for us. As I stated before, the one desertion caused the other. Mankind's desertion of God, symbolized by the disciples forsaking the Lord in Gethsemane, was responsible for the Father's desertion of Jesus on Calvary. It was the price the triune God had to pay to save us from our sins.

Because that desertion saves us, we are happy about it. Because God forsook Jesus He will never forsake us. Because Christ was alone, horribly and terribly alone, on a cross of long ago, you and I will never be alone, neither in this life nor the next. God will always be with us.

31

Chapter Two

Creativity Through More Frequent Use of Biblical Metaphors and Images of the Gospel

The Son of God became flesh, He lived about 33 years on our earth, He suffered hell and death on a cross, He rose again, He returned to heaven—these are the principal literal saving facts as the Scriptures present them.

In addition, the Bible frequently presents the Gospel-event metaphorically. It uses figures of speech, word pictures, images, rhetorical devices—in varying degrees of "metaphoricalness"—to describe the meaning and significance of Christ's saving acts. It will broaden our homiletical horizon and provide us a greater variety of ways to tell "the old, old story" if we become increasingly aware of these Biblical metaphors.

The Gospel-Event Itself Not a Metaphor.

A preliminary caution: The above does not mean that the Gospel-event itself is a metaphor. It isn't. It happened. It occurred in history. It's factual. It's actual. It's literal. There was a Jesus who was born and lived and died and rose again; this series of historical happenings is as capable of verification as any other historical happenings of equal antiquity. The birth and crucifixion of Jesus, for example, are as "real" and as "solid" as the Battle of Hastings and the defeat of the Spanish Armada. The neglect and/or denial of this truth is the heresy of our times. The ever present danger attending our otherwise legitimate metaphorical approach to the Gospel is to reduce to mere metaphors those *literal, utterly historical* Gospel-events that the Bible occasionally describes metaphorically. That is, we may conclude falsely that what the picture words are describing are themselves mere pictures. To illustrate, we may be tempted to treat the combination of metaphorical and literal Gospel that we find in the Bible as if it were an onion. If we regard the inner layers, the literal Gospel-events, as no more substantial than the outer layers, the metaphors for those Gospel-events, we peel them all away until we are left with nothing. The more appropriate procedure is to treat the combination of metaphorical and literal Gospel we find in the Bible as if it were an apple; we regard the metaphors for the Gospel-events as tasty, nutritious outer layers, but ultimately we arrive at a hard, irreducible core—the literal Gospel-events—which cannot be peeled away. While the Bible contains many word pictures richly descriptive of God's tender relationship with us, the Scriptural accounts of His Son's incarnation, life, death, resurrection, and ascension are *not* word pictures. They do not constitute a "pretty story" of how God feels about us. They are not mythological representations of God's state of mind. Rather, they are fact, very fact of very fact, historical not "made."

Why God Uses Gospel-Metaphors

Why does God use metaphors for the Gospel? Why doesn't He "just stick to the facts?"

My first reaction to this question is to look for the answer in the nature of language itself. In discussing the history of language, C. S. Lewis points out that "words did not start by referring merely to physical objects and then get extended by metaphor to refer to emotions, mental states and the like. On the contrary, what we now call the 'literal and metaphorical' meanings have both been disengaged by analysis from an ancient unity of meaning which was neither or both."[1] In short, our classifications "literal" and "metaphorical" are, like so many educationally helpful tools, partial oversimplifications. They are convenient categories, to be sure, but they are not mutually exclusive. As valuable as our awareness of this truth may be, however, we have no choice, once we are committed to language, but to employ the imprecise classifications as precisely as we can and to continue to discuss and use metaphor as if there were such an entity existing in a pure state and clearly distinguishable from its opposite, the literal. Even the most ardent literalist will find metaphor unavoidable. To quote Lewis again:

> But very often when we are talking about something which is not perceptible by the five senses we use words which, in one of their meanings, refer to things or actions that are. When a man says that he grasps an argument he is using a verb (*grasp*) which literally means to take something in the hands, but he is certainly not thinking that his mind has hands or that an argument can be seized like a gun. To avoid the word *grasp* he may change the form of expression and say, 'I see your point', but he does not mean that a pointed object has appeared in his visual field. He may have a third shot and

say, 'I follow you', but he does not mean that he is walking behind you along a road. Everyone is familiar with this linguistic phenomenon and the grammarians call it metaphor. But it is a serious mistake to think that metaphor is an optional thing which poets and orators may put into their work as a decoration and plain speakers can do without. The truth is that if we are going to talk at all about things which are not perceived by the senses, we are forced to use language metaphorically. Books on psychology or economics or politics are as continuously metaphorical as books of poetry or devotion. There is no other way of talking, as every philologist is aware.[2]

My point is that once God in His wisdom committed Himself to language as a means to communicate His saving love, He simultaneously committed Himself to the use of metaphor. When words are used, metaphor is inevitable. I hasten to add that this outcome is not at all unfortunate. It is cause for rejoicing. Our language is the richer for it. Metaphor helps rather than hinders communication. In brief, metaphor is a necessary good.

But there are even better, more helpful answers to the question why God uses metaphors for the Gospel. Though God has not told us His reasons, I believe that the God-conceived, God-executed, God-communicated plan of salvation for the human race is so colossal that it defies the capacity of language to contain it and to convey it. Hence, God pulls out all linguistic stops in order to convey it to human minds and human hearts. He comes at it from every possible angle. Although language is not equal to the beatific Gospel it describes, nevertheless it is the vehicle God chose to describe it, better, no doubt, than any other vehicle God might have chosen. So God exploits the medium He selected. He taps its maximum potential. Biblical metaphors, figures of speech, images, and rhetorical devices to communicate the Good News are the delightful outcome of God's mining the medium of language for all it is worth.

Not mutually exclusive from the reason just given is the supposition that God uses Gospel-metaphors in order to reach all kinds of people. What may not be effective on this particular person might be effective on another. Whereas a certain culture may be impervious to one approach, it may be open to another. At the risk of irreverence, I suggest that in using Gospel-metaphors God is employing an "if-this-doesn't-work-try-that" approach to human perception of His saving love. The Gospel-metaphor of the Good Shepherd or of the sacrificial Lamb may not be especially meaningful to us who are both centuries and miles away from shepherds and their flocks. But to a nomadic poeple "watching their flocks by night," to a culture steeped in the religious ritual of sacrificing lambs, such Gospel-metaphors were highly effective. The picture of salvation in terms of thirst-quenching water may not particularly move those of us who routinely take a drink of water from a nearby water fountain, perhaps even unconscious at the time of the thirst that impelled our action. But to desert-dwellers, ever on the lookout for water and ever hoping that the oasis they finally find will not prove to be a mirage, the water metaphor is certainly meaningful. A Gospel-metaphor that modern men and women can appreciate is the Biblical imagery of arbitration or mediation. When there is a labor strike nowadays, a mediation board negotiates between labor and management. When teachers threaten to walk out on the school administration that employs them, an arbitrator is appointed. For people accustomed to this kind of negotiation, the Biblical representation of Christ as the "mediator between God and men" is extremely valuable. To put it more reverently than earlier, I am suggesting that in His use of Gospel-metaphors God is being "all things to all men" that He "might by all means save some" (1 Cor. 9:22).

Whatever His reasons, the fact remains that in the Scriptures God describes the Gospel metaphorically as well as literally, and we are the richer for His having done so. Let us now look at some of these metaphors in detail. The list that follows is by no means complete and is intended as an appetizing sample rather than as an exhaustive analysis. Some of the metaphors and images overlap; they are not always mutually exclusive. Some of the examples cited are more clearly metaphorical than others. Finally, not all of them will be equally meaningful to the reader.

Metonymy and Synecdoche

I begin with a couple of instances that are so frequent in the Bible and so familiar to the Christian that most of us are unaware of their metaphorical aspects. (It seems to be a linguistic fact that if we use a metaphor long enough, we begin to regard it as literal.) My first example is from 1 Corinthians 1:18 and Ephesians 2:16, both of which highlight the role of "the cross" in God's plan of salvation and on the basis of which we often say, "We are saved *by the cross*." Meaningful as this statement is, we do not mean it literally. To be sure, the crucifixion is literal, no question about that! But we certainly do not mean to say that a particular piece of wood shaped like a cross is what saves us. (If we do mean that, then we start making pilgrimages to acquire "a true piece of the cross," or we start wearing a cross around our neck like a rabbit's foot.) Recast, our confession "We are saved by the cross" means "We are saved *by what happened on the cross.*" Our original statement is an instance of a common linguistic shorthand called metonymy, a device in which one thing stands for another. For instance, when we turn on our radio or television in the morning we may hear the newscaster say, "The White House announced this morning that the national deficit this year will be larger than anticipated." We don't exclaim, "What! The White House can't talk!" Rather, we understand what is meant, namely, that *the President* in the White House has made an announcement. "White House" is shorthand for "the President in the White House." One thing, a building, evokes an idea associated with that building, its customary occupant. Likewise, the cross evokes an idea associated with it: the crucifixion and damnation of our Lord.

My second example could be taken from any number of Bible passages, but 1 John 1:7 will serve the purpose. "The *blood* of Jesus Christ His Son cleanseth us from all sin" (emphasis added). To be sure, the blood of Jesus Christ was literally shed. (Nothing metaphorical about that. It happened, and it hurt, and it cost Him His life!) But in this passage the literal word "blood" is also being used metaphorically. The metaphorical device is called synecdoche, in which the part stands for the whole (or vice versa). For instance, the common nautical cry "All hands on deck!" means "All sailors on deck!" The part, "hand," stands for the whole, "sailor." (How tragic it would be if a sailor, not understanding everyday English usage, would take this order literally, lop off his hand, and heave it up on deck!) A more objectionable instance of synecdoche occurs frequently on television: "The program will continue after this word from our sponsor." "Word?" It always turns out to be "word*s*"—too many words. Again the part stands for the whole. So it is with the use of the word "blood" in the passage cited. The blood is just a part of the *total* sacrifice that Jesus made in our behalf in His suffering and damnation and death, a truth of which we are subtly reminded by the familiar words of the explanation to the Second Article of the Apostles' Creed: "who has redeemed me...with His holy, precious blood *and* with His innocent suffering and death" (emphasis added). But even though the blood is only a part of that total sacrifice Jesus underwent in our behalf, the usage of the word "blood" calls to mind that total sacrifice. One of the means of grace, the Lord's Supper, capitalizes on this particular Biblical metaphor. Although this sacrament too provides us with the literal blood of Christ "in, with, and under" the literal wine it supplies, that presentation graphically calls to mind the entire passion suffering and substitutionary sacrifice of our Lord.

Familiar Gospel-Metaphors

If it is the Lord's Supper that mines the blood metaphor for all it is worth, the other sacrament, Baptism, capitalizes on the next Biblical metaphor we will consider, namely, washing (e.g., Is. 1:18 and especially Titus 3:4-6). As water washes away dirt, so Baptism, because it encapsulates the Gospel-event, washes away our sin.[3] To be sure, our sins are literally removed, eliminated, from the sight of God. But to say that they are "washed away" is a metaphorical way of describing that literal phenomenon. (Frankly, it is hard to find an altogether literal way of describing the literal fact; even my words above, "removed" and "eliminated," are not entirely free of metaphor.) Nevertheless, "washing" is a superbly simple and graphic metaphor. Even a child reluctantly washing his hands before dinner can "redeem the occasion" by associating that unwelcome activity with the blessing of Christ's sacrifice on the cross, the washing away of our sins.

Overlapping with the blood metaphor is the lamb metaphor. The Bible often portrays Jesus as the lamb sacrificed for our sins (e.g., Is. 53:7; 1 Peter 1:18-19). Since in the act of sacrificing the lamb blood is shed, the two metaphors are not mutually exclusive. Again we need to distinguish carefully between what is literal and what is metaphorical. The sacrifice that Jesus made is literal, but, of course, He is not a lamb—that is metaphor. Here for the first time in our list we have no trouble recognizing a metaphor as a metaphor. The incarnation means that Jesus became literal man, not literal lamb. Some of us may find it difficult to preach on the lamb metaphor, not merely because it is alien to our contemporary experience, but also because the metaphor has become homiletically hackneyed. Yet what an ecstatic moment that must have been in the history of God's chosen people when John the Baptist identified an approaching stranger on the banks of the Jordan River with "Behold the Lamb of God, which taketh away the sin of the world" (John 1:29). Suddenly the hopes and aspirations associated with all the years of repeated sacrifice of lambs found their fulfillment.

To position the next Gospel-metaphor—Jesus as the Good Shepherd (e.g., Ps. 23; John 10:1-16)—right after discussion of the lamb metaphor may appear to be "mixing" the metaphors. The Bible confronts us with both of these metaphors, not to "mix" them, but to capture two different facets of God's relationship with us through Christ. The lamb metaphor accents the purity and meekness of Christ as well as His sacrificial death. The shepherd metaphor accents the tender concern and protective leadership of Christ. Despite their different emphases, the two metaphors do have something in common: the sacrificial death of Jesus in our behalf. John 10:11 reminds us that the shepherd, like the lamb, "giveth his life for the sheep."

Gospel-Metaphors with Universal Application

Less alien to our largely urban society than the sheep and shepherd metaphors are the food and water metaphors for the Gospel. After all, hunger and thirst are universal needs.

Nowhere does the Bible make fuller use of the food metaphor for the Gospel than in the sixth chapter of John's gospel. The high spot of this chapter is Jesus' assertion, "I am the bread of life: he that cometh to Me shall never hunger" (v. 35). Note that this claim is made right after the feeding of the five thousand, at a time when the people were naturally thinking of bread. Be it reverently said, Jesus "exploits" the situation; He presents the Gospel to these people in the metaphor of bread. Jesus' procedure in this incident provides an obvious precedent for pastors today in their ministry, namely, to present the Gospel as much as possible in terms of their listeners' situation and understanding. In this instance Jesus has not only supplied us with an additional metaphor to enrich our Gospel-preaching but has also given us a practical homiletical tip on how to use it.

There are three unique values in the Gospel-metaphor of food. First, it implies the dual life dimension of the Christian experience. In becoming Christians we receive from God a kind of life *additional to* the bodily life we have also received from Him (through our parents). That additional life is the life of God. Every Christian enjoys *two* kinds of life, bodily and spiritual. Truly he is born and then "born again" (John 3:3-6). Endowed with two kinds of life, it stands to reason that a Christian needs *two* kinds of food or "bread." He needs bread to sustain his bodily life, a need that God is well aware of since He Himself has urged us to pray, "Give us this day our daily bread." But as Jesus made clear during His temptation in the wilderness, man cannot live by bread alone (Matt. 4:4). To sustain his spiritual life he needs "the Bread of Life," Jesus Himself, as He is offered through means of grace.

This is the second unique value in the Gospel-metaphor of food: it tells us something about the character of the means of grace (Baptism, the Lord's Supper, and the spoken Word). They do more than inform us—they feed us. They do more than give information, ideas, concepts, and principles—they impart life. The means of grace are the means of life. This is vividly clear in the Lord's Supper. We usually associate life with the ingredients of food and drink and with the activities of eating and drinking. That is precisely what we have in the Lord's Supper: the ingredients of food and drink (bread-body and wine-blood) and the activities of eating and drinking. The Lord's Supper makes it especially clear that in all the means of grace we are absorbing not merely ideas but primarily spiritual life and nourishment.

This same accent surfaces to a surprising degree even in the spoken Word. Despite the verbal, intellectual character of the spoken Word, despite its obvious association with information, ideas, concepts, and principles, it is interesting to notice how often the Bible describes the spoken Word in images of food and/or life. Some examples: "Thy words were found, and I did eat them" (Jer. 15:16); "Man shall not live by bread alone, but by every word that proceedeth out of the mouth of God" (Matt. 4:4); "Of His own will begat He us with the word of truth" (James 1:18); "As newborn babes, desire the sincere milk of the word, that ye may grow thereby" (1 Peter 2:2); "And I took the little book out of the angel's hand, and ate it up; and it was in my mouth sweet as honey; and as soon as I had eaten it; my belly was bitter" (Rev. 10:10). Add to this list of Bible passages a familiar prayer of the church: "Blessed Lord, who has caused all Holy Scriptures to be written for our learning, grant that we may in such wise hear them, read, mark, learn, and inwardly *digest* them…" (emphasis added).

38   The third unique value in the Gospel-metaphor of food has been

implicit in the discussion of the other two values: it clarifies the nature of Christian faith. Christian faith is not merely information about, understanding of, and agreement with an idea or belief or philosophy or set of rules or code of principles. It is more than that; it is a *life,* a throbbing, pulsating life. It is alive, dynamic, intimate, involving us emotionally as well as intellectually, permeating not just our head but our whole being. Indeed, Jesus once likened believing in Him to eating and drinking Him and added that apart from such believing "ye have no *life* in you" (John 6:53, emphasis added). Striking as is this way of describing our faith relationship with the Lord we love, it is not so farfetched when we consider that a parent sometimes says of a child, "I love him so much that I could eat him up."

The water metaphor, though obviously more meaningful to nomadic man miles away from a desert oasis than to modern man mere steps away from a water cooler in the hall, is still useful today, for thirst is a universal need. This metaphor is surprisingly frequent in the Old Testament (e.g., Ps. 36:8; 46:4; 65:9; Is. 43:19; Ezek. 47:1-12). In the New Testament it is coupled with the food metaphor in the sixth chapter of John's gospel (e.g., v. 35) and is especially prominent in our Lord's conversation with the woman at the well in John 4:1-30. Once again notice our Lord's wisdom in adapting His presentation of the Gospel to the specific needs of the individual in question. Drawing water may have been a daily chore for this woman. What does Jesus do? He presents the Gospel to her in the metaphor of water. "Whosoever drinketh of this water shall thirst again: But whosoever drinketh of the water that I shall give him shall never thirst; but the water that I shall give him shall be in him a well of water springing up into everlasting life" (John 4:13-14). Salvation is a water that not only relieves immediate thirst but also provides permanent satisfaction. This is an attractive and economical metaphor, for it says so much with so little and says it well besides. With its wealth of theology expressed in non-theological language, the precedent for creative preaching is obvious.

In earlier discussion of the washing metaphor I pointed out how the water of Baptism dramatizes the significance of that particular metaphor. The water of Baptism also dramatizes the significance of the metaphor under consideration here. Even as water satisfies thirst and sustains life, so Baptism, because of the Gospel-event it encapsulates, satisfies our spiritual thirst and sustains in us the life of God. "For by one Spirit we are all baptized into one body...and have been all made to *drink* into one Spirit" (1 Cor. 12:13, emphasis added).

There is a common sermon illustration that somehow has remained effective despite its commonness, an illustration that gets homiletical mileage out of the water metaphor. It relates as follows: On account of their sins all people were dying of spiritual thirst, and there was no water of salvation available; the reservoir of salvation, so to speak, was empty, bone-dry. But Christ came and by His saving acts replenished the reservoir of salvation.

Thanks to Him there was now an abundance of water in the reservoir for everybody, not only enough to go around but plenty to spare. Yet the people are still dying of spiritual thirst because they have no ability to obtain the water of salvation so abundantly available. So God's goodness goes farther: having already replenished the reservoir with water, He now pipes the water as well. The Holy Spirit is His agent; the means of grace are the pipes. The water of salvation is channeled directly to individual people. Still the process threatens to break down because each individual needs to turn on the faucet if he is to drink, but he neither wishes nor is able to do this. Nevertheless, God's goodness goes farther still: through the agency of the Holy Spirit and the instrumentality of the means of grace, He persuades and enables the individual to turn on the faucet and drink—and live forever.

Gospel-Metaphors Especially Appropriate to Contemporary Man

The fact that "whatsoever things were written aforetime were written for *our* learning" (Rom. 15:4, emphasis added) is especially evident in the next two metaphors we consider: mediation and covenant. These are uniquely effective for modern man. Since these two concepts are a peculiar blend of literal and metaphorical elements, it is perhaps more accurate to speak of them as Gospel-images rather than as Gospel-metaphors. What we have here are literal truths conveyed through the language of negotiation and contract. The old contract (the first covenant between God and man) has been broken by man. His sin has nullified that contract. The party of the first part (God) and the party of the second part (people) are at odds with each other. Enter Jesus, the Mediator (1 Tim. 2:5), who arbitrates between the two parties. He reconciles them (2 Cor. 5:18; Eph. 2:14). By His atonement on the cross He effects "at-one-ment." As a result, God gives us a new contract or covenant, which is even better than the first (Luke 22:20; Heb. 8:6 and 9:15). Mediation leads to contract; there is a cause and effect relationship between the two images. The very structure of our Bible reflects these Gospel-images; there is an "Old Testament" (i.e., an "Old Contract") and a "New Testament" (i.e., a "New Contract"). To put it in contemporary political terminology, through Jesus God has given us "a new deal." To a society steeped in the process of arbitration and contract negotiation, the Biblical cause and effect Gospel-images of mediation and covenant are most meaningful and effective.

Gospel-Images for Justification and Sanctification

Closely associated with the legal language of negotiation and contract is the legal language of the courtroom so often used in the Bible to describe the Gospel-event and its significance, what theologians call "forensic justification." While by no means exclusive to Paul, the metaphor is a Pauline favorite (e.g., Rom. 8:1, 33; 2 Cor. 5:19). Here again the language used defies precise classification. The Gospel-truth communicated, our Jesus-given new status with God, is hard, tangible fact, but that fact is conveyed to us through courtroom imagery. We are the prisoner before the bar. We have committed heinous crimes. We are guilty, guilty as sin, and we can enter no other plea. God, the righteous judge, is about to declare us guilty and sentence us to eternal death. But Jesus is our lawyer, our advocate (1 John 2:1), who pleads for us. He breaks precedent and goes farther in His effort to save us than any lawyer has ever been known to do. He not only takes our part—He takes our place. He assumes our guilt and shoulders our sentence. He wins acquittal for us. God declares us righteous —and our lawyer guilty. God sets us free—and bundles our lawyer off to the place of execution.

What is so valuable about this approach to the Gospel-event is that it clarifies precisely what saves us and what does not. Our eternal salvation depends upon an alien righteousness rather than upon our own. It depends upon a righteousness credited to us by God on account of Jesus rather than upon a righteousness manufactured by us or in us. The Bible is doubly insistent in showing that good works do not save; it points out that neither our self-manufactured good works nor *even* the good works God Himself manufactures in us through the Holy Spirit can save. God, to be sure, is interested in the production of good works in us, so interested that that is one of the reasons He sent Jesus to our earth. But these good works are not a cause of salvation; rather, they are a product of it. God *declares* us righteous through Christ, and He *makes* us righteous in Christ. Both of these stirring facts are true, but our eternal salvation is entirely accomplished the moment God has declared us righteous. The minute He *says* it is so, it *is* so—no matter how guilty we are (from our point of view) at the time He says it. (Remember who it was to whom Jesus said, "Today shalt thou be with Me in paradise.") The beauty of the courtroom imagery for the Gospel-event is that it sharply distinguishes between justification and sanctification.

If the previous Gospel-imagery clarifies where good works do not belong, namely, in the area of salvation, the Gospel-imagery we turn to now clarifies where good works *do* belong, namely, in every aspect of our lives. The images I have in mind are those of redemption and ransom (e.g., Matt. 20:28; 1 Cor. 6:19-20; 1 Peter 1:18-19). How these images accent the significance of good works for everyday life will become clear in the remaining paragraphs of this section.

Both the redemption and the ransom images for the Gospel are instances of highly metaphorical language being nudged toward literalness through frequent and habitual usage. Although the connotations of the two images are slightly different—those of "ransom" being more negative, suggesting that a "kidnapping" has taken place—they have enough in common with each other to justify my treating them together. Both "redeem" and "ransom" suggest a purchase price paid to recover property. It is interesting to note that in its translation of 1 Peter 1:18-19 the Revised Standard Version has substituted the word "ransom" for the word "redeem" used in the King James Version. This substitution suggests that even in the minds of Bible translators the two words are practically interchangeable. Thus, to say that Christ has "redeemed" us—or "ransomed" us—is to say in either case that we are the property for which He has paid the purchase price of damnation and death.

Even more important than the "togetherness" of the redemption and the ransom images is the "togetherness" of God's justification and sanctification goals for us. As we saw in our consideration of courtroom imagery, the Bible often distinguishes sharply between justification and sanctification, between faith and good works, in order to clarify precisely that we are saved only through the former. But just as often the Bible presents justification and sanctification as a unity, as two equivalent thrusts of one divine plan, in order to show that God's work is one even as He is one, to keep before our minds the importance of good works to God, and to demonstrate the interdependence of saving faith and good works in the Christian life.

Where the one is, the other must also be. Even though we are saved through faith, and through faith alone, yet "faith without works is dead"—in short, is not faith. While it is true that faith is cause and good works result, yet a greater than a cause-effect relationship is here. They are an entity, two sides of the same God-given coin. Note, for instance, the interchangeableness of faith and good works in Romans 10:9-10. In verse 10 Paul reverses the order in which he presents them in verse 9, and even more surprisingly his first order is not the logical or systematic one—he puts result before cause, the cart before the horse! Titus 2:14 says that Christ "gave Himself for us, that He might redeem us from all iniquity, and purify unto Himself a peculiar people, zealous of good works." Notice how this passage not only equates God's justification and sanctification goals but also mentions them in the same breath. These goals are a unity, two aspects of one divine mission.

The redemption and ransom images for the Gospel capture this unity. They "put Humpty-Dumpty back together again." True, they do this not overtly or directly, but implicitly. Why does one redeem or ransom property, like a field, for example? To recover or salvage it, to be sure. But more than that: to improve the property, to clear it of litter and refuse, to cultivate it and make it bear fruit. Both goals, salvaging and fruit-bearing, are implicit in the purchase of the property. Likewise, God's justification and sanctification goals for us are implicit in His purchase of us through Christ. God buys us so that we might be saved and so that we might do good works. Because the redemption and ransom images imply both of these goals and present them as equivalent aspects of one divine plan, they assign good works a significant role in Christian living. Like our salvation—which they never effect but which they always accompany—our good works are a major thrust of God's eternal design. They decidedly belong in every dimension of our life.

Waning Gospel-Metaphors Worth Salvaging

Next let us consider three Gospel-images rapidly waning in contemporary usage. The first of these is what has been called the "classic" presentation of the atonement (e.g., Gen. 3:15; Luke 11:21-22; 22:53; Col. 1:12-13). The "classic" approach pictures our salvation primarily in terms of an epic, cosmic, cataclysmic struggle between "two mighty opposites":[4] the antagonist, Satan, representing the kingdom of darkness, and the protagonist, Jesus, representing the kingdom of light.[5] The plan of salvation is more than a matter between a holy, loving God and a sinful, rebellious people. The devil is involved too. (I suspect it is forgetfulness of the devil that is largely responsible for contemporary disuse of the "classic" approach to the Gospel.) The plan of salvation involves a struggle bigger than any one of us. It began long before we appeared on the scene, and mopping up operations will continue long after our earthly exit. It is a struggle outside our self and outside our planet. John Milton's *Paradise Lost* and John Bunyan's *Pilgrim's Progress* are literary representations of the Bible's "classic" depiction of the atonement. J. R. R. Tolkien's *Lord of the Rings* trilogy and C. S. Lewis' space trilogy and *Chronicles of Narnia* are recent attempts to revive modern awareness of the epic struggle between God and Satan for the prize of the human soul and have done much to reduce that forgetfulness of the devil so dangerous to contemporary society.

It is certain that the Lord Jesus never lost sight of Satan as His principal antagonist. When the motley crew of soldiers drew near to arrest Him in Gethsemane, Jesus looked beyond them. He looked beyond the quisling, Judas, who had guided them, and beyond the conniving churchmen, Annas and Caiaphas, who had sent them out. They were not the enemy—at least not the ultimate one. Satan was. It was he who was pulling the strings, using as puppets rather than partners the human participants in Jesus' passion suffering, and Jesus clearly identified him. "This is your hour," Jesus cried, "and the power of darkness" (Luke 22:53). As the passion hours wore on the showdown between Jesus and Satan intensified, climaxing on the cross when Jesus cried out, "My God, My God, why hast Thou forsaken Me?" Satan must have "rejoiced in iniquity" and twitched his tail in glee at that moment when it appeared that civil war had broken out in the camp of his adversary and that God's house was divided against itself. Perhaps symbolic of this "apparent" victory for the kingdom of darkness was the phenomenal darkness that covered the earth during Jesus' crucifixion. In accordance with ancient prophecy (Gen. 3:15) Satan was truly bruising Jesus' heel. But Satan was forgetting the remainder of that prophecy,

43

namely, that his own head was about to be crushed, that he would be bested in this epic confrontation, that his momentary gain would prove to be his ultimate undoing. For through this "heel-wounding" ordeal Jesus delivered the whole human race from the bondage of Satan, and by His powerful resurrection from the grave Jesus became the victor in His classic conflict with the prince of darkness.

Two values of homiletical import accrue from a fuller understanding of this partly literal and partly metaphorical "classic" representation of the atonement. One is a greater appreciation for the doctrine of Christ's descent into hell. On occasion we may be tempted to view the ecumenical creeds as according that doctrine a degree of importance out of proportion to the rather minimal Scriptural treatment of it. But given the "classic" presentation of the atonement, the doctrine of Christ's descent into hell clearly "belongs" and "makes sense." If indeed Jesus and Satan have "squared off" in mighty battle, a battle whose issue seemed momentarily in doubt when Satan was bruising Jesus' heel on Calvary, it is "meet, right, and salutary" that when Jesus' powerful resurrection to life crushed Satan's head our Lord travel to the camp of the enemy to apprise him of his defeat. In the afterglow of His triumphant return to life, it was fitting for Jesus to inform Satan and his damned crew that He had won the battle and that God had accomplished His mission.

The other value of the "classic" representation of the atonement is an increased appreciation of the role of prayer and of God's Word in Christian experience. The origin of "the human predicament" is ultimately outside our self and outside our planet. While our sinful flesh is an enormous part of our problem, it is by no means the whole of our problem. Satan has a hand in it too. "We wrestle not against flesh and blood, but against principalities, against powers, against the rulers of the darkness of this world" (Eph. 6:12). Likewise, the solution to our problem is ultimately outside our self and outside our planet. There is more to salvation than "finding one's self," achieving self-awareness, or making a trip to a counselor's office or a psychiatrist's couch. Helpful as these practices may be, ultimately we must lift up our eyes unto the hills from whence cometh our help and remind ourselves that our help cometh from the Lord, who made heaven and earth (Ps. 121:1-2). The realization will impel us to prayer, to resort to that vehicle that has traveled to outer space long before the advent of space technology, to go beyond our self and our world and through prayer tap the power of Him who rules the worlds. Further, the realization will impel us to listen with ever increasing fervency to that message from outer space, also predating space technology, the very Word of God, which alone can provide the help we so desperately need.

The second in the group of Gospel-images waning in contemporary usage is the Second Adam image. Occasionally the Bible presents Christ as if He were another Adam, a "second" Adam, but a better and more effective

Adam than the first one. Both are representative men; what each does individually affects the human race collectively. Sometime after his creation the first Adam was tempted by Satan, succumbed, and sinned. The consequences were devastating—and universal. In, with, and under Adam's sin, we sinned and acquired the capacity for further sin. In, with, and under Adam's guilt, we were guilty. In, with, and under Adam's death, we died. Centuries later another Adam appeared on the scene, Christ Jesus, and repaired the ruins made by the first Adam. Like the first Adam, He was tempted by Satan, but He triumphed. The results were blessed—and again universal. In, with, and under His victory, we are victorious. In, with, and under His righteousness, we are righteous (Rom. 5:19). In, with, and under His resurrection, we shall be resurrected (1 Cor. 15:21-22). The Second Adam gives us a fresh start and, in effect, pulls us along with Him. By His power we hop onto His bandwagon. "If any man be in Christ, he is a new creature: old things are passed away; behold, all things are become new" (2 Cor. 5:17).[6]

The third in the group of the Gospel-images waning in contemporary usage is the "name" metaphor. Periodically the Bible claims that it is the "name" of Jesus that saves. "There is none other name under heaven given among men, whereby we must be saved" (Acts 4:12). "Whosoever shall call upon the name of the Lord shall be saved" (Rom. 10:13). In this instance the reason for the declining usage is clearer than in the previous two cases. The slippage is largely the result of linguistic changes beyond our control. There was a time when people immediately understood the Bible passages just cited. Today those passages may puzzle us at first. "What's in a name?" we may be tempted to ask facetiously.[7] For today a name is primarily a tag by which we differentiate one person from another. But such was not always the case. Years ago a name involved one's honor, reputation, integrity, personality, ancestry, and descendants. Years ago a name was something one staked his life on, took oaths on, or fought duels over. Often a name reflected one's vocation. Modern names like "Smith," "Miller," and "Sawyer" are vestigal testimonies to this fact.

So it is with the name of God. It involves His whole person: His nature, His character, etc. When Moses asked God what he should tell the Israelites concerning who had sent him, God replied, "I AM THAT I AM... Thus shalt thou say unto the children of Israel, I AM hath sent me unto you" (Ex. 3:14). The name of God involves also His function, His vocation if you will. The angel said to Joseph concerning the child to which Mary was to give birth: "Thou shalt call His name JESUS: for He shall save His people from their sins" (Matt. 1:21). We have already discussed how one of Jesus' names, "the Word," demonstrated His function from eternity toward God His Father, namely, that of revealing and describing Him. In the light of the foregoing Gospel insights that the "name" metaphor supplies, it is evident that pulpit use of it is worth revival. If the preacher is careful to remove the initial bewilderment that it may cause his listeners, he will discover that this metaphor will do much to freshen his presentation of the Gospel.

A Useful Gospel-Metaphor Seldom Used

What distinguishes the next Biblical metaphor for the Gospel from the previous three (characterized by declining usage) is its almost total neglect in the history of preaching, past and present alike. That Gospel-metaphor is the picture of Christ as the Bridegroom and of the church as His bride. The continual homiletical disregard of this metaphor for the communication of the Gospel is surprising, not only because of the frequency of the metaphor in the Bible (e.g., Ps. 45; Song of Sol.; Is. 61:10; 62:5; Jer. 3; Ezek. 23; much of Hosea; the parables of the 10 virgins and the king's marriage feast; the well-known passage on marriage in Eph. 5:22-33; and numerous instances in Rev.) but also because of the remarkable usefulness of the metaphor.

Christ is the Bridegroom and we become His bride. "With His cross He us weds." What is so valuable about this metaphor is the wealth of theological truth it so economically conveys. To begin with, the Bridegroom-bride metaphor evokes a truth central to our faith: it is Christ who takes the initiative in our relationship with Him. In the conduct of courtship and marriage in contemporary society, it may no longer be the case that the bridegroom is the initiator and that the bride plays a largely passive role. But society still pays lip service to the convention that it is the bridegroom who does the courting and wooing and asking. Certainly this is the case with Christ and us; in this instance the convention holds. "Ye have not chosen Me, but I have chosen you" (John 15:16). "Herein is love, not that we loved God, but that He loved us" (1 John 4:19).

Further, the Bridegroom-bride metaphor connotes the intimacy of our relationship with Him. In human perception there are few relationships more intense and more tender than the love between a newly married man and woman. The love between Christ and us is similarly intense and tender, only more so.

It is common knowledge that in marrying someone we marry his or her family too. To love our spouse means to love them. So it is in our relationship with Christ, our Bridegroom. To love Him means to love His family: every snob on the hill and every bum in the gutter, the politician afar off and the inlaw close at hand. "If a man say, I love God, and hateth his brother, he is a liar" (1 John 4:20). Our vertical relationship with Christ automatically involves us in a horizontal relationship with people. On Judgment Day our Husband will remind us that to have loved Him during our earthly life meant that we loved His family too. "Inasmuch as ye have done it unto one of the least of these My brethren, ye have done it unto Me" (Matt. 25:40).

Finally, the Bridegroom-bride metaphor implies the reality of eternal bliss in heaven. When two people marry, it is their expectation that they will "live happily ever after." To be sure, even under the most ideal conditions we recognize that this wish is hyperbolic because the marriage relationship ends at death. But there is no danger of hyperbole when we associate the wish with our marriage to Christ. In *that* marriage we do indeed "live happily ever after." There is no "until death do you part" clause; in fact, death only intensifies and solidifies the relationship between us and our Bridegroom.

The especially remarkable feature of the Bridegroom-bride metaphor is its economy. It conveys maximum meaning with minimum words. Many substantive truths of our theology are implicit in the metaphor, subtly conveyed to the listener in the speaking of the metaphor and unconsciously absorbed by him in the hearing of it.

The Clothing Metaphor

Often associated with the Bridegroom-bride metaphor for the Gospel is the clothing metaphor. The bride adorns herself for the wedding, and her exotic wardrobe is the gift of the Bridegroom (e.g., Is. 61:10; Rev. 21:2). Equally often, the clothing metaphor is associated with the washing metaphor, just as in everyday life getting dressed is a predictable sequel to getting washed. We even frequently associate the two activities in our speech; the combination "washed and dressed" is an idiomatic phrase. So the Christian after having his sins washed away in Baptism gets dressed with Christ (e.g., Gal. 3:26-27). Sometimes the clothing metaphor appears by itself, independent of either the wedding or the washing imagery (e.g., Zech. 3:3-4; Rom. 13:14).

Whether the clothing metaphor appears in conjunction with another metaphor or on its own, its value is delightfully obvious. It provides an economical way of communicating a crucial aspect of the Gospel, namely, that we are saved by an alien rather than by an indigenous righteousness. It is not our own goodness but rather the goodness of Christ with which God garbs us that makes us right with God. "Jesus, Thy blood and righteousness/My beauty are, my glorious dress" is the way a familiar hymn puts it. A common prayer for communicants requests Jesus to "take off from them the spotted garment of the flesh and of their own righteousness, and adorn them with the garment of the righteousness purchased with Thy blood." It was the failure to put on this garment of Christ's righteousness that got a guest into trouble in one of our Lord's parables (Matt. 22:11-14). Might there not even be a foreshadowing of our need for God's garbing us in Christ's righteousness in the fact that God, following the fall of man into sin, made coats of skin for Adam and Eve *after* their own awkward attempts to cover their nakedness with fig leaves? (Compare Gen. 3:7 with Gen. 3:21.)[8]

The Apostle John's Contribution

It is the apostle John who provides us with some of our favorite Gospel-metaphors. Besides his accent on Jesus as the Word, the Lamb of God, and the Good Shepherd (already discussed), he supplies the unique metaphors of Jesus as the highway to heaven (John 14:6), the door to eternal life (John 10:9), the vine by which we bear fruit (John 15:5), and even as a variety of magnet drawing all men unto Himself (John 12:32).

What is helpful about these designations is that they are clearly metaphors. We have no trouble recognizing them as word pictures, a recognition difficult in some of the previous metaphors discussed. Not even the most ardent literalist is in danger of interpreting the incarnation to mean that Jesus became a door or a vine!

What is even more helpful about these metaphors supplied by John is their attractive economy. The door and highway metaphors accent the exclusivity of Jesus as the entrance and way to heaven—a cardinal Christian truth, but expressed apart from abstract, theological-sounding language. The vine metaphor says in a phrase or two what often requires paragraphs in our sermons, namely, that we need the power of the Gospel as much for sanctification as for justification; that we do good works "by grace alone" as well as get saved "by grace alone."

Old Testament Metaphors for the Gospel

It should come as no surprise that the Old Testament, in keeping with the concreteness and vividness of its language, should supply us with a host of Gospel-metaphors. Besides the ritualistic use of a scapegoat (Lev. 16:7-10), so rich in vicarious implications, and the frequency of the "branch" and "root" metaphors (Is. 11:1; Zech. 3:8), so closely allied to the vine metaphor already presented, the Old Testament books picture God as our rock (Ps. 31:3), our fortress (Ps. 71:3), our tower and our shelter (Ps. 61:3), our keeper and our shade (Ps. 121:5), our shield, buckler, and horn of salvation (Ps. 18:2), our city (Ps. 48), our home (Ps. 90), our refuge and the everlasting arms underneath us (Deut. 33:27), an eagle whose wings bear us up (Ex. 19:4) and cover us with feathers (Ps. 91:4) and under which we take refuge (Ps. 57:1).

Plainly these metaphors are too numerous to discuss in detail. Let me take just one of them, that of God as an eagle with its supportive and protective wings and feathers, and briefly comment on its homiletical potential. Given an awareness of this Old Testament metaphor, the preacher suddenly has an "Aha!" experience when in his New Testament reading he encounters the wistful cry of Jesus over Jerusalem: "O Jerusalem, Jerusalem, thou that killest the prophets, and stonest them which are sent unto thee, how often I have gathered thy children together, even as a hen gathereth her chickens under her wings, and ye would not!" (Matt. 23:37). Richly suggestive in its own right of the tender love of Jesus, the New Testament metaphor of the hen becomes doubly effective when coupled with the familiar Old Testament metaphor of the eagle. The combination reassures us that Jesus is indeed "the same yesterday, and to day, and for ever" (Heb. 13:8). Here is not only a creative sermon idea but also a powerful tribute to the unity of the Old and New Testaments.[9]

Chapter Three

Creativity Through the Use of Gospel-Handles

In this chapter I introduce the concept of the "Gospel-handle." As far as I know, the term is my own coinage. If the phrase itself is not original, at least the specific meaning I have attached to it is. While there are no books or articles dealing with the subject, I have discovered creative preachers now and then using Gospel-handles without being aware of either the term or what it is specifically they are doing. What I have done is given a name to a practice that comes more or less naturally to preachers with a capacity for creativity.

What is a "Gospel-handle"? A "Gospel-handle" involves the selection from a Biblical sermon text of a word (or words) which in itself contains no Gospel but which is used as an approach, transition, or handle to an account of the Gospel outside the text. Often the Gospel-handle is a prominent expression in the Biblical sermon text which stands out in the listener's memory, perhaps because of its unusualness or repetition. The preacher, then, exploits that word, using the listener's consciousness of the word and nudging him toward the Gospel. He takes the listener "where he's at" to get at the Gospel. Thus the use of a Gospel-handle need not be contrived; if anything, it is a "natural" transition to the Gospel in that it gets to the Gospel via a bridge already built into the listener's mind. Insofar as the word or words used are from the text, the practice is textual, but insofar as the account of the Gospel employed is outside the text, the practice is non-textual.

Certain assumptions that I consider valid and important lie behind this definition—and behind the use of Gospel-handles. These assumptions are so inextricably interwoven that it is difficult to separate them from one another and present them in proper sequence. One assumption is that if a given Biblical sermon text contains no Gospel (a rare occurrence, incidentally), the preacher must import the Gospel from elsewhere in the Bible. This assertion involves another assumption, namely, that *the main business of preaching is to preach the Gospel.* When a preacher expounds a Biblical text, he does so not merely to expound that particular text, but, above all, to proclaim the Gospel. Bible-preachers are basically Gospel-preachers; in their weekly preaching they continually use *a* word of the Scriptures to get at *the* Word of the Scriptures, Jesus Christ Himself. It is bad if a preacher fails to preach his text, but it is even worse if he fails to preach the Gospel. To use theological jargon, a preacher must be committed to the Scriptures as the formal principle of his theology and to the Gospel as the material principle. But his commitment to the formal principle is not an end in itself; it is a means to an end. That commitment exists so that the preacher might facilitate his commitment to the material principle, the Gospel. Finally, behind all these assertions is the assumption that our Lord Jesus Himself supplied us with the cardinal hermeneutical principle, the chief rule of Biblical interpretation, when He said, "Search the Scriptures... they are they which testify of Me" (John 5:39).

Why use Gospel-handles? For three reasons: (1) to get to the Gospel when the Biblical sermon text itself contains little or no Gospel; (2) to provide an alternate approach to the Gospel in an overly familiar text; and (3) to provide within the same sermon "extra" Gospel in addition to that explicitly supplied by the text.

Admittedly, the device is a two-edged sword. It can be harmful as well as helpful, depending upon how one employs the technique. Usage of the device can be irresponsible or tasteless, but it need not be. Given loyalty to the Scriptures, enthusiasm for the Gospel, a desire to help people, and a reasonable skill with words, the preacher can use Gospel-handles "to the glory of God and the welfare of people," and he will find the device homiletically productive.

What are the possible weaknesses or dangers in the use of Gospel-handles? The principal one is contrivance, that is, manipulating the sermon text by forcing it to say something it does not. While one might be tempted to argue that the end justifies the means, that manipulating a text to arrive at the Gospel is the very stuff of preaching, still one must practice responsible exegesis. Therefore, it is desirable in the use of Gospel-handles to avoid both contrivance itself and the appearance of contrivance. One of the most common forms of contrivance is allegorizing, in which the literal meaning of Scripture is considered secondary to its deeper, mystical meaning. Careful and skillful use of words can usually avert the charge of allegorizing. That is, instead of saying that a given word or phrase in a Biblical text "means," "stands for," or "symbolizes" a specific Gospel truth, the preacher rather says that a given word or phrase in a text "calls to mind," "reminds him of," or "suggests" a specific Gospel truth. Instead of making claims, the preacher makes connections. I am not implying that the solution to the problem rests on a mere verbal technicality. The solution ultimately lies in the God-given sanctification of the preacher himself. The preacher, given such sanctification, will struggle to find those words to communicate the glorious Gospel of the Scriptures without violating the particularity of the text under consideration. He will be creative without being irresponsible.

Another possible weakness or danger in the use of Gospel-handles is sensationalism and/or tastelessness. Haddon Robinson tells the story of a preacher who in eagerness to emphasize the attribute of God's omnipresence said, "God is even in the trash can!" Robinson rightly comments that however accurate the assertion is, it is inappropriate.[1] But in this example it was neither the idea of God's omnipresence nor the wish to communicate the idea that was faulty; rather, the tasteless way in which that legitimate idea and desire were expressed was objectionable. Experience with student assignments involving Gospel-handles has led me to conclude that seldom is an idea intrinsically poor, beyond verbal redemption. What is required in most every instance is skill in the choice and use of the words with which that idea is presented. Even more urgent is the God-given sanctification to direct such skill. In the end the preacher's attitude will determine whether or not he will be guilty of sensationalism. If a preacher means to show off with a Gospel-handle, that is probably the impression he will project. If he means to glorify God and help people with a Gospel-handle, that too will be the impression projected. Where there's a will, there are the words to communicate that will.

Offsetting the negative possibilities just mentioned are the many positive features of Gospel-handles that will "freshen" our Gospel preaching. Sometimes the device is the only way, short of arbitrary importation, to bring the Gospel to a text that contains no Gospel. Or sometimes the device provides an alternate approach to the Gospel in a familiar text that does contain the Gospel. The technique provides opportunity in a sermon for "extra" Gospel without incurring the risk of sounding repetitious. It may smoothen the transition to the Gospel so that the Gospel's placement will not seem awkward and its timing predictable. Above all, the Gospel-handle technique will sensitize the preacher to the Gospel-potential of every text that comes under his scrutiny. He will develop a Gospel awareness, sniffing every Biblical text for its traces of Gospel, searching the Scriptures because he is convinced that they are they which testify of Jesus. The technique will help the preacher to treat the Scriptures, not as a religious scrapbook containing edifying bits and pieces, but as a tightly integrated testimony to the Good News of God's mighty acts of salvation through Jesus Christ.

Finally, there seems to be Biblical precedent for the practice—not for the specific technique, but for the principle behind it, namely, to get to the Gospel in whatever legitimate way we can. If it were not for the fact that we have grown accustomed to it, that "it's in the Bible," and that no less a person than St. Paul himself did it, wouldn't we feel uncomfortable about Paul's Gospel treatment of the Old Testament incident alluded to in 1 Corinthians 10:4, where he claims that the rock that followed the Israelites and from which they drank was no less a person than Christ Himself? How about the Gospel mileage Paul derives in Galatians 4:21-31 from the Hagar-Ishmael-Isaac relationship of the Old Testament? Wasn't Paul "allegorizing"? Aren't we sometimes uneasy at the method by which St. Matthew extracts Messianic significance from what appear to be obscure, isolated excerpts from the Old Testament? Wouldn't the more traditional homileticians among us think him guilty of undue liberties if it were not for the fact that he is under the protective umbrella of divine inspiration? Look at our Lord's remark in John 2:19: "Destroy this temple, and in three days I will raise it up." This is the closest thing to a Gospel-handle I have found in the Scriptures. In this passage our Lord uses the word "temple," which seemingly contains no Gospel—or at least is misunderstood by his hearers as containing no Gospel but simply constituting a reference to the temple in Jerusalem—as an approach, a transition, a handle to the Gospel. The word "temple," as the Holy Spirit explains in 2:21, becomes a way of referring to the resurrection itself, a high spot in the literal Gospel!

I certainly do not point to these Scriptural usages to cast Paul, Matthew, and our Lord in an unfavorable light, nor to declare a field day for creatively dubious exegesis in our sermon work. But I point them out to demonstrate the desirability, even necessity, of "erring" in a Gospel-direction in our preaching. Richard Lischer says it well:

> If preaching did nothing more than restate the ideas of sacred texts, theology would have nothing to do, and the text-to-sermon manual would speak the final word to preachers. But preachers are charged with *proclaiming the gospel in texts, by means of texts, and in faithfulness to texts* ... I am not issuing a license for the preacher to ride rough-shod over the particularity of texts...I am inviting preachers to understand their task as broader and more demanding than the serial restatement of a pericope's religious ideas.[2]

Dr. Lischer goes on to point out that even "Luther pressed texts, sometimes demanding more than they had to give, that they might *necessitate* Christ."[3]

Having said all this, I can empathize with the pastor who may experience some discomfort in the employment of Gospel-handles. But that discomfort may not be altogether bad. For out of the tension between creativity and responsibility will more likely come a product that will strike the proper balance between sensationalism and dullness, and one that will simultaneously interest listeners and glorify God. Work through the following examples with an open mind and a wary eye. Through it all I am convinced that Gospel-handles used responsibly will not only put zest into our preaching but also help us carry out our commitment to preach nothing "save Jesus Christ and Him crucified" (1 Cor. 2:2).

For the sake of convenience I am presenting Gospel-handles under five different categories: (1) the use of a single word from a Biblical sermon text; (2) the use of a phrase; (3) the use of a sentence; (4) the use of a metaphor; and (5) the use of a rhetorical device. It is obvious that the last two categories can overlap somewhat with the first three. All the examples grouped under these categories apply only to the Gospel section of a sermon; they usually involve only one or more paragraphs of a sermon, not the entire sermon.

Gospel-Handles Based on a Single Word in the Biblical Sermon Text
Hebrews 12:18-24
Gospel-Handle: "mount" (v. 18)

18 For ye are not come unto the mount that might be touched, and that burned with fire, nor unto blackness, and darkness, and tempest,
19 And the sound of a trumpet, and the voice of words; which voice they that heard intreated that the word should not be spoken to them any more:
20 (For they could not endure that which was commanded, And if so much as a beast touch the mountain, it shall be stoned, or thrust through with a dart:
21 And so terrible was the sight, that Moses said, I exceedingly fear and quake:)
22 But ye are come unto mount Sion, and unto the city of the living God, the heavenly Jerusalem, and to an innumerable company of angels,
23 To the general assembly and church of the firstborn, which are written in heaven, and to God the Judge of all, and to the spirits of just men made perfect,
24 And to Jesus the mediator of the new covenant, and to the blood of sprinkling, that speaketh better things than that of Abel.

The word "mount" ("mountain" in most translations) stands out in this pericope because of its concreteness and repetition (vv. 18, 20, 22). Unfamiliar as the passage is to most listeners, even a child will remember after one hearing the word "mount." Asked to summarize what he has just heard, the child might say, "Oh, yes, I remember. It was all about mountains, a couple of them, one scary, the other a nicer mountain. Let's see— what were their names again?" While the Gospel-handle need not be a prominent or memorable word, it is fortunate when it is since that makes the transition to the Gospel just that much easier and more natural. In this particular pericope there is plenty of explicit Gospel for the preacher to mine, notably verse 24, which contrasts the respective persons and sacrifices of Jesus and Abel. I would suggest that the preacher mine this contrast for all it's worth since the account of the Gospel in this epistle selection is hardly an overly familiar one. But the Gospel-handle "mount" provides opportunity for additional Gospel and especially for Gospel that can be encapsulated in the sermon's very theme and parts. Throughout this text there is an elaborate contrast between the terrors of Mount Sinai (vv. 18-21) and the delights of Mount Zion (vv. 22-24). What accounts for the contrast? Is it not the event that occurred on another "mountain," Mount Calvary? Therefore, why not tell a story of *three* mountains? Let me suggest the following theme and parts as an approach to a sermon on this text.

From Mt. Sinai via Mt. Calvary to Mt. Zion

I. Sinai: the mountain that signifies what our relationship with God would be had it not been for Jesus.

II. Calvary: the mountain that makes the difference in our relationship with God.

III. Zion: the mountain that signifies what our relationship with God is now, thanks to Jesus.

Note in the development above how the word "mount," which contains no Gospel whatever, is used as a bridge or handle to an account of the Gospel, Jesus' crucifixion on Calvary, outside the text.

Matthew 21:28-32

Gospel-Handle: "son" (v. 28)

28 But what think ye? A certain man had two sons; and he came to the first, and said, Son, go to work to day in my vineyard.
29 He answered and said, I will not: but afterward he repented, and went.
30 And he came to the second, and said likewise. And he answered and said, I go, sir: and went not.
31 Whether of them twain did the will of the father? They say unto Him, The first. Jesus saith unto them, Verily I say unto you, That the publicans and the harlots go into the kingdom of God before you.
32 For John came unto you in the way of righteousness, and ye believed him not: but the publicans and the harlots believed him: and ye, when ye had seen it, repented not afterward, that ye might believe him.

Note again in this pericope that the word chosen to function as a handle to the Gospel is a prominent and memorable word, the word "son." If the listener remembers anything at all from a superficial hearing of the text, it will probably be the word "son." Asked to summarize what he has heard, the listener may reply: "Oh, that was a story about two sons, neither

55

one of them much good, but one of them somewhat better than the other, and I guess the idea is that we are to be like the lesser of the two evils presented."

Before using this particular Gospel-handle, the preacher needs to be aware of two problems unique to the parable of the two sons. The one problem is minor: the order of the sons. (Compare, for example, the New English Bible translation of this passage with that of King James.) This difference is the result of a textual variant that need not concern us here, but whatever version the preacher uses, his identification of the two sons will have to be consistent with that version to prevent audience confusion.

The other problem is a weightier one. Is the parable discussing justification or sanctification? Is it telling us how we are saved, or is it urging us to do good works? Or is it, perhaps, dealing with both areas? I think a case can be made for either justification or sanctification. In terms of first impressions the parable appears to be discussing sanctification. After all, the question asked is: Which of the two boys did the will of his father? Doing God's will is something we naturally associate with good works. The parable unquestionably has a sanctification thrust. The interpretative principle prompting this conclusion is that the simplest explanation is most likely to be the correct explanation.

But in terms of integrating the end of the parable with its beginning, justification appears to be the thrust of the parable. To the discerning reader the end of the parable at first does not appear to harmonize with the start of the parable. Verses 28-31a seem to talk about sanctification, but suddenly verses 31b-32 switch to justification, discussing such things as "repenting" and "believing" and "going into the kingdom of God." What's going on here? Suddenly the reader realizes that the lack of harmony he sees in the parable is his own fault, that in reading verses 28-31a he too hastily jumped to the conclusion that the parable was going to discuss sanctification when, in fact, as verses 31b-32 make clear, the parable was headed for a justification goal.

The publicans and harlots (v. 32) were like the one son (vv. 28-29) who at first refused to work in his father's vineyard but eventually repented and complied with his father's command. The Pharisees, the addressees of Jesus' parable, were like the other son (v. 30) who appeared obedient to the father's command but ultimately failed to follow through. The Pharisees may have appeared to be better than the notorious publicans and harlots. But ultimately the publicans and harlots, because they repented of their sin and believed in Jesus, were the ones who were going into the kingdom of God before the Pharisees. The publicans and harlots were "doing the will of God" by being caught up in God's will to save. It occurs to the reader that "the will of God" discussed in the parable may be His *saving* will, that will described in 1 Timothy 2:4, "Who will have all men to be saved, and to come unto the knowledge of the truth." "To do God's will," as advocated by the parable of the two sons, means, then, to be saved, to be apprehended by God's saving will, as were the notorious publicans and harlots mentioned in verse 32.

Personally, I see no objection to either of these interpretations—or to a combination of the two—but the use of the Gospel-handle "son" is primarily serviceable only if the parable is viewed as having a sanctification thrust. Actually, the parable of the two sons is a story without a hero. The one son is better (or at least less evil) than the other, but neither one is particularly admirable. Hypocrisy may be more contemptible than rebellion, but both are bad. Our mission is to avoid the sins of both sons, to say "Yes" to God's imperative (unlike the one son) and then do it (unlike the other son). How can we do this? We can't. We're powerless, helpless. We can't do God's will; as a matter of fact, we don't even want to. That's the ugly consequence of the sin-power in our lives. God is telling us to go into His vineyard to work, and we are utterly devoid of the ability and even the desire to do so.

Nevertheless, we can say "Yes" to God and do His will. How? By means of the third Son, the Son of God, the one the parable does not talk about but the one who is telling the parable. He is the solution to our problem. As the Son of God, Jesus both said "Yes" to His Father and then "did it." "Lo, I come to do Thy will, O God" (Heb. 10:9). "My meat is to do the will of Him that sent Me, and to finish His work" (John 4:34). "Father, if Thou be willing, remove this cup from Me: nevertheless not My will, but Thine, be done" (Luke 22:42). "He humbled Himself, and became obedient unto death, even the death of the cross" (Phil. 2:8). What Jesus did is more than a model; it is a means. His obedience unto death empowers us with obedience. Because of Jesus' atoning life, death, and resurrection, we can now say "Yes" to God and do His will. Thanks to Jesus, God "worketh in [us] both to will and to do of His good pleasure" (Phil. 2:13). We "can do all things through Christ which strengtheneth [us]" (Phil. 4:13). "I am the vine, ye are the branches: He that abideth in Me, and I in him, the same bringeth forth much fruit: for without Me ye can do nothing" (John 15:5).

There is, to be sure, adequate Gospel in the parable; one does not have to go outside it, as I have done in my use of the Gospel-handle "son." Verse 32 of the text abounds in Gospel, especially if the parable is viewed as having a justification thrust. According to that verse God accepts publicans and harlots into His kingdom. That is fabulous Gospel, a stirring tribute to the grace of God. Even the phrase "the way of righteousness" in the same verse can be given a forensic meaning; it can be understood as "the way of *Christ's* righteousness," the righteousness God credits to us when we are brought to faith in Christ as our Savior. I am not suggesting that the preacher ignore the Gospel that the text provides. But I am suggesting that he can supplement and enrich that text-supplied Gospel through the use of the Gospel-handle "son," especially if his sermon has a sanctification objective.

I am also suggesting that he can use the handle "son" as an alternate approach to the Gospel the third or fourth time he preaches on this parable and feels that the approach to the Gospel provided by the text has become too familiar to his audience.

Exodus 20:1-6

Gospel-handle: "thy" (vv. 2 and 5)[4]

1 And God spake all these words, saying
2 I am the Lord thy God, which have brought thee out of the land of Egypt, out of the house of bondage.
· 3 Thou shalt have no other gods before Me.
4 Thou shalt not make unto thee any graven image, or any likeness of any thing that is in heaven above, or that is in the earth beneath, or that is in the water under the earth:
5 Thou shalt not bow down thyself to them, nor serve them: for I the Lord thy God am a jealous God, visiting the iniquity of the fathers upon the children unto the third and fourth generation of them that hate Me;
6 And shewing mercy unto thousands of them that love Me, and keep My commandments.

This text provides two obvious approaches to the Gospel. The first is the rich description of God's mercy in verse 6. The second is the recital of God's deliverance of Israel from Egypt, "out of the house of bondage," in verse 2. In his use of the latter approach the preacher usually engages in moderate and unobjectionable "allegorizing" by pointing out that for us today "the house of bondage" is sin.

The Gospel-handle "thy" provides additional opportunity for the Gospel. Note that God describes Himself throughout this passage as "the Lord *thy* God," not as "the Lord *the* God." The unobtrusive word "thy" makes all the difference, especially in verse 5, where God is so awesomely described as "a jealous God," and One "visiting the iniquity of the fathers upon the children unto the third and fourth generation of them that hate [Him]." In this "desert" of awe and terror there is an "oasis" of tenderness and intimacy: God calls Himself "*thy* God." The word "thy" indicates a relationship between God and us. It is not the relationship we would expect in such a context—one of distance and fear—but rather a relationship of closeness and love. God is not merely *the* God—He is *our* God! We are not His pawns or puppets or playthings, not even merely His creatures. We are rather His people, special people in fact, "a chosen generation, a royal priesthood, an holy nation, a peculiar people" (1 Peter 2:9), "kings and priests unto God" (Rev. 1:6). We belong to God and God belongs to us, for He is "the Lord *thy* God." It is Jesus, of course, who has brought about this relationship. As He Himself so tenderly reminded His disciples through Mary Magdalene immediately after His resurrection, "I ascend unto My

Father, and *your* Father; and to My God, and *your* God" (John 20:16; emphasis added).

In some respects this particular Gospel-handle is atypical. To begin with, the word functioning as the handle is not a prominent word as in the previous two examples; rather, it is an inconspicuous word, eminently unnoticeable. Further, it may be argued that the word "thy" does not constitute a genuine Gospel-handle because the word actually seems to contain Gospel rather than merely connect us with Gospel elsewhere. One may insist that what we have here is simply a product of discerning exegesis rather than of creative impulse. Whatever our conclusion, the fact remains that it is a superb avenue to the Gospel because it is so delightfully simple and uncontrived. Once the student had brought it to my attention, I marveled that I had never thought of it myself in all my prior exposure to this common phrase in the Old Testament, "the Lord thy God."

1 Samuel 4:19-22
Gospel-Handle: "Ichabod" (v. 21)[5]

19 And his daughter in law, Phinehas' wife, was with child, near to be delivered: and when she heard the tidings that the ark of God was taken, and that her father in law and her husband were dead, she bowed herself and travailed; for her pains came upon her.
20 And about the time of her death the women that stood by her said unto her, Fear not; for thou hast born a son. But she answered not, neither did she regard it.
21 And she named the child Ichabod, saying, The glory is departed from Israel: because the ark of God was taken, and because of her father in law and her husband.
22 And she said, The glory is departed from Israel: for the ark of God is taken.

A Gospel-handle is particularly welcome in the homiletical treatment of this text because the text appears to contain no Gospel. It is a "bad news" text, heaping tragedy upon tragedy. Eli's two sons die in battle and Eli himself dies at the report of their death. One of his daughters-in-law, pregnant, goes into labor upon the same report and dies in childbrith. Israel loses a major battle. Worst of all, the pagan enemy captures the ark of God. Where is the "good news" in this recital of "bad news"?

It lies in the name given by the dying mother to her child, "Ichabod." As verse 21 explains, the name signifies that "the glory is departed from Israel." In preaching on this text the parish pastor would probably develop the Law portion of his sermon by delineating (1) how the glory of God departed from the family of Eli; (2) how the glory of God departed from the nation of Israel; and bringing the point home, (3) how the glory of God departed from the people in his audience because of their sins. **59**

But then the Gospel parallels appear. We are reminded of another occasion where the glory of God departed: from Jesus suspended on the cross. In His hour of greatest need Jesus turned to His Father for help and God was gone. "My God, My God, why hast Thou forsaken Me?" Instead of the pillar of fire signifying God's presence (as in Old Testament times), there was now a phenomenal darkness signifying God's absence. The sinless Jesus had been made sin for us; that's why the glory of God departed from Him in that awful moment. Bearing our sins, Jesus was in God's eyes "a worm, and no man," "numbered with the transgressors," "smitten of God, and afflicted." In fact, the preacher might say that Jesus became Ichabod for us; the glory of God departed from Him rather than from us because Jesus had assumed the ignominy of our sins. Because Jesus did this each of us is now back in the glory of God, basking in His love and goodness.

Let me make two concluding observations. First, as creative as the above treatment of "Ichabod" is, it is simultaneously responsible. No claim is made that the name "Ichabod" contains Gospel or constitutes a reference to Christ and His work. Such a claim would at best be fanciful exegesis. But a connection is made between the name "Ichabod" (which means no more than the text says it means) and the Gospel-event on the cross. Bizarre as that connection may seem to some readers, what choice does the preacher have? Once he is committed to preaching on this text, he is committed to preaching the Gospel "by hook or by crook," that is, by natural transition or by arbitrary importation. The handle "Ichabod" provides the necessary "hook" for the Gospel. In this instance, where there appears to be no explicit Gospel, a textual sermon is not enough. In this case one cannot preach a merely textual sermon and at the same time be loyal to his Scriptural commitment to know nothing "save Jesus Christ, and Him crucified." To be faithful to that commitment the preacher has two choices: either arbitrarily introduce the Gospel or use the convenient bridge to the Gospel that the word "Ichabod" provides.

As a second observation note how essential an awareness of the full literal Gospel is to this particular Gospel-handle. Without that awareness the preacher could not conceive of this creative approach to the Gospel. If one does not know about Jesus' experience of damnation on the cross, he is unlikely to make a connection between that experience and the departure of God's glory spoken of in our text. To reiterate a point made earlier: An understanding of the full literal Gospel is a prerequisite for the creative devices presented in this book.

Gospel-Handles Based on a Phrase in the Biblical Sermon Text

Mark 9:43-48

Gospel-Handle: "cut it off" (vv. 43 and 45)

43 And if thy hand offend thee, cut it off: it is better for thee to enter

into life maimed, than having two hands to go into hell, into the fire
that never shall be quenched:
44 Where their worm dieth not, and the fire is not quenched.
45 And if thy foot offend thee, cut if off: it is better for thee to enter
halt into life, than having two feet to be cast into hell, into the fire
that never shall be quenched:
46 Where their worm dieth not, and the fire is not quenched.
47 And if thine eye offend thee, pluck it out: it is better for thee to
enter into the kingdom of God with one eye, than having two eyes
to be cast into hell fire:
48 Where their worm dieth not, and the fire is not quenched.

With the possible exception of the expressions "life" and "kingdom of God" in this pericope, there is little explicit provision for Gospel. An opportunity for Gospel lies in the phrase "cut it off." The Gospel-handle in this instance is typical because the phrase contains no Gospel in itself and because the phrase is a memorable one, being both graphic and repeated.

What is remarkable about this pericope is the picture of repentance that it provides, a picture that is a stark corrective to our current anemic versions of the repentance process. Repentance in this text is described as a drastic, radical, revolutionary action. Repentance is not merely a cavalier promise to turn over a new leaf. It does not merely consist of New Year's Day resolutions made in a moment of painful sobriety. Repentance according to Mark is more like an amputation than anything else. It is something like cutting off a hand (v. 43) or a foot (v. 45) or plucking out an eye (v. 47). Repentance hurts—like an amputation. It is not entered into lightly or flippantly—no more than an amputation is.

In fact, the action required is so drastic and radical that we can't do it. "Cut it off!" God demands of us concerning the sin in our lives. But we can't "cut it off." For this thing called sin is bigger than any one of us. The very thing we need to remove is precisely the thing that saps us of the power to remove it. God has demanded of us the impossible. If there is to be surgery of sin, we cannot perform it. Only Jesus, the Great Physician, can "amputate" our sins.

He can do it because of what happened to Him on the cross. Jesus can "cut off" our sins because He Himself, bearing our sins, was "cut off" from God, "cut off out of the land of the living" in the language of Isaiah 53:8. The Son of God was "amputated" from the heavenly family: "My God, My God, why hast Thou forsaken Me?" At the cross God looked at His Son, laden with our sins, and abandoned Him, in effect saying, "If Thy Son offend Thee, cut Him off!"

What is unique about this otherwise typical Gospel-handle is that it deploys the power of the Gospel into an area of sanctification (sorrow over sin and accompanying amendment) where even the most Gospel-conscious of us tend to omit or minimize the Gospel and resort to moralizing.

Note again the key role played by the full literal Gospel in the development of this particular Gospel-handle.

Gospel-Handle: "prepare a place" (v. 2)

1 Let not your heart be troubled: ye believe in God, believe also in Me.

2 In My Father's house are many mansions: if it were not so, I would have told you. I go to prepare a place for you.

3 And if I go and prepare a place for you, I will come again, and receive you unto Myself; that where I am, there ye may be also.

4 And whither I go ye know, and the way ye know.

5 Thomas saith unto Him, Lord, we know not whither Thou goest; and how can we know the way?

6 Jesus saith unto him, I am the way, the truth, and the life: no man cometh unto the Father, but by Me.

Ideal for an Ascension Day sermon, this text assures us that even though Jesus has left our world and returned to His home in heaven, He still is vigorously active in our behalf. In addition to ruling the world from God's right hand and interceding to God for us whenever we sin (divine activities described elsewhere in the Bible), Jesus according to this pericope is busy preparing a place for us in heaven. "In My Father's house are many mansions.... I go to prepare a place for you" (v.2).

Think for a moment of the significance of this activity: preparing a place for us. In human relationships when one of us is invited to be a guest in someone else's home, we might indulge in the platitude "Don't go to any fuss or bother." Yet it pleases us when we arrive to discover that our hostess has gone to fuss and bother: the room has been cleaned, the bedding changed, everything freshened and tidied. She has indeed prepared a place for us. It's all very flattering. It means that our hostess considers us important and our stay at her house a matter of significance. She wants everything to be shipshape so that nothing will disappoint us when we come.

Our Lord's assertion that in heaven He is preparing a place for us has similar significance. By His crucifixion and resurrection He has made it possible for us to get to heaven. (Here we incorporate—rather than omit—the superbly explicit Gospel that the text provides in verse 6: "I am the way, the truth, and the life: no man cometh unto the Father, but by Me.") And, really, that's plenty. What more can we expect than that Jesus should live on our earth, die, and rise again so that we might go to heaven? But Jesus doesn't stop there. He does more than expected. Not only does He make it possible for us to get to heaven but He also prepares a place for us there. He goes to fuss and bother. He engages in "heavenly housework," so to speak. It's all very flattering. We're special in His sight, "a chosen generation," "the apple of His eye," "kings and priests unto God," "the bride of the Lamb." He longs for our arrival; He can't wait till we get there. He wants everything shipshape when we arrive; He makes sure that there will be no disappointment when we reach our heavenly mansion. All these stirring implications can be unpacked from the simple assertion "I go to prepare a place for you."

What is unique about this Gospel-handle when coupled with the delightful Gospel of verse 6 is that it captures the extra Gospel, the bonus Gospel of the text. It captures the gratuitous, the superfluous, the prodigal aspect of the Christian Gospel—the very thing that makes the Gospel so "Gospel-ish." It "lays Gospel unto Gospel." It provides "Gospel in full measure and running over." It reminds us that ours is a Savior who never quits in His lavish outlay of goodness; a Savior who when asked to give one coat gives two; a Savior who when requested to walk with us one mile walks an extra mile; a Savior who not only prepares the way for us but also prepares a place for us.[6]

Genesis 18:23-24, 26, 32

Gospel-Handle: "fifty righteous" (v. 24)/"ten righteous" (v. 32)

23 And Abraham drew near, and said, Wilt Thou also destroy the righteous with the wicked?
24 Peradventure there be fifty righteous within the city: wilt Thou also destroy and not spare the place for the fifty righteous that are therein?
26 And the Lord said, If I find in Sodom fifty righteous within the city, then I will spare all the place for their sakes.
32 And he said, Oh let not the Lord be angry, and I will speak yet but this once: Peradventure ten shall be found there. And He said, I will not destroy it for ten's sake.

Although this familiar Old Testament story contains no reference to the saving role of Christ, there is plenty of Gospel in it, what might be called "attitudinal Gospel," that is, an account that highlights God's disposition to save, His inexhaustible mercy and patience, and His incapacity to find "pleasure in the death of the wicked" (Ezek. 33:11). There is further opportunity for Gospel in the relationship that surfaces between Abraham and God. The fact that a creature can negotiate with the Creator, actually badger and nag Him (so politely yet insistently, so respectfully yet stubbornly), argues an intimacy and boldness made possible only by the saving work of Christ. Thanks to the future action of Jesus, Abraham was one of those fortunate people who could approach God "as dear children approach their dear father." It is the careful yet persistent execution of this role by Abraham that makes the reading of this Old Testament story such a delightful experience. In my opinion, no alternate approach to the Gospel in this narrative should omit these obvious Gospel facets but rather build on them.

The alternate approach suggested by the Gospel-handle "fifty righteous"/"ten righteous" consists of the contrast between the situation in our text and the circumstance described in Romans 5:18-19: "Therefore as by the offence of one judgment came upon all men to condemnation; even so by the righteousness of one the free gift came upon all men unto justification of life. For as by one man's disobedience many were made sinners, so by the obedience of one shall many be made righteous." Abraham bargained with God to spare Sodom if but 50 righteous could be found in the city. Ultimately, he pushed God to agree to spare the city if only 10 righteous could be located. But it didn't work. Not even that minimal number could be found, and Sodom and Gomorrah were destroyed.

Our world in its generations following Sodom and Gomorrah has fared better than those wicked cities, even though it has been every bit as evil and the prospect of finding any righteous people in it has seemed even more hopeless. "There is none righteous, no, not one" (Rom. 3:10). But now comes the Good News corrective to our dismal outlook. God found one exception to the rule, not 50, not even 10, just one righteous man in our world. Yet because of that one God proved willing to spare our world. That one righteous man was the Lord Jesus Himself. While not of our world He was in our world for 33 years by virtue of His incarnation and virgin birth. He was perfect, sinless. He kept all of God's laws. He met all of God's demands. He did what He promised at His baptism: He fulfilled all righteousness (Matt. 3:15). Because He did and because God graciously regards His accomplishment as our accomplishment, our world has been spared. "God will have all men to be saved" (1 Tim. 2:4). He is "not willing that any should perish, but that all should come to repentance" (2 Peter 3:9).[7]

Matthew 10:34-37

Gospel-Handle: "set a man at variance" (v. 35)

34 Think not that I am come to send peace on earth: I came not to send peace, but a sword.

35 For I am come to set a man at variance against his father, and the daughter against her mother, and the daughter in law against her mother in law.

36 And a man's foes shall be they of his own household.

37 He that loveth father or mother more than Me is not worthy of Me: and he that loveth son or daughter more than Me is not worthy of Me.

This text is a hard saying. It upsets our customary notions about Jesus and His religion. As the Prince of Peace He was the One at whose birth the angels sang, "On earth peace, good will toward men." Yet in this text He says, "Think not that I am come to send peace on earth: I came not to send peace, but a sword" (v. 34). He who has commanded us in His Law to love father and mother and has urged us to "follow peace with all men" (Heb. 12:14) now says, "I am come to set a man at variance against his father, and the daughter against her mother, and the daughter in law against her mother in law" (v. 35). Normally, living at peace with people is the divine rule, the virtuous course of action. No one is to regard our text as a divinely decreed holiday from that commendable path. Our text does not contradict or eliminate the divine directive to live peaceably with all men. But it does amend and modify it. It points out divine exceptions to the divine rule. There are times, such as when "we ought to obey God rather than men" (Acts. 5:29), that the virtuous alternative is to live at variance with people rather than at peace with them. There are times, such as when we have a choice between the two goods of loving God and loving parents, that loving God is the higher good (v. 37). In short, there are occasions when the proper course of action is for a man to be set "at variance against his father, and the daughter against her mother, and the daughter in law against her mother in law."

The prime instance of this virtue of living "at variance" (i.e., when it is a virtue), Exhibit No. 1, is the relationship of Father and Son at Calvary. There Father was set at variance against Son. There one might say that God put principle above person. Jesus had been described by the Father Himself as His "beloved Son" in whom He was "well-pleased." Father loved Son, and the feeling was mutual. But when Jesus voluntarily took our sins upon Himself, God turned away from His Son in holy abandonment because of the iniquity He saw on Him. Father was set at variance against Son. Jesus discovered an ironical application of His words in verse 36 that "a man's foes shall be they of his own household"—His own Father had forsaken Him at that critical moment when He was made sin for us. Because of this mighty act of divine love, we and all other people are no longer at variance with God but at peace with Him.

What happened at Calvary, however, is more than an exhibit of the virtue of putting principle before people (i.e., when it is a virtue). It is the energy for that virtue. What transpired on the cross is more than a model. It is a means. Whenever in our daily living we are faced with the difficult alternative of obeying God rather than men, of simultaneously loving father, mother, son, daughter and yet loving God above all, we draw our strength from the Gospel-event on Golgotha. We can practice the virtue of living at variance with others (i.e., when it is a virtue) because at the cross Father was set at variance against Son. We can endure the discomfort that our Christian faith sometimes entails, the discomfort of discovering that "a man's foes shall be they of his own household," because—and only be-cause—Jesus on the cross also discovered, in a sense, that "a man's foes shall be they of his own household."

Of all the examples of Gospel-handles presented so far, this one is perhaps the most vulnerable to abuse. Care must be exercised at every point to clarify that the Matthew passage does not even remotely allude to the Gospel-event on Calvary. To suggest that it does would be faulty exegesis. But to make an association between the Matthew passage (which means no more than it says) and the Gospel-event on Calvary is appropriate for that preacher who is determined "not to know any thing…save Jesus Christ, and Him crucified" and who searches the Scriptures because "they are they which testify of [Him]."

Gospel-Handles Based on a Sentence in the Biblical Sermon Text
Matthew 20:1-2, 6-12, 16

Gospel-Handle: "The last shall be first, and the first last" (v. 16)[8]

1 For the kingdom of heaven is like unto a man that is an householder, which went out early in the morning to hire labourers into his vineyard.
2 And when he had agreed with the labourers for a peny a day, he sent them into his vineyard.
6 And about the eleventh hour he went out, and found others standing idle, and saith unto them, Why stand ye here all the day idle?
7 They say unto him, Because no man hath hired us. He saith unto them, Go ye also into the vineyard; and whatsoever is right, that shall ye receive.
8 So when even was come, the lord of the vineyard saith unto his steward, Call the labourers, and give them their hire, beginning from the last unto the first.
9 And when they came that were hired about the eleventh hour, they received every man a penny.
10 But when the first came, they supposed that they should have received more; and they likewise received every man a penny.
11 And when they had received it, they murmured against the goodman of the house,
12 Saying, These last have wrought but one hour, and thou hast made them equal unto us, which have borne the burden and heat of the day.
16 So the last shall be first, and the first last.

Of all the texts so far subjected to the Gospel-handle technique, this one is perhaps the least in need of that approach, for the parable oozes with Gospel. Although it says nothing about Jesus' saving acts, it abounds in "attitudinal Gospel"; it is an engaging picture of that glorious "unfairness" of God and His topsy-turvy way of dealing with people that theologians call "grace." No number of sermons on this text can exhaust the Gospel opportunities it provides.

Yet the Gospel-handle "The last shall be first, and the first last" is one of the delightful options available. Notice that this sentence frames the parable, not only concluding it in verse 16 but also preceding it in the last verse of the previous chapter. So positioned, the sentence brings the story into sharper focus, even as a frame serves a portrait. And thus repeated, the statement is memorable even after minimal exposure to the parable. But the repetition has interpretative as well as mnemonic significance. "Pay attention to what an author repeats" is a familiar interpretative principle applied to secular literature. Thus, if Salinger speaks frequently of a turned-around cap or Hemingway alludes often to rainy days, there is likely to be some symbolic or thematic significance to the repetition. The principle is applicable to Biblical literature as well. The very fact that the sentence, "The last shall be the first, and the first last," is repeated—and all the more so because it is repeated before and after the story—increases the likelihood that it has something to do with the meaning of the story. Hence its use as a Gospel-handle is not so likely to come off as arbitrary, contrived, or forced.

So it is no surprise that there is a connection between this sentence and certain facets of the story, like the amount and order of pay. Equal pay accorded unequal labor (vv. 9 and 10) is as topsy-turvy as the "first-last, last-first" principle, and paying those laborers first who were hired last (v. 8) is a remarkably literal application of the principle.

But there is an even more profound connection between the sentence and the story, a connection that leads us to the very core of the Christian Gospel. What is true of the order of pay is true of the Lord Jesus and us as well. Jesus was "first" in the kingdom of heaven, the only begotten Son of God, "the heir of all things," "the brightness of His glory," "the express image of His person," "so much better than the angels," seated "on the right hand of the Majesty on High" (Heb. 1:2-4), "who being in the form of God thought it not robbery to be equal with God" (Phil. 2:6), of whom the Father repeatedly said, "This is My beloved Son in whom I am well pleased." Yet this Jesus, who was "first" in the kingdom of heaven, became "last." He exchanged the security of life in heaven for the insecurity of life on earth; there was no room for Him in the inn, and, unlike the foxes and birds, the Son of man had "not where to lay His head" (Matt. 8:20). He "made Himself of no reputation, and took upon Him the form of a servant" (Phil. 2:7). He not only died, but died disgracefully: "He humbled Himself, and became obedient unto death, *even* the death of the cross" (Phil. 2:8, emphasis added). In the language of Psalm 22 He was "a worm, and no man; a reproach of men, and despised of the people." In the language of Isaiah 53 He "was despised, and we esteemed Him not," "smitten of God, and afflicted," "brought as a lamb to the slaughter," "numbered with the transgressors"; "it pleased the Lord to bruise Him" and "put Him to grief." Made our sin and made our curse for sin on the cross, Jesus was forsaken by God—the ultimate indignity. At that moment in the eyes of the Father, the

Son was like those carcasses spoken of in the last verse of Isaiah, "an abhorring unto all flesh." Truly Jesus, the first, had become last.

Because Jesus, the first, became last, we, who deservedly are last because of our sins, have now become first in the kingdom of heaven. Once "not a people" at all, we are now "the people of God" (1 Peter 2:10): the "elect of God," "a chosen generation," "a royal priesthood," "a holy nation," "the apple of God's eye," "kings and priests unto God." Because of what Jesus has done he who is least in the kingdom of God is now greater than John the Baptist (Luke 7:28). Here is the very heart of the Christian Gospel: we who are last have become first because He who was first became last.

James 5:1-6

Gospel-Handle: "Ye have condemned and killed the just" (v. 6)[9]

1 Go to now, ye rich men, weep and howl for your miseries that shall come upon you.
2 Your riches are corrupted, and your garments are motheaten.
3 Your gold and silver is cankered; and the rust of them shall be a witness against you, and shall eat your flesh as it were fire. Ye have heaped treasure together for the last days.
4 Behold, the hire of the labourers who have reaped down your fields, which is of you kept back by fraud, crieth: and the cries of them which have reaped are entered into the ears of the Lord of sabaoth.
5 Ye have lived in pleasure on the earth, and been wanton: ye have nourished your hearts, as in a day of slaughter.
6 Ye have condemned and killed the just; and he doth not resist you.

This text appears to be entirely Law. It is a scathing indictment of the wealthy among James's addressees for reveling in their riches and for abusing the poor and innocent. The last verse, the Gospel-handle "Ye have condemned and killed the just," seems to climax James's castigation of some of his readers. Hence, in this heavily Law-oriented pericope a Gospel-handle is most welcome, perhaps even imperative.

The Law-climax, "Ye have condemned and killed the just," turns out to be the Gospel-opening. On its first level it applies to James's addressees: they have condemned and killed righteous people. On another level, since "whatsoever things were written aforetime were written for our learning" (Rom. 15:4), James's indictment applies to us also: we have abused and mistreated innocent people. On still another level the assertion applies to God: He too, in a sense, has "condemned and killed the just" in the person of His own innocent Son, and He did it so that we might have life and have

68

it more abundantly (John 10:10). Suddenly we are surprised by Gospel in a passage that at first appeared to contain only Law!

Since there is an exegetical ambiguity in the sixth verse, it is possible that the Gospel can be found in the text itself rather than by means of a Gospel-handle. Is the term "just" in the statement "Ye have condemned and killed the just" singular or plural in meaning? Does it refer to an individual person or to a class of people? Since the Greek original for the word is generic, it is permissible to translate the word "just" either way: "Ye have condemned and killed the just (person)" or "Ye have condemned and killed the just (people)." The Good News Bible and the Living Bible opt for the plural; the former has "innocent people" and the latter has "good men." The Revised Standard Version chooses the singular; it says, "the righteous man," although that rendering, possibly generic, can still be given a plural sense as well. King James leaves it open; it simply uses the adjective "just" and lets the reader supply the missing noun, either singular or plural. If the Good News Bible and Living Bible are correct, then a Gospel-handle is desperately needed for proper homiletical handling of this Law-oriented text.

Martin Franzmann, however, in his commentary on this passage, argues that the term "just" is a reference to the Lord Jesus Himself, and not merely a term for a certain class of people. His argument is reinforced by the sentence that follows in verse 6, "he doth not resist you," a statement suggestive of Isaiah's well-known description of the Messiah as "a sheep before her shearers is dumb, so He openeth not His mouth" (Is. 53:7). If Dr. Franzmann is correct, the Gospel, as is so often the case, lies in the text itself, and releasing it is largely a matter of exegesis. Thus the Gospel-handle approach is no longer crucial to the proper homiletical treatment of this text.

While eliminating the need for a Gospel-handle, Dr. Franzmann's insight simultaneously justifies a specific application of the Gospel-handle as described above. If "just" is a reference not merely to a person or persons but to Jesus Himself, then to apply the statement "Ye have condemned and killed the just" to God's treatment of Jesus as well as to the addressees' and our treatment of Jesus is no longer so far-fetched as it may initially appear to be. While still playing with the word "Ye" in the statement, the Gospel-handle is no longer manipulating the word "just."

John 1:45-51

Gospel-Handle: "Behold an Israelite indeed, in whom is no guile!" (v. 47)[10]

45 Philip findeth Nathanael, and saith unto him, We have found Him, of whom Moses in the law, and the prophets, did write, Jesus of Nazareth, the son of Joseph.

46 And Nathanael said unto him, Can there any good thing come out of Nazareth? Philip saith unto him, Come and see.

47 Jesus saw Nathanael coming to Him, and saith of him, Behold an Israelite indeed, in whom is no guile!

48 Nathanael saith unto Him, Whence knowest Thou me? Jesus answered and said unto him, Before that Philip called thee, when thou wast under the fig tree, I saw thee.

49 Nathanael answered and saith unto Him, Rabbi, Thou art the Son of God; Thou art the King of Israel.

50 Jesus answered and said unto him, Because I said unto thee, I saw thee under the fig tree, believest thou? thou shalt see greater things than these.

51 And He saith unto him, Verily, verily, I say unto you, Hereafter ye shall see heaven open, and the angels of God ascending and descending upon the Son of man.

The text supplies ample opportunity for preaching the Gospel: (1) mention of Christ as the fulfillment of Old Testament prophecy (v. 45); (2) the reference by Christ to His mighty saving acts in His promise to Nathanael that he will "see greater things than these" (v. 50); and (3) the description of the communion between heaven and earth that Christ effects (v. 51).

An excellent opportunity for preaching alternate or additional Gospel lies in the sentence serving as the Gospel-handle: "Behold an Israelite indeed, in whom is no guile!" It is a simple enough remark, actually nothing more than a divine compliment to the integrity of the man approaching the Savior. What a fine tribute to Nathanael by the omniscient Jesus, who searches and knows the hearts of men: "Behold an Israelite indeed, in whom there is no guile!"

Even the most ardent literalist should have no trouble understanding this tribute to Nathanael as hyperbole, that is, legitimate exaggeration for the sake of effect. In an absolute sense Jesus' observation is not true. The virtuous Nathanael was also a sinner, nor did Jesus' compliment mean to deny this basic theological truth. His remark was simply a way of saying that among men Nathanael was an exceptional person, head and shoulders above others when it comes to sanctification. But perfect? Of course not. No one is, not even such a decent person as Nathanael.

Right? Wrong! In another sense—the Gospel sense—Jesus' compliment of Nathanael is absolutely true, lacking hyperbole altogether. By virtue of comparing spiritual things with spiritual things, interpreting Scripture with Scripture, we suddenly realize that our Gospel-handle takes us to the very heart of the Christian Gospel itself: forensic justification. When we draw a line from this passage to the saving act of Jesus on the cross, it dawns upon us how delightfully true Jesus' tribute to Nathanael is. Because of what Jesus did on the cross God has declared Nathanael righteous, absolutely righteous, as righteous as Christ Himself is righteous. There is not a smidgin of hyperbole in God's assessment of Nathanael.

Nor is there hyperbole in God's assessment of us, for on the cross Jesus took the blame for our sins too. He of whom it is written, "neither was any deceit in His mouth" (Is. 53:9), assumed our deceit. He of whom it is said, "neither was guile found in His mouth" (1 Peter 2:22), took upon Himself our guile. Because He did God has declared us righteous and can now say of us as He did of Nathanael: "Behold an Israelite indeed, in whom there is no guile!"

John 11:5-6 (RSV)
Gospel-Handle: the entire text

To provide variety in mode of presentation and to demonstrate the homiletical utility of the Gospel-handle technique, a sermonette rather than an explication appears below. This is a homily that was addressed to a seminary community. The Gospel-handle consists of the contrast between the first and the second sentences of the text. The specific connection between that contrast and the Gospel-event occurs in the second last paragraph of the sermonette that follows.

> John 11:5-6—"Now Jesus loved Martha and her sister and Lazarus. So when He heard that he was ill, He stayed two days longer in the place where He was."

Now isn't that something? Jesus loves Lazarus. Lazarus gets sick. So Jesus stays away. So Jesus stays away! What a lame and impotent conclusion! Jesus loves Lazarus. Lazarus gets sick. So Jesus stays away. What a classic *non sequitur*! Think of how this would sound if you heard it anywhere else than from the sacred pages of a book you have revered since childhood. For instance: Joe is my colleague and friend—Joe needs help on a committee assignment—so I don't assist him. For instance: I like Ken—Ken needs money—so I refuse to loan him five dollars. Either this is nonsense or this is some divine paradox that passes all human understanding. Quite a word, that word "so."

Obviously, I'm here today to cast my vote for the latter alternative, namely, that our text verbalizes divine truth, not nonsense. There's a heap of theology in that word "so." You know the clichés as well as I do. "God's ways are not our ways"; "Whom the Lord loves He chastens"; "All things work together for good to them that love God." And even though they're clichés they're true. Put our text into the context of these well-known sayings and it looks entirely different. Jesus loves Lazarus—Lazarus gets sick—so Jesus stays away. Jesus knew what He was doing. His peculiar conduct wasn't cold and loveless, not at all. True, Lazarus died. But look what came of it. Martha and Mary were strengthened in their faith as a result of their brother's resurrection. A large number of Jews were persuaded of Jesus' Messiahship. And Lazarus himself was equipped with a tremendous piece of empirical evidence regarding the truth of his religion. Jesus did love by staying away.

To be sure, our Lord doesn't always work in this seemingly perverse way. The Bible is teeming with examples of God blessing those whom He loves. Jesus loves Peter—Peter's mother-in-law gets sick—so Jesus heals her. Jesus has compassion on the multitudes—the multitudes are hungry—so Jesus feeds them. That's the way it usually is: Jesus' love is expressed in an obvious and normal fashion requiring no explanation or apology.

Another thing: many of our misfortunes are self-inflicted, not God-sent. Let us not say when we have failed to prepare for a class: "Jesus loved me—so my lecture fell through." Let us not say when we have burned the candle at both ends night after night: "Jesus loved me—so He sent me mononucleosis." "What a man sows he reaps," and there's no sense in trying to explain that away.

Nevertheless, the truth of our text remains. Sometimes Jesus loves us and then stays away. We should be aware of this. For instance, when sickness occurs. Or when a member of our family dies. Or when a planned publication falls through. Or when a hoped-for promotion fails to materialize. Or when salary fails to match not only merit but even need. Or when the work-load seems out of proportion to our capacity to carry it. As bad as these things look, we ought to be suspicious. Appearance isn't always reality. Conceivably these misfortunes could be tokens of God's love. We might just be in the company of Lazarus and his sisters. Jesus loves—so Jesus stays away. And that's mighty good company to be in. Sooner or later the truth will out; the reality of Jesus' love will emerge from its cloud cover.

All these strange dealings of God toward us are part of a pattern, a pattern pieced out during our Lord's stay on earth. At the Jordan God said of Jesus, "This is my beloved Son in whom I am well pleased." On Calvary Jesus said, "My God, My God, why hast Thou forsaken Me?" Here too God loved and God stayed away. He forsook His beloved Son. That too was peculiar conduct, but that too was love. Not only was Jesus resurrected to greater glory than ever as a sequel to God's abandonment of Him, but, above all, we and all men were saved. Jesus loves Lazarus—Lazarus gets sick—so Jesus stays away. Jesus loves me—I have a need—so Jesus stays away. Really these are but miniatures of God's treatment of Jesus on the cross. They are Calvary-in-little. No wonder our afflictions are called crosses.

In fact, these afflictions are more than representations of Calvary. Connected with God's Word, they are channels for Calvary. When God loves us in this strange fashion, we are more than reminded of the cross. We are made recipients of the cross and its blessings: salvation and new creature-hood. That is blessedness indeed! If then you have troubles (and who of us doesn't?), try to view them as channels for God's love. Doing so may or may not make the troubles easier to bear. But it surely can make you a child of God.

Gospel-Handles Based on a Metaphor in the Biblical Sermon Text
Isaiah 22:15, 19-25
Gospel-Handle: "nail" (vv. 23 and 25)

15 Thus saith the Lord God of hosts, Go, get thee unto this treasurer, even unto Shebna, which is over the house, and say,

19 And I will drive thee from thy station, and from thy state shall He pull thee down.

20 And it shall come to pass in that day, that I will call my servant Eliakim, the son of Hilkiah:

21 And I will clothe him with thy robe, and strengthen him with thy girdle, and I will commit thy government into his hand: and he shall be a father to the inhabitants of Jerusalem and to the house of Judah.

22 And the key of the house of David will I lay upon his shoulder; so he shall open, and none shall shut; and he shall shut, and none shall open.

23 And I will fasten him as a nail in a sure place; and he shall be for a glorious throne to his father's house.

24 And they shall hang upon him all the glory of his father's house, the offspring and the issue, all vessels of small quantity, from the vessels of cups, even to all the vessels of flagons.

25 In that day, saith the Lord of hosts, shall the nail that is fastened in the sure place be removed, and be cut down, and fall; and the burden that was upon it shall be cut off: for the Lord hath spoken it.

Basic to the search for the Gospel in this text is the double application of much Old Testament prophecy. By this is meant that God's prophet would make a prediction that would have two fulfillments: an immediate, often secular fulfillment; and then a remote, more spiritual or Messianic fulfillment. The prophecy in our text is a case in point. At first it seems to predict nothing more than the fall of one statesman and the rise of another. But all of a sudden we begin to realize that it's talking about Christ too.

Initially, this text appears to be merely a story about two statesmen, Shebna and Eliakim. At the time of the prophecy Shebna held a high office in the king's palace. It appears that the job went to his head, for Isaiah informs us that Shebna strutted around with his chariots and built himself a magnificent tomb high on a mountainside where everyone could see it. Because Shebna forgot God, Isaiah prophesied that God would remove him from his high office. However, Isaiah uses a more picturesque word than "remove"; he says that God would pick up Shebna like a ball and throw him far away into another country. At this same time there was a stalwart man of God named Eliakim. Isaiah prophesied that he would be elevated to the high position from which Shebna had fallen. As long as he remained a stalwart man of God, Eliakim's position would be secure; nothing could shake him. He would be as permanent a fixture in the king's palace as a nail

73

pounded into the castle wall. In Isaiah's own hard-to-beat language: "I [God] will fasten him as a nail in a sure place" (v. 23).

Accustomed to the double application of much Old Testament prophecy, conservative scholarship has treated this passage from Isaiah as a Messianic prophecy, regarding Eliakim as a type of Christ. Isaiah wasn't merely predicting the honors that would be heaped upon Eliakim nor merely describing the blessings resulting from his good conduct in office. He was also predicting the honors that God would confer upon Jesus and describing the blessings arising from His gracious rule. Just as the government would be committed into Eliakim's hand (v. 21), so also for Christ "the government shall be upon His shoulder" (9:6). In verse 22 Isaiah prophesies, "And the key of the house of David will I lay upon his shoulder; so he shall open, and none shall shut; and he shall shut, and none shall open." Isaiah wasn't referring here merely to the palace keys that Eliakim would have in his keeping, but more importantly to the keys to heaven that Christ would possess. When in verse 23 Isaiah uses the striking metaphor of a nail fastened in a sure place, he was indicating more than simply the security that Eliakim would enjoy in the king's palace. He was describing the rights, the status, the permanence that Christ would enjoy in His Father's mansions. In summary, Isaiah in this text is prophesying not only about a minor official of long ago but primarily about the Messiah. As far as you and I are concerned today, it is Christ, not Eliakim, who is that nail fastened in a sure place spoken of in verses 23 and 25.

What has just been presented is a familiar "typological" approach to Gospel in Old Testament prophecy. The last verse of the text, however, has something unusual to say about the nail fastened in a sure place, material that not only increases the probability that this is indeed a Messianic prophecy but also enriches the Gospel already presented. Verse 25: "In that day...shall the nail that is fastened in the sure place be removed, and be cut down, and fall; and the burden that was upon it shall be cut off." In this concluding verse Isaiah seems to leave behind the immediate, secular application of his prediction and concentrate exclusively on its more remote, Messianic application. Here he states that the nail fastened in a sure place would be removed and would fall. Something else, a burden, would fall with it. To the best of our knowledge Eliakim did not experience such a fall, so verse 25 may not apply to him at all. But it most certainly applies to Christ.

Its metaphor of the nail suggests a beautiful explication of God's act of salvation. Christ was the nail fastened in a sure place. Loved by God His Father and equal with Him, Christ had a permanent place in His Father's house. But according to verse 25, Christ as the nail fastened in a sure place was removed and cut down. The dislodgement began when He left His Father's abode to come down to our planet and experience our problems and hardships for 33 years. And never was that "nail in a sure place" more truly removed and cut down than when Jesus was suspended from a Roman cross on a little knoll outside Jerusalem. For there not only enemies poked fun at Him and soldiers executed Him, but, worst of all, His Father deserted Him and damned Him.

Why did the Father do this to His beloved and sinless Son? Why was that "nail in a sure place" suddenly removed and cut down? Verse 25 provides the reason: because of a burden that hung upon that nail. That burden was our sin. Since Christ bore that burden, God executed and damned Him; He removed and cut down that "nail in a sure place." Because our sins got between Christ and God, there is no longer anything to get between us and God. Nothing stands in our way. We are sure of God's affection, now and forever. Indeed, if we push our metaphor even farther, each of us is now a nail fastened in a sure place.

One concluding caution is in order. Edifying as the preceding approach may be, the preacher dare not be dogmatic about the association of the "burden" in verse 25 with "sin." What makes that association tenuous is the fact that in verse 24 the burden (at least in King James) is described as "the glory" rather than as something shameful (like sin). The Good News Bible and Revised Standard renderings of verse 24 may help the preacher surmount the difficulty: the former translates verse 24, "But all the relatives and dependents will become a *burden* to him" (emphasis added); and the latter, "And they will hang on him the whole *weight* of his father's house" (emphasis added). Clearly the connotations of "burden" and "weight" are more negative than those of "glory," thereby strengthening the association of the burden in verse 25 with sin. But nothing in the text warrants an absolute, dogmatic association.

Luke 23:27-31

Gospel-Handle: "green tree"/"dry [tree]" (v. 31)

27 And there followed Him a great company of people, and of women, which also bewailed and lamented Him.

28 But Jesus turning unto them said, Daughters of Jerusalem, weep not for Me, but weep for yourselves, and for your children.

29 For, behold, the days are coming, in the which they shall say, Blessed are the barren, and the wombs that never bare, and the paps which never gave suck.

30 Then shall they begin to say to the mountains, Fall on us; and to the hills, Cover us.

31 For if they do these things in a green tree, what shall be done in the dry?

Unless expanded, this text contains scant Gospel. The scene is sordid: Jesus on His way to the place of execution, hooted and jeered at by the accompanying throngs and compelled to carry the instrument of execution,

His own cross. The tone is harsh: Jesus' words to the woman may at first sound vindictive, like the bitter cry of an utterly disillusioned man. Therefore, any route to the Gospel in this somber pericope will be welcome. Normally the pastor preaching on this text would get at the Gospel by reminding his listeners where Jesus is going, namely, to the cross from which He will save the world. But that too is imported Gospel, just as in the case with Gospel-handles. However, the Gospel-handle provides a more natural transition to the Gospel. Such a handle lies in the metaphors of the green tree and the dry tree provided in verse 31.

What prompted the tears of the women is hard to say: perhaps the quiet and gentle bearing of Jesus; perhaps their knowledge of His innocence; perhaps the sight of the cruelties inflicted upon Him as well as their awareness of even greater cruelties in store for Him at the place of execution. Whatever the cause, the tears of these women were genuine. They unquestionably felt sorry for Jesus. They meant to be sympathetic.

Yet Jesus rejected their tears. In some rather harsh language He told these women to weep for themselves, not for Him. They were to weep because in the terrible days that lay ahead their own city, Jerusalem, would be besieged by the Roman armies and destroyed. So terrible would those days be that being childless would actually be a blessing and being covered by mountains would be better than facing the sufferings of that siege. In those impending events lay an appropriate cause for tears.

These were not the vindictive words of a man disillusioned with life and bitter toward people. We can be sure of this because just a little later this same Jesus asked His Father to forgive His executioners and promised eternal life to one of the criminals put to death with Him. Jesus' words in our text were harsh because He wanted to make unmistakably clear to these women that their sympathy was not enough. Their sympathy was overly preoccupied with the manifestation of Jesus' physical suffering and not sufficiently concerned with the cause of that suffering, namely, their own sins. Further, they failed to realize the higher purpose of the scene going on before their eyes: Jesus was not merely on His way to suffer and die but was, above all, on His way to save people—including these women. Throughout the ages these daughters of Jerusalem have served as a symbol of a particular brand of sympathy called sentiment, which overemphasizes the physical suffering of Jesus and overlooks the grand purpose of that suffering. Accordingly, as much as Jesus may have humanly appreciated the tears of these women, He was compelled to reject them as woefully inadequate and emblematic of a wrong reaction toward Him and His work.

The corrective to their misapprehension can be found via the Gospel-handle technique in Jesus' parting remark to them: "If they do these things in a green tree, what shall be done in the dry?" Let the "green tree" stand for Jesus, who was sinless, pure, innocent. (The word "green" today yet carries a connotation of innocence.) Let the "dry tree" stand for the

Israelites, the women, and us, who are all sinful, corrupt, and guilty. There is Scriptural warrant for this latter connection in Jude 12, which includes the dry tree metaphor among its other ear-filling designations for sinful people. It calls them "clouds…without water, carried about of winds; *trees whose fruit withereth, without fruit, twice dead, plucked up by the roots;* Raging waves of the sea, foaming out their own shame; wandering stars, to whom is reserved the blackness of darkness for ever" (emphasis added). The point is that if Jesus as the sinless "green tree" is about to be executed, what is bound to happen to the sinful "dry tree"—like the Israelites, the women in our text, and ourselves? Far worse things, to be sure! That is the obvious answer expected.

But that is not the answer given. Actually, the text doesn't answer the question at all. But the Gospel surely does. Its answer: nothing ultimately will happen to us dry trees—except heaven—because the green tree, Jesus, became the dry tree in our place and suffered the fate of the dry tree in our place. He was made sin for us and suffered the curse for sin, namely, death and hell. Therefore, heaven rather than hell is what happens to us dry trees. Indeed, if we push our metaphor even farther, each of us is now a green tree in the sight of God because we have been credited with Christ's own righteousness. That is what the women in our text needed to see, and that is what we can convey effectively to our listeners through usage of the Gospel-handle "green tree"/"dry tree."

Any pastor using this Gospel-handle should be aware of an exegetical difficulty in the text. Does the Greek word for "tree" refer to *two* trees, a green tree and a dry tree, or to only *one* tree, a green tree that becomes dry? Both translations of the original are possible. The Living Bible opts for two trees: "For if such things as this are done to Me, the Living Tree, what will they do to you?" Good News, on the other hand, settles for one tree: "For if such things as these are done when the wood is green, what will happen when it is dry?" If the word for "tree" is translated as only one tree, a green one that becomes dry, then our Gospel-handle cannot be used, for to associate Jesus with the green tree would involve incorrectly portraying Jesus as an originally innocent person who gradually became a sinner.

Despite the risk involved in importing the Gospel into this text, the preacher must be aware of the even greater risk of not importing the Gospel at all. As indicated earlier, this pericope contains no explicit Gospel; it is a Law text. Using a purely textual approach in preaching on this pericope, despite the customary integrity of this methodology, will result in a Law sermon—and nothing more. If the goal of one's sermon is to provide an historical answer to Jesus' question, "What shall be done in the dry [tree]?", the result will be a description of the destruction of Jerusalem in 70 A.D. This treatment of the text is good—as far as it goes. But it doesn't go far enough. To demonstrate from this text that what a man sows he reaps is a valid application of the text. But to stop with that application is a damnable misuse of the Scriptures. Law-preaching as a preliminary to Gospel is always in order. But Law-preaching by itself is never in order. It is better to import the Gospel through the use of a Gospel-handle than to leave a sermon devoid of Gospel out of rigid allegiance to strictly textual preaching.

Matthew 7:6

Gospel-Handle: "that which is holy...pearls"[11]

6 Give not that which is holy unto the dogs, neither cast ye your pearls before swine, lest they trample them under their feet, and turn again and rend you.

The student author of this Gospel-handle reverently suggested that in one sense God did not heed His own advice recorded in this verse; in the Gospel event God did not practice what He preached in our text. In sending His Son to our world, God gave "that which is holy" to "dogs" and cast His "pearl" before "swine."

The initial results were in keeping with the outcome described in our text: people "trampled" Jesus under their feet, "turned against" God, and attempted to "rend" Him. When the Son of God arrived there was no room for Him in the inn. "He was in the world, and the world was made by Him, and the world knew Him not" (John 1:10). He was "despised and rejected of men...we hid as it were our faces from Him; He was despised, and we esteemed Him not" (Is. 53:3). All who saw Him laughed Him to scorn and shot out the lip (Ps. 22:7). Men mocked Him, whipped Him, slapped Him, spat upon Him, crowned Him with thorns, and nailed Him to a cross. While He was dying they gambled for His clothing. Truly, when God gave "that which is holy" (the sinless Jesus) unto "dogs" and cast His "pearl" (His own beloved Son) before "swine," the outcome was altogether in keeping with God's own unerring prediction.

But by the agency of another "that is holy" (the Holy Spirit) and the instrumentality of another "pearl" (God's Word), God brings into being a glorious exception to the rule spelled out in our text, that glorious exception called faith by which we are converted from the "dogs" and "swine" we are by nature to people who are able to accept "that which is holy," God's "pearl," His Son, as our Lord and Savior. "But as many as received Him, to them gave He power to become the sons of God, even to them that believe on His name" (John 1:12).

This Gospel-handle should constitute only a brief portion of a sermon on this text and should never be represented as an explication of the text. In addition, the creative insight the preacher provides must be worded as reverently and responsibly as possible. Yet despite these qualifications, the association between the Law-message of the text and the Gospel-event is a valid and edifying connection in the pastor's task to preach Christ and Him only.

Luke 13:6-9

Gospel-Handle: "fig tree" (v. 6)[12]

6 He spake also this parable; A certain man had a fig tree planted in his vineyard; and he came and sought fruit thereon, and found none.
7 Then said he unto the dresser of his vineyard, Behold, these three years I come seeking fruit on this fig tree, and find none: cut it down; why cumbereth it the ground?
8 And he answering said unto him, Lord, let it alone this year also, till I shall dig about it, and dung it:
9 And if it bear fruit, well: and if not, then after that thou shalt cut it down.

In explicating a parable we customarily avoid pressing its details for meaning. We find *the* point of comparison and subordinate its other points to that. Nevertheless, it is sometimes appropriate to interpret parabolic detail so long as that interpretation reinforces the main point of the parable rather than upstages it, so long as it does not contradict any truth taught clearly and directly elsewhere in the Bible, and so long as it does not violate the canons of good taste. While there can be dangers in both directions, I believe that today our Lord's parables suffer more from under-interpretation than from over-interpretation. It is my experience that those who suggest that it is "allegorizing" to explicate parabolic detail are at the same time tolerant of such explication so long as it is familiar and conventional, not new and creative.

Thus, none of us are alarmed at the identification of the "certain man" in our parable as God, of the "fig tree" as people, and of the "fruit" expected from the tree as faith and/or good works. These are familiar, almost unavoidable associations in the treatment of this parable and all in good taste. None of them contradicts any clear doctrine of Scripture, and each is useful in accenting the point of the parable which is God's expectation of us to bear the fruit of faith and/or good works and His infinite care and patience in assisting us to meet His expectation.

For a preacher to associate the vinedresser of the parable with Christ in His intercessory role may give us pause momentarily, but we gladly go along with the association for the sake of the Gospel, as long as its proponent does not go so far as to say that the vinedresser "represents" or "is" Christ. For a preacher to associate the "dung" of the parable by which the vinedresser fertilizes the fig tree with the principal saving acts of Christ may cause in us mixed reactions: joy over the additional provision for Gospel that its proponent finds in the parable, but uneasiness over flirtation with bad taste and with excessive interpretation.

The Gospel-handle "fig tree" takes a different—and utterly unexpected—approach to supplementary Gospel in this parable. After conventionally associating the fig tree with us, it creatively associates the fig tree with Christ. Conventional parabolic interpretation suggests that Christ *pleads* for the fig tree, but the creative Gospel-handle suggests that Christ *becomes* the fig tree in our place. Given this approach, Christ endures God's curse of the fig tree for not bearing fruit (detailed in Matt. 21:19 and Mark 11:13-14, 20-21)[13] but also bears the fruit of righteousness for God, fruit which we appropriate through faith. In effect, the handle enhances the Gospel in the parable, not by *improving* upon the Gospel in the parable but by *adding* to the Gospel in the parable.

So long as its proponent does not claim that this is what the parable of the fig tree is saying and so long as this Gospel-handle supplements rather than supplants the Gospel the parable contains, I have no objection to the process; in fact, if the handle occurred in the third or fourth sermon I happened to hear on this text, I might even welcome the change.

Gospel-Handles Based on a Rhetorical Device in the Biblical Sermon Text

It is not uncommon for some in the secular world to speak of the Bible as "great literature." While agreeing with this observation, Christians are not always pleased at this tribute to the artistic quality of the Scriptures. However well-intended and complimentary the remark is, Christians realize that it can represent an inadequate view of the Bible as *merely* literature and *nothing more than* literature. Christians are convinced that the Bible is much more than a work of art, far more than a literary masterpiece. They know the Scriptures to be more than a collection of profound insights attractively stated by highly skilled and competent men. Christians recognize that the Bible is *God's* Word, that it is a collection of human writings enjoying an advantage shared by no other literary work in all the world no matter how great. That is the advantage of verbal inspiration by God with its logical concomitant, inerrancy. "Holy men of God spake as they were moved by the Holy Ghost" (2 Peter 1:21). Hence the Bible is in a class by itself. It must be approached with a different set of presuppositions. To treat it merely as literature is to mistreat it.

Nevertheless, we need to remember that the Bible is also literature. To a high degree the Bible contains many of the ingredients common in literary masterpieces: anthropomorphism, dramatic irony, hyperbole, metaphor (in the narrow sense), metonymy, paradox, parallelism, simile, and synecdoche to name a few. Three of these, metonymy, synecdoche, and metaphor (in the narrow sense), have been discussed previously. To be sensitive to the presence of these rhetorical devices is not only to do justice to the literary merit of the Scriptures but also to enrich one's own response to the Scriptures. To miss their presence is in a sense to mistreat the Scriptures. Several published authors have expressed themselves on this thought. "Is it not equally wrong to handle the Scriptures unaesthetically as to handle it untruthfully?"[14] "Christians ought not to tolerate a double standard in worship—namely, zeal for the truth in doctrine and disregard of the truth in art."[15] "Belief in the authority of the Bible will not by itself be sufficient for understanding it if the reader ignores the literary principles that underlie the Bible and determine much of its meaning."[16]

One rhetorical device which occurs surprisingly often in the Bible is dramatic irony, a literary device that is a source of much pleasure and meaning to the reader particularly of Greek and Elizabethan drama. In dramatic irony two ingredients are usually present: (1) the speaker's words are true in either a greater or a different sense than he intends them—he has no idea how truly he speaks; (2) the listener or reader is better aware of certain circumstances than is the speaker—he knows something the speaker doesn't.

Some examples from secular masterpieces may help us better understand dramatic irony. In Sophocles' *Oedipus Rex*, Oedipus, ruler of Thebes, denounces the unknown murderer of King Laius by crying out:

> ...if he ever tread my hearth and I
> Know it, be every curse upon my head
> That I have spoke this day.[17]

Little does Oedipus know at the time as does the audience that the unknown murderer is he himself, and that he is pronouncing his dire curses upon his own head. For prior to his arrival at Thebes, Oedipus had killed a stranger in a violent quarrel who was none less than King Laius himself.

In Shakespeare's *Twelfth Night*, Duke Orsino addresses Cesario not knowing as the audience does that he is really a she in male disguise—Viola:

> For they shall yet belie thy happy years
> That say thou art a man. Diana's lip
> Is not more smooth and rubious; thy small pipe
> Is as the maiden's organ, shrill and sound,
> And all is semblative a woman's part.[18]

In attributing feminine characteristics to Cesario, the Duke does not realize how truly he speaks—Cesario is a woman! A moment later the Duke commissions Cesario to woo the Lady Olivia in his behalf and promises:

> Prosper well in this,
> And thou shalt live as freely as thy lord
> To call his fortunes thine.[19]

The Duke is not aware as is the audience that Viola *will* call his fortunes hers **81** someday, not as the recipient of the generous reward he intended when he made the promise, but as the Duke's lawful wife. Unwittingly, the Duke is "prophesying" his own marriage to Viola!

In *The Picture of Dorian Gray* by Oscar Wilde, Dorian Gray, impressed by the magnificent portrait Basil Hallward has painted of him, comments: "Why did you paint it? It will mock me someday—mock me horribly!"[20] Dorian here is expressing the conventional fear that many of us have about portraits and photos, namely, that years later we will be appalled by the painful contrast between the unchanging youthfulness of the picture and the advancing age of the subject. As the novel unfolds it appears that Dorian's fear is unfounded, for in his particular case there is a reversal: it is the portrait that grows old and wrinkled while he himself with the passage of years remains inexplicably young. Nevertheless, it ultimately turns out that Dorian's fear is not groundless, for as the reader of this familiar tale knows, the portrait *does* mock him—mock him horribly—in that it records every wicked deed and thought of which Dorian is guilty. Even though Dorian retains his youth his portrait is a hideous memento of his sinfulness, a conscience made visible, a relentless nemesis hounding Dorian incessantly in his pursuit of pleasure. Despite all the unexpected developments in the novel, Dorian's conventional fear is realized—but in an unconventional, unforeseen manner. His words turned out to be true in a different way than he meant when he spoke them—hence the dramatic irony.

Three obvious instances of dramatic irony in the Bible come to mind. The first occurs in the encounter between Nathan and David. After David's adultery with Bathsheba and his murder of her husband, the Lord sends Nathan to the King. When Nathan tells his story of the rich man who bypassed his own flocks to appropriate the sole lamb of a poor neighbor in order to feed a guest, David cries out in anger: "As the Lord liveth, the man that hath done this thing shall surely die" (2 Sam. 12:5). Little does David realize at the moment as does the reader that he is pronouncing judgment upon himself. Nathan's "Thou art the man" (v. 7) captures the irony of the pronouncement in all of its intense drama, and the reader finds in it a safety valve, an outlet for feelings crying for release.

A second obvious instance of Biblical dramatic irony occurs in John 11:49-51. The chief priests and Pharisees are discussing their perennial problem of Jesus, a problem intensified by His most recent miracle of raising Lazarus from death. Suddenly Caiaphas, the high priest, proposes a solution. "It is expedient for us," he asserts, "that one man [meaning Jesus] should die for the people, and that the whole nation perish not." He, of course, meant something nasty and selfish, that it would be to the political advantage of the Jewish nation if Jesus could be sacrificed to the Roman overlords so that Roman attention to Jesus would take the heat off the chief priests and Pharisees. But as verse 51 indicates, Caiaphas was not aware of the full import of his words. His sinister suggestion turns out to be glorious prophecy. It *is* "expedient," that is, spiritually advantageous, that one person, Jesus, should die for the people so that they would not need to perish in hell. As the spiritual heirs of Jesus' life-giving death, we know something that Caiaphas didn't—hence the dramatic irony.

A third obvious instance of Biblical dramatic irony arises in the Emmaus episode (Luke 24:13-35), and its presence there is certainly one of the factors that makes the reading of that account such a pleasurable experience. When Cleopas in verse 18 asks the stranger who has just joined the twosome, "Art thou only a stranger in Jerusalem, and hast not known the things which are come to pass there in these days?", little does he know as does the reader that he is addressing the very person to whom all these things had happened! When Cleopas continues in verse 21 with the complaint, "But we trusted that it had been he which should have redeemed Israel: and beside all this, today is the third day since these things were done," the irony becomes almost unbearable. For we know what Cleopas doesn't know: Jesus has risen on the third day and has redeemed Israel, not in the political sense Cleopas had in mind but in the spiritual sense God had in mind.

Particularly the last two of these three instances of Biblical dramatic irony indicate that there is a basic difference between Biblical dramatic irony and much of the dramatic irony in secular literature. Usually, the dramatic irony in secular literature is grim, painful, and shattering. But Biblical dramatic irony almost always highlights God's grace and goodness. If there is a surprise it is a pleasant one. If there is an unforeseen second level of meaning in one's words, that level of meaning is a pleasurable one. Biblical dramatic irony is blessed rather than cruel. It dramatizes the plan of salvation. It reveals a powerful and gracious God ever at work bringing His good out of man's evil, accomplishing His wisdom despite or even through man's ignorance. Typical as many of the Biblical instances of dramatic irony are, they are atypical in respect to their pleasant outcome. Scriptural dramatic irony is dramatic irony *with a difference.*

This basic difference in Biblical dramatic irony is evident in the instances that follow.[21] While the presence of dramatic irony in these instances may not be overt, even the suspicion of its presence in the following passages will help us to find the Gospel in them and therefore prove to be an enriching and rewarding experience. Such an approach of finding dramatic irony in Scripture is in keeping not only with the familiar reminder of the Sunday collect "that Thy Word, as becometh it, may not be bound, but have free course and be preached to the joy and edifying of Christ's holy people"[22] but it also is in keeping with our Lord's own hermeneutical directive in John 5:39: "Search the Scriptures; for in them ye think ye have eternal life: and they are they which testify of Me."

Psalm 88:9-12

Gospel-Handle: dramatic irony

9 Mine eye mourneth by reason of affliction: Lord, I have called
daily upon Thee, I have stretched out my hands unto Thee.
10 Wilt Thou shew wonders to the dead? shall the dead arise and
praise Thee? Selah.
11 Shall Thy lovingkindness be declared in the grave? or Thy faith-
fulness in destruction?
12 Shall Thy wonders be known in the dark? and Thy righteousness
in the land of forgetfulness?

In this passage the psalmist nags God for His apparent neglect of
him. Almost "blasphemously" (be it reverently said) he fires questions at
God that expect a negative answer in each case. "Wilt Thou shew wonders
to the dead?" (Hardly!) "Shall the dead arise and praise Thee?" (Fat
chance!) "Shall Thy lovingkindess be declared in the grave?" (I doubt it!)
"Shall Thy wonders be known in the dark?" (No, no, a thousand times no!)
How does one bring the Gospel into a sermon on this text? There seem to
be two superb possibilities.

One is to point out that this very "nagging" the psalmist indulges in
is, thanks to Jesus and His sacrifice on the cross, indicative of the intimacy
that now exists between us and God. We can now approach Him "as dear
children approach their dear father." What the psalmist does is similar to
what others in Scripture have done: the Syrophoenician woman who
matches wits with our Lord; the importunate widow who pesters the unjust
judge till she gets what she wants; the friend who stops by at midnight for
bread even though the occupants of the house are in bed; and those violent
people in Matthew 11:12 who take the kingdom of heaven by force.

A second and even better way to bring the Gospel into a sermon on
this text is to recognize the presence of dramatic irony in it. As citizens of
the New Testament and children of the resurrection, you and I know that
the psalmist's sarcastic and desperate remarks had an outcome not foreseen
by him at the time. His arrogant questions, to which he thought only
negative answers were possible, have (surprise, surprise!) received positive
answers, gloriously positive answers. "Wilt Thou shew wonders to the
dead?" (Indeed, Christ has: to Lazarus, Jairus' daughter, the widow of Nain's
son, and others.) "Shall the dead arise and praise Thee?" (Indeed, such is
our hope now that Christ has risen.) "Shall Thy lovingkindness be declared
in the grave?" (Oh, yes, there above all!) "Shall thy wonders be known in
the dark?" (To be sure! Even there, even there!)

Matthew 27:24-25

Gospel-Handle: dramatic irony

24 When Pilate saw that he could prevail nothing, but that rather a

tumult was made, he took water, and washed his hands before the multitude, saying, I am innocent of the blood of this just person: see ye to it.

25 Then answered all the people, and said, His blood be on us, and on our children.

This passage provides the most interesting possibility of dramatic irony in the entire Scriptures. In fact, unless one suspects the presence of dramatic irony in this text, it is difficult to derive Gospel from it all. Nowhere do we find the people of Christ's day giving expression to a more frenzied, more fanatical hatred for Jesus than in this particular passage. Faced with a ticklish problem, Pontius Pilate resorts to a time-tested gimmick: passing the buck. Taking water and washing his hands, he insists, "I am innocent of the blood of this just person: see ye to it." Pilate is saying here, "If there's any blame in connection with this affair, I'm free of it; you people take it." And they take Pilate's offer. They are willing to assume all the blame. So much do they hate Jesus that they will gladly suffer any consequences that might result from killing Him. In fact, for all they care any such consequences may extend to succeeding generations of Jews too. That doesn't make any difference. "His blood be on us, and on our children," the people scream. Seldom has hatred been more intense.

Too many preachers in developing a sermon on this text are content to detail how this self-imposed curse came true in Jewish history.[23] Too many pastors are quick to infer from this text the moral: "Whatsoever a man soweth, that shall he also reap" (Gal. 6:7). Certainly this is a legitimate application of the text, good as far as it goes. But if it goes no farther, if it is the *only* application of the text, then it fails to meet the preacher's most fundamental obligation: to use *a* word of the Bible to get at *the* Word of the Bible, Jesus Christ.

The possibility of dramatic irony in this passage provides the preacher with just the opportunity he needs to get at the Gospel. "His blood be on us, and on our children." Jesus' enemies intended these words to be a self-imposed curse: "We and our children accept the consequences of His murder." But without the Jews ever intending it, these words in the light of the Gospel contain a blessing too. Christ's blood *is* on us and on our children, that is, in a saving sense. His blood is on us and on our children just as the blood of the Passover lamb was on the doorposts of the houses of the Israelites prior to the exodus, saving the occupants from the destruction wrought by the Lord at that time. The benefits of Christ's blood are on us and on our children. The wonderful blessings of eternal salvation in heaven and the opportunity for goodness in everyday life which Christ won for us through the shedding of His blood are available to all people of all generations, including those Jews who meant something quite different when they screamed, "His blood be on us, and on our children." Peter says that we were redeemed "with the precious blood of Christ" (1 Peter 1:19). Paul says that in Him "we have redemption through His blood, even the forgiveness of sins" (Col. 1:14). John says that "the blood of Jesus Christ His Son cleanseth us from all sin" (1 John 1:7).

All the Biblical writers testify to the blessings that come to us from Christ's blood. His blood is on us and on our children—in the best sense of the phrase. That is the central truth of the Christian religion. Ironically, a frenzied, fanatical mob may have given voice to it on a Friday morning of long ago.

John 4:44

Gospel-Handle: dramatic irony

44 For Jesus Himself testified, that a prophet hath no honour in his own country.

Though it is difficult to classify this passage as an instance of dramatic irony, it has perhaps the greatest Gospel potential of the three examples cited so far. In this text Jesus concedes "that a prophet hath no honour in his own country." At first blush this passage means that great men are seldom if ever accorded the honor they deserve in their home environment, an observation so often confirmed by human experience that it has almost become a cliché. One way to redeem this cliché and unpack its potential for Gospel is to be sensitive to the possible irony in the passage. Let it be noted, however, that it can hardly be called dramatic irony since the omniscient Jesus would assuredly not be unaware of the possibly higher level of meaning His words contained.[24]

At any rate, there is no more dramatic instance of the truth of Jesus' observation "that a prophet hath no honour in his own country" than at the cross. In the hour of His utmost need Jesus turned to His home, heaven, the eternal abode of both Him and His Father, only to discover that His Father had forsaken Him. He was indeed without honor in that terrible moment when, sinless as He was, He was made sin for us and made the curse for our sin. During the throes of damnation in our place Jesus was "Exhibit No. 1" of a prophet being without honor in His own country.

Genesis 6:5-7 and 8:21

Gospel-Handle: anthropomorphism

Another rhetorical device appearing in Scripture that can be used as a Gospel-handle is anthropomorphism. One encounters anthropomorphism whenever human characteristics are attributed to God. The Gospel-handle of anthropomorphism serves to resolve a paradox in the following text. But it does more than that: It takes us directly to the significance of the incarnation in God's saving plan. To provide variety in mode of presentation and to demonstrate the homiletical utility of Gospel-handles, a sermonette rather than an explication appears below.

> Genesis 6:5-7—"And God saw that the wickedness of man was great in the earth, and that every imagination of the thoughts of his heart was only evil continually. And it repented the Lord that He had made man on the earth, and grieved Him at His heart. And the Lord said, I will destroy man whom I have created from the face of the earth."

> Genesis 8:21—"And the Lord said in His heart, I will not again curse the ground for any more for man's sake; for the imagination of man's heart is evil from his youth; neither will I again smite any more every thing living, as I have done."

Did anything strike you as strange when I read these two texts together? Did you notice it? The reason that God advanced for not sending another flood was the same reason that He gave for sending the flood in the first place: man's depravity. That's curious, isn't it? Noticing that "the imagination of man's heart is evil from his youth," God resolves to wipe man out with a flood. After it is all over God resolves never to send another such disaster. Why not? Because "the imagination of man's heart is evil from his youth." Very interesting, isn't it?

A resolution of this paradox can be found in the anthropomorphic language of our text. Most of us encountered that mouthful of a word called "anthropomorphism" already back in catechism days. When, for instance, we read in our Bible history stories that "it repented the Lord that He had made man on the earth, and it grieved Him at His heart," the pastor, perhaps eager to unload this big word from his repertoire, laid it on us. "That's an anthropomorphism," he told us with a degree of unpardonable pride. "That Lord who is the same yesterday, today, and forever doesn't really, of course, change His mind," he continued; "it just looks that way to us. That's a human way of speaking. God is pictured as a man, as one who walks and talks and gets angry and makes up and repents and so on, so that we who are mere men can better understand who He is and what He's about. You see, whenever human form or human characteristics are attributed to God, that's an anthropomorphism. Got it?" Well, we had it all right. We hurried home from instruction and tried to impress our folks by casually inserting the word into our table chatter.

But I wonder if the anthropomorphism in our text isn't even deeper than that. It isn't just a matter of God feeling sorry He had made man in the first place. It's as if God were initially committed to a trial and error approach, as if He were testing an hypothesis. Man's incredible wickedness had stirred up His holy ire. Something must be done about it. How about a law and order approach? How about destroying the human race, saving only the cream of the crop? Let's try it. Enter the flood. But after it's all over, the beat goes on: "the imagination of man's heart is [still] evil from his youth."

It just didn't work. Human depravity is still with us. So abandon the hypothesis. We'll have to try something else.

Now I've made God sound so human that my description is more than anthropomorphic—it's incorrect! So I hasten to add that of course this isn't the way God went about it. He doesn't formulate, test, and abandon hypotheses. He doesn't learn from experience. He doesn't try first one thing and then another. He knows what He's doing at all times and in all places. In fact, He knew all along, right from the start. There's plenty in the Bible to support this.

Nevertheless, God might have had His holy writer picture it that way, as if He were committed to a trial and error approach. He might have inspired this anthropomorphic representation for a very good reason. And that is to set us up for, prepare us for the approach that did work, the plan that God—no, not eventually but rather eternally—came up with: the Christ approach, the Gospel approach.

Here is where revelation became really anthropomorphic, super-anthropomorphic. God sent His Son in the form of a man, literally! He took on flesh and blood. He had arms, legs, nose, ears, complexion, speech, height, weight, the whole works. He shared our life; He shared our death; He took upon Himself our damnation. No mere verbal representation this! No mere imagery here! God became man. This was for real. And this was something for which we need not apologize. For this we shout "Hallelujahs." Blessed anthropomorphism!

Blessed primarily because it worked. Oh, to be sure, depravity is still with us. The imagination of our heart is still evil from our youth. But God, through our faith in the God-Man whom He sent, chips away at it, whittling away at it. Day after day, month after month, year after year, God works on us through Christ, not only lessening the evil it is certain we brought into this world but also replacing it with good, His good. If it repents Him that He made man, He now remakes man in Christ. If it grieves Him that He created us, He now recreates us in Christ. To be sure, only in heaven will He complete the process. Only then will we be perfect. But in the meantime God is continually refining us into the image of His dear Son, Jesus Christ.

No wonder God promised in our text not to send another flood and curse again the ground for man's sake. He doesn't have to. To relapse into my all too human way of speaking, He has hit upon the right approach. He has come across the solution. In terms of a familiar car ad, He has "found a better idea." Or in the more traditional—and acceptable—language of St. Paul, He has found a "better way." That way is Christ.

Chapter Four

Creativity Through the Use of New Sermon Approaches and Formats

In this chapter I discuss a variety of creative sermon approaches and formats and provide sermon models exemplifying them. After presentation of a number of multiple text arrangements and some sermon approaches involving a variety of literary genres, the chapter continues with a briefer consideration of the following sermon approaches and formats: extended analogy, role playing, dialog, letter format, inversion, cliché redemption, word study, grammar, logic, and mathematics.

The sermon models selected to exemplify these creative approaches and formats were preached in a variety of settings: a few in parish situations; some in small group meetings; many in an academic environment. Sermons chosen from the last two settings will reflect their environment in their brevity, in the kinds of problems discussed, and in the occasional academic character of the language employed. In an attempt to gather the most effective sermon models possible, I have in some instances borrowed the sermons of others. Appropriate credit for the sources of these sermons has been provided in the endnotes.

I offer two suggestions about your use of the creative sermon approaches and formats that follow. First, use them only occasionally. In my experience the kind of creativity represented by these sermon approaches and formats is effective in inverse proportion to its frequency. Used sparingly, these approaches and formats can stimulate and edify. Used too frequently, however, they can tire people and lose their effectiveness. Second, use these creative sermon approaches and formats only where a good pastor-people relationship exists. To establish such a relationship requires sanctification and time. I would discourage the novice from extensive use of these creative sermon approaches and formats. The danger is that if the audience concludes that the preacher is showing off or trying to impress them, his creative efforts will be futile no matter how well they are done.

Multiple Texts

Of all the creative modes discussed in this chapter, the multiple text format enjoys the advantage of being the most palatable to Christian audiences because there is nothing even remotely bizarre or sensational about the approach. Pastors, too, will find the format advantageous. Since intelligence has sometimes been defined as the capacity to see relationships, the multiple text format is particularly accessible to the preacher whom God has gifted with intelligence and who is thoroughly familiar with his Bible. For example, something he reads in 2 Peter may call to mind something he read in Joshua. What he reads may echo or parallel what he remembers, or it may contrast to it, seem to contradict it, or seem to be in some other kind of relationship with it (cause and effect, question and answer, problem and solution, etc.). Bringing the two texts together will often generate a creative sermon. When a text from one part of the Bible is juxtaposed with a text from another part of the Bible, creativity is a frequent outcome.

Such an approach to preaching is in keeping with the hermeneutical directive to interpret Scripture with Scripture and helps fulfill the pastor's role as systematician. In the multiple text approach the Christian preacher is performing a marriage between widely scattered Biblical texts, joining together what God in His Holy Word has—in terms of location at least—put asunder; and, consistent with our analogy, the result is often a new family of Biblical insights. So brought together, the texts prove fruitful and multiply. To change the metaphor, the dialectic arising from the side by side placement of multiple texts may result in a synthesis, in a creative insight not present—or at least not perceptible—in either text by itself. To return to our initial point, to arrange such a dialectic, to perform such a marriage, requires considerable and increasing familiarity with the Scriptures.

Conceivably a pastor may sometimes feel uneasy about synthesizing scattered Bible passages to serve as a sermon text, especially if that synthesis has not been suggested to him by the pericopes assigned for a given Sunday. He may fear that he is manipulating the Bible passages he has selected, that he is arranging them to make the Bible say what he wants it to say. He may suspect himself of approaching the Scriptures with a preconceived notion and then positioning his multiple text choices in such a way that they buttress that preconceived notion. Since preachers too are a part of a fallen world, such manipulation is a possibility, and the pastor does well to be constantly on his guard.

But the conscientious pastor need not be unduly fearful about the multiple text approach to preaching. Much depends upon the source of what has been called his "preconceived notion." If that notion is of the devil, the world, or one's flesh, the juxtaposition of multiple texts is poor homiletical procedure. But his "preconceived notion" may have had its origin in the Scriptures themselves; the preacher may have gotten his idea from his previous Bible reading. If such is the case the homiletical procedure is valid.

We appear to have here a homiletical variant of the age-old question: Which came first, the chicken or the egg? Seldom can even the most conscientious of us approach a Biblical sermon text—including one assigned to us by a pericope—in a vacuum, entirely devoid of personal input. Even in the most ideal conditions in our sermon preparation, it is inevitable that we bring something to the text as well as derive something from the text. But bringing something to the text is not necessarily bad. What is crucial is the origin and/or character of what we bring to the text. Is our input the product of previous reading of the Scriptures? If not that, is our input at least in agreement with the Scriptures or not in contradiction to them? It is possible to think we are bringing something of ourselves to a sermon text when, in fact, what we bring is God's gift to us through our previous use of His Word and His gracious direction of our life experiences centered in that Word. In summary, the more we read in the Scriptures, the more we understand what we read. The more we "dwell richly in the Word" (Col. 3:16), the more meaning we see in a specific Word of God serving as a sermon text. There is a give and take, a mutual interaction, between our study of texts and our previous Bible reading. The relationship snowballs. In this area too our Lord's words apply: "Whosoever hath, to him shall be given; and whosoever hath not, from him shall be taken even that which he seemeth to have" (Luke 8:18).

The main advantage I see in the multiple text approach is that it constitutes a superb demonstration of the unity of Scripture. Preachers often talk about that unity, sometimes perhaps in the hope that their talking will make it so in the perception of their lay people. But isn't it psychologically more effective to *demonstrate* that unity rather than merely talk about it? To find an Old Testament truth echoed or paralleled in the New Testament, to wrestle with a Scriptural paradox and resolve it with the Scriptures, to see scattered parts of the Bible in a variety of logical relationships, what could be better proof of our claims about the unity of the Bible? In the occasional use of the multiple text approach, the preacher and his listeners will experience the pleasant surprise of discovering that what they have repeatedly expressed their allegiance to, the unity of Scripture, is indeed perceptibly true.

New Testament Echoes of an Old Testament Text

In this first subdivision of our presentation of the multiple text sermon formats, we see a text in the New Testament simply echoing or paralleling a text in the Old Testament. There is no particular logical or sequential relationship between the two texts; the one merely seems to be a reverberation of the other. But it is a reassuring reverberation, a process by which God "makes our assurance doubly sure." The echo sustains us in our conviction that the theology of the New Testament is integrally related to that of the Old Testament. The parallel helps us to see in that collection of writings we call the Scriptures, composed by various people at various times in history, the sort of unity and consistency we might expect if, as the Scriptures claim, they have an ultimate common author, God Himself, who has ultimately one purpose: to save and sanctify fallen humankind.

Let me provide some brief examples of a New Testament passage echoing an Old Testament verse. In Psalm 56:8 God's providential care for us is described with the metaphor of tears: "Thou tellest my wanderings: put Thou my tears into Thy bottle: are they not in Thy book?" This can be coupled with that same providential care for us described in Matthew 10:30 with the metaphor of hair: "But the very hairs of your head are all numbered." When the psalmist asks (116:12-13), "What shall I render unto the Lord for all His benefits toward me?" he answers, "I will take the cup of salvation." Taken together, the question and answer surprise us with the truth that God wants us to repay Him for all His blessings to us by simply accepting another blessing from Him, the blessing of salvation! The thrill is even greater when we find this same surprise in the New Testament echo of this Old Testament truth, John 6:28-29. Here some followers of Jesus, eager to show their gratitude to God for His goodness toward them, ask, "What shall we do, that we might work the works of God?" Jesus' astounding answer is: "This is the work of God, that ye believe on Him whom He hath sent." In other words, we work for God by letting Him work for us, by letting Him work that faith in Jesus in our hearts by which we receive another gift from Him, the gift of eternal life. The point of both passages: for all His goodness toward us God would appreciate it very much if we would give Him an opportunity to be even better toward us. The fact that Joshua's spies to Canaan are welcomed in Jericho by a harlot seems to foreshadow the warm reception to be given to Jesus (Joshua's namesake) centuries later by publicans and harlots. In both cases the so-called fools of this world are wiser than the so-called wise; "and base things of the world, and things which are despised, hath God chosen, yea, and things which are not, to bring to nought things that are" (1 Cor. 2:28). In the chapter dealing with Biblical metaphors for the Gospel, I called attention to the added significance that Jesus' cry over Jerusalem (Matt. 23:37) acquires when we realize that His metaphor of a hen gathering her chickens under her wings echoes the Old Testament metaphor of an eagle whose wings bear us up (Ex. 19:4) and whose feathers cover us (Ps. 91:4) and provide us refuge (Ps. 57:1). It is fascinating to pursue the theological implications of the parallel between

Jacob's compliment to Esau (Gen. 33:10) "I have seen thy face, as though I had seen the face of God" and John's promise to us (1 John 3:2) that someday we shall behold the face of God: "When He shall appear, we shall be like Him; for we shall see Him as He is."

The sermon below capitalizes on another New Testament echo of an Old Testament truth. I have selected this particular parish sermon as a model not only because it demonstrates a parallel between passages widely separated in the Scriptures, but also because it doubles as a model for the presentation of the full literal Gospel, of the Gospel in terms of Christ's damnation.

> Exodus 32:31-32—"And Moses returned unto the Lord, and said, Oh, this people have sinned a great sin, and have made them gods of gold. Yet now, if Thou wilt forgive their sin—; and if not, blot me, I pray Thee, out of Thy book which Thou hast written."

> Romans 9:3—"For I could wish that myself were accursed from Christ for my brethren, my kinsmen according to the flesh."

We observe Lent in order to become more aware of God's love for us through Christ. One way to achieve this increased awareness is to describe that love. Various descriptions are possible. The most familiar one, no doubt, is the description of Christ's intense physical suffering. Our two texts, however, suggest a somewhat unusual way of describing God's love for us through Christ. They show the ultimate extreme to which that love went. I submit their approach today, supremely confident that it can increase our awareness of God's love for us through Christ.

"Greater love hath no man than this, that a man lay down his life for his friends," Jesus once said. He meant that there is no more effective way for a person to show his love for another than by dying for him, dying in his place so that he might live. That is the supreme sacrifice, the most that a person can do. All of us, perhaps, know of instances in which someone made this supreme sacrifice: laying down his life for another. Maybe we read in the newspaper once of a mother who threw herself into the path of an oncoming car and thereby saved her child. Or possibly some of us remember that high school classic, *A Tale of Two Cities* by Charles Dickens, in which one man volunteered to be guillotined in the place of another. Nothing could be more heroic.

Our Lord Jesus made this supreme sacrifice. He lay down His life for us. He was crucified for us, executed in our place. In fact, He "went His own saying one better" because He lay down His life, not for friends, but for enemies, for decidedly unlovable people. St. Paul expressed his astonishment this way: "For scarcely for a righteous man will one die: yet peradventure for a good man some would even dare to die. But God commendeth His love toward us, in that while we were yet sinners, Christ died for us" (Rom. 5:7-8).

Yes, Jesus went this far: He lay down His life for us. But really, He went even farther. Laying down His life for us was an extreme that Jesus went to, true, but it was not *the* extreme that He went to. Our two texts today suggest that Jesus' love for us drove Him even farther than laying down His life for us. The sacrifice He finally made was even greater than what we would ordinarily call the supreme sacrifice.

What was that sacrifice? We said a moment ago that giving his life for another is the most a person can do. That is correct: dying for another is the most we humans can do. Our power to help others does not extend beyond this point. We can help our fellowmen in many different ways, even to the extent of dying so that they might live, but beyond that—we're helpless. There is nothing more that we can do.

People have realized this limitation; in fact, they have chafed under it. There have been times in the history of our world when people have wished it were possible to do more. Moses was one of these. He had been up on Mt. Sinai conversing with God and receiving the Ten Commandments from Him. Upon his return he discovered his followers singing and dancing and, of all things, worshiping a golden calf, and doing so at the instigation of one who certainly should have known better, Aaron. Moses became very angry with the Israelites, even to the extent of breaking the two stone tablets he carried, grinding the golden calf into powder, then making the people drink it with water, and finally supervising a slaughter of his idolatrous countrymen. But the next day we see another side of Moses' character. Realizing the heinous sin committed by his followers, he pleads to God for their forgiveness. He recognizes that this will be hard for God to do. "Oh, this people have sinned a great sin, and have made them gods of gold," he admits. But then he adds: "Yet now, if Thou wilt forgive their sin—; and if not, blot me, I pray Thee, out of Thy book which Thou hast written." Moses doesn't request God merely to let him die for his countrymen. He goes farther: he asks to be damned in their place, to have his name blotted from the book of eternal life and transferred to the list of all those headed for damnation. So great is Moses' love for the Israelites that he implores God to let him suffer the hell that they had coming for their idolatry.

St. Paul was another example of this type of love. Among other things in his letter to the Romans, he discusses the fate of his countrymen, the Jews, many of whom were rejecting Christ. Paul pulls no punches. He points out the inevitable damnation they will experience if they persist in this rejection. But he points it out with sorrow, not with glee or with a holier-than-thou or an I-told-you-so attitude. "I have great heaviness and continual sorrow in my heart," he begins. And now listen to this: "For I could wish that myself were accursed from Christ for my brethren, my kinsmen according to the flesh." Paul doesn't merely wish to die for his countrymen; he realizes that that couldn't help them as far as their escaping hell is concerned. No, like Moses, he wishes to be damned for his country-men, "accursed from Christ." So great is his love for them that if it were possible he would suffer their hell.

Ah, but there was the catch: if it were possible. But it wasn't possible. Neither Moses nor Paul could do what he wished because both of them were sinful. Therefore, if they suffered hell it could only at best count for themselves, certainly not for anyone else. The assistance Moses and Paul wished to give was simply beyond human power to give. God so much as told Moses that such help was out of the question when He said, "Whoso-ever hath sinned against Me, him will I blot out of My book." Paul himself seemed to realize the impossibility of carrying out his wish when he pointedly said, "I *could* wish"; that is, I'd wish to be accursed from Christ for my countrymen if only such a wish could do any good, but of course it can't. "Greater love hath no man than this, that a man lay down his life." That is the most a person can do. Beyond that he has no power to help.

Moses and Paul were not the only ones to entertain this wish. At some point in the divine plan this unbelievable wish was expressed also by Christ Jesus. There came a time in that world beyond all worlds when God the Son approached God the Father with the request that He might be blotted out of the book of life, that He might be accursed of God for us, sinners and enemies of the heavenly family—so great was Jesus' love for us. His Father also so loved us that He accepted the offer of His Son and sent Him to our world to carry out His wish.

You see, Christ could carry out this wish. That's why God sent Him. Like Moses and Paul, Christ wished to suffer hell for others. But unlike Moses and Paul, Christ was able to do what He wished. For He was the Son of God. He was pure and holy; there was no sin in Him. If He were to suffer hell, it could count for others since He had no sins of His own. All of which is just another way of expressing the familiar truth that "not man could save man but only God could save man."

What amazes us, however, is not simply that Christ could do what He wished, but that He did it. He did it! There are many amazing things in the life of Jesus of Nazareth: the lowly manner of His birth; His humble up-bringing; His exposure to temptation and human problems; His patient endurance of persecution, misunderstanding, and disappointment; His suf-fering, particularly during the last week of His life; His cruel and humiliat-ing mode of death. But topping all of these, more amazing than any of these, is this: on the cross He permitted Himself to be blotted out of the book of life and accursed of God for us, so that we might live in heaven forever. Innocent as He was and loved of the Father as He was, Jesus, nevertheless, let Himself be made sin for us and be made the curse for sin in our place. He suffered our hell. No cry of despair in all history has ever equaled the despair of Christ's cry on the cross, "My God, My God, why hast Thou forsaken Me?" Greater agony there has never been. Greater love there has never been. It was "the extremest of extremes" to go to, "the supremest of supreme sacrifices" to make. It amazes us that Christ wished to suffer our hell; it amazes us that He could suffer our hell; it amazes us most of all that He did suffer our hell.

We are told in the account of Christ's crucifixion that when He voiced this cry of despair, "My God, My God, why hast Thou forsaken Me?" many of the people in the vicinity failed to understand what He meant. Today we definitely do not want to share their ignorance. We want to understand. For a time Christ is blotted out of God's book of life. He is accursed of His Father. He tastes the hell, the forsakenness of God, that is the wages of sin, and He does it that we might live: live here "unto Him who died for us and rose again" and live there "in His Father's mansions." That is the extreme to which God's love for us went. That is the sum and substance of Lent. This is what it's all about. This is the thing above all things that we want to know. The Scriptures assure us that it's worth the knowing.

Cause and Effect

In this subdivision of our presentation of multiple text sermon formats and in the subdivisions that follow, we see a relationship emerge when one text is juxtaposed with another. That is, the second text is not merely parallel to the first; the one text is not simply an echo, reverberation, or repetition of the other. Rather there is some logical or sequential relationship between the two texts, such as cause and effect, contrast, paradox, question and answer, problem and solution, or multiple aspects of a given truth.

The logical relationship between multiple texts we are presently considering is cause and effect, a relationship that is self-explanatory. One of my students a few years ago did a study on Genesis 3:17-18 and Matthew 27:29 suggesting a cause and effect relationship between the thorns mentioned in the first passage (God's description to Adam and Eve of the curse of sin) and the crown of thorns that Jesus wore (mentioned in the second passage). Even more provocative than his suggestion that sin was the cause and Jesus' suffering the result was the symbolism he found in Jesus' crown of thorns. Since thorns (like the thistles and other items mentioned in the Genesis passage) were part of the curse of sin and since Jesus wore a crown of thorns, it follows that His action signified that He was taking upon Himself our curse of sin. In other words, the crown of thorns is a metaphorical way of dramatizing the literal truth described in Galatians 3:13: "Christ hath redeemed us from the curse of the law, being made a curse for us."

When Matthew 26:56 and Matthew 27:46 are placed side by side, there seems to be at first nothing more than a repetition, a certain action (forsaking Jesus) occurring twice. In the first passage we see the disciples forsaking Jesus, and in the second passage we see God forsaking Jesus. But ultimately there is a cause and effect relationship between the two incidents. It is because people deserted God that it became necessary for God to desert His Son—to save people from the consequence of their desertion. A sermon exploring that cause and effect relationship was included in the second chapter of this book. Its inclusion there demonstrated the homiletical treatment of Christ's damnation on the cross. The same sermon doubles as a model for multiple texts in a cause and effect relationship (cf. pp. 29-31).

Contrast

Like the cause and effect relationship, the contrast relationship between multiple texts is self-explanatory, and of all the multiple text relationships possible, it is the easiest to find in the Bible and the easiest to deal with in a sermon. Contrast, for example, Ephesians 2:1 and Romans 6:2; the one speaks of death *in* sin, the other of death *to* sin. (The little prepositions make all the difference in the world!) Look at the different use to which water is put in John 13:5 and Matthew 27:24: Jesus uses water to wash His disciples' feet, signifying His humility and His eagerness to serve; but Pilate uses water to evade responsibility, signifying his cowardice and his political ambition. How different from each other the attitudes toward sin expressed in 1 Timothy 1:15 and Jude 13: Paul is sorrowing over sin and honestly confessing it, but the people Jude describes are reveling in their sin and brazenly flaunting it. How different in tone and spirit is our Lord's use of numbers in Matthew 18:22 from Lamech's use of numbers in Genesis 4:24: Lamech wishes to be avenged "seventy and sevenfold" while Jesus urges us to forgive "seventy times seven." How different is man's relationship to the tree of life described in Revelation 22:1-4 and that described in Genesis 3:22-24, a difference than can be accounted for only by the Gospel-event.

This brief homily below, delivered at a joint faculty meeting, contrasts two kinds of faith.

> John 6:37—"Him that cometh to Me I will in no wise cast out."
>
> 2 Timothy 1:12—"I know whom I have believed, and am persuaded that He is able to keep that which I have committed unto Him against that day."

The two texts I just read seem to show the two extremes, the two poles, of Christian faith. The one seems to describe a minimum faith—if I may put it that way: "Him that cometh to Me I will in no wise cast out." The other seems to describe a maximum faith: "I know whom I have believed, and am persuaded that He is able to keep that which I have committed unto Him against that day." One text pictures the spark of faith; the other text pictures the rock of faith. The one faith sounds like a faith of desperation; the other faith sounds like a faith of certainty. In the one case faith seems wavering; in the other case faith seems heroic.

Now why bring this to your attention? I can think of two good reasons, only one of which I'm going to dwell on today. Juxtaposing these two texts could provide a challenge, urging us to get with it, to grow in faith, to move farther from our *terminus a quo* and get closer to our *terminus ad quem.*

But suppose we regard that as material for some future devotion. Rather than challenge you today, let me juxtapose these two texts to comfort you. If you're like me, I'm sure you aspire to the one faith but are forever settling for the other. The stronger faith is the ideal we shoot for (and, oh, how we yearn for it!), but the weaker one is the reality that we all too often find in our everyday lives (but, oh, how we thank God for even that reality!). How often have I longed to join Paul in that bold statement, "I know whom I have believed, and am persuaded that He is able to keep that which I have committed unto Him against that day." There have been moments (ah, blessed moments!) when I have succeeded. But all too often it didn't ring true. Just when I was fantasizing about being martyred for my faith in a lion-packed arena, the crowds hushed in admiration, and the music of "Pomp and Circumstance" in the background, there came a stab of pain in the back and I panicked with the fear of surgery, or there came a payment due notice and I wondered how I could possibly pay the bill, or one of the children slurped his soup and I was quickly transformed from the great in faith of my daydream to the great with anger of my workaday world. It was then, in that moment of truth, painful, naked truth, that there stole upon my senses like a breath of fresh air, like an oasis in the desert, the reassurance of the words of Jesus, "Him that cometh to Me I will in no wise cast out."

That's the beauty of our God. He'll let me squeak by. He'll accept me even though I don't come to Him till the ship is sinking. He'll take me, yes, even blundering, stumbling, idiotic me, with all my weaknesses bared and all my pretensions exposed. Jesus' death and resurrection have that much power. We are indeed saved by grace and by grace alone! Oh, the comfort this sweet sentence gives: "Him that cometh to Me I will in no wise cast out."

Paradox

One of the most interesting multiple text arrangements is that of paradox, juxtaposing Biblical texts that seem to contradict or negate each other, but which when studied carefully yield a profound truth. There is something inherently creative in the process. Often a text will open up when compelled to defend itself against another text. In tension there is truth. Truth, of course, must be our goal, not tension or contradiction. The danger in the approach is to arrive at no solution at all or to attempt a false solution by carefully rigging the riddle to make everything turn out all right in the end (knocking down a straw man).

There is a surprising amount of paradox in the Bible, both within texts and between texts. Perhaps the best-known example of paradox within a text is Jesus' statement "He that findeth his life shall lose it: and he that loseth his life for My sake shall find it" (Matt. 10:39). Another well-known paradox is Jesus' promise "Come unto Me, all ye that labour and are heavy laden, and I will give you rest. Take My yoke upon you...and ye shall find rest unto your souls. For My yoke is easy, and My burden is light" (Matt. 11:28-30). Less familiar but every bit as intriguing is Jesus' observation "Whosoever hath, to him shall be given; and whosoever hath not, from him shall be taken even that which he seemeth to have" (Luke 8:18).

Even more intriguing are the paradoxes that exist between texts. A classic paradox results when Mark 9:40 and Luke 11:23 are placed side by side. In the former Jesus says, "He that is not against us is on our part"; in the latter Jesus says, "He that is not with Me is against Me." Juxtaposing John 7:34 and John 12:26 gives rise to another fascinating paradox. When Jesus tells us in the first passage, "Where I am, thither ye cannot come," we despair of reaching heaven. When Jesus assures us in the second passage, "Where I am, there shall also My servant be," we revel in heaven's accessibility. A preacher's effort to resolve this paradox can result in a superb Law-Gospel sermon. He can move his hearers from the shocking realization that because of their sins they are unable to be with Jesus in heaven to the thrilling conviction that because Jesus has made them right with God they are indeed able to spend eternity with their Lord. One of my favorite Biblical paradoxes—because it supports my earlier claim that from tension there often emerges profound truth—occurs in Jesus' words to Martha in John 11:25-26: "He that believeth in Me, *though he were dead*, yet shall he live: And whosoever liveth and believeth in Me *shall never die*" (emphasis added). One verse speaks of death occurring; the next verse speaks of death *not* occurring. Attempts to resolve this paradox will lead one to the discovery of the important Scriptural truth that there are two kinds of death, physical and spiritual, as well as two kinds of life, physical and spiritual.

One of the sermons included in Chapter Three to demonstrate the homiletical utility of a Gospel-handle can also serve as a model for multiple texts in a paradoxical relationship (cf. pp. 85-88).

Question and Answer

One of the relationships possible in a multiple text arrangement is a question and answer format. The two examples that follow are from other homiletics texts. Question: "What is man, that Thou art mindful of him?" (Ps. 8:4). Answer: "The Spirit Itself beareth witness with our spirit that we are the children of God" (Rom. 8:16). Question: "If a man die, shall he live again?" (Job 14:14). Answer: "He that believeth in Me, though he were dead, yet shall he live" (John 11:25).

The model below is excerpted from a sermon delivered to a pastors' conference. As will become evident, the sermon deals not merely with the respective contents of the question and the answer but primarily with a pastoral approach that can be inferred from the manner in which our Lord answers the question directed to Him. That very inference demonstrates once more the creative potential of a multiple text approach to preaching. Rather than incorporate the entire sermon, I have included only that portion relevant to the question and answer format.

> Luke 10:29 (the question): "But he, willing to justify himself, said unto Jesus, And who is my neighbor?"

> Luke 10:36 (the answer): "Which now of these three, thinkest thou, was neighbor unto him that fell among the thieves?"

I have always been fond of the story of the Good Samaritan, but at the same time I have sometimes been tempted to regard the story as grossly irrelevant. Be it reverently said, the Lord Jesus never really answered the lawyer's question. He asked, "Who is my neighbor?" and Jesus replied (in effect), "You be a neighbor." It appears as if the Savior missed the point completely.

Technically beside the point—yes. Actually, however—no. Oh, I guess that even technically the question was answered. At least I've always been told that the answer to the lawyer's question, if not directly given in the story, is at least implied, namely, that a neighbor is whoever is in need. But let us not defend our Lord too eagerly, lest in our doing so we miss the very jolt He intended for us. Technically, Jesus didn't answer what was asked; rather, He answered what needed answering. Searching for a neat, precise doctrinal formulation for the concept of "neighbor," the smart-aleck lawyer was forgetting to be one. This was his crying need. At the risk of apparently skirting the issue, Jesus spoke to the issues of life and death. You see, there are sometimes matters more important than the particular matter raised.

Actually, this is old hat for most of us. Every prof knows that not every question asked in the classroom reflects a thirst for knowledge; it may only be a ruse for delaying the inevitable quiz or for seeking relief from furious note-taking. It's likewise a truism of counseling that not every complaint by the patient reflects the true state of affairs. When he says, "I'm fatigued," he may be saying, "I'm vocationally mixed-up." When he says, "I want to quit my preparation for the ministry" (for example), he may only be confessing, "I haven't been getting enough sleep lately." This is true even on a simpler level. If you are fixing a flat tire and a passerby asks, "Do you have a flat?" you don't rudely reply to what appears to be an unnecessary question; instead, you understand the query as an offer to be of service. If a girl remarks, "Isn't it a pretty moon tonight?" her boyfriend understands that question sufficiently well to avoid launching, by way of reply, into a discourse on astronomy.

But we are getting far afield. To get to the point, might not our text be confronting us with a divine approach that we would do well to emulate? It is not always enough to answer the question; we must answer the question behind the question. It is not always sufficient to deal with the stated need; we must deal with the needs behind the apparent need. When a fellow Christian comes to you with the question, "Have I committed the sin against the Holy Ghost?" a doctrinal explanation or a comforting reassurance may not be the answer; his needs might be psychiatric. When a youth takes an unequivocal pro-integration position, do not rejoice with the angels too quickly at the measure of the man's faith; he could conceivably be a rebel without a cause in search of a cause. When a church officer enumerates a fellow member's crimes toward himself and then asks you what quirk in that member's constitution makes him do such awful things, risk a long shot: avoid the question and lecture the man evangelically about the need of forgiving "seventy times seven." When a building committee member beefs too vehemently and continuously about a particular location or a specific building plan, you should at least be aware of the possibility that he may be seeking pocketbook protection. And when a lady says, "I don't like to gossip but…," you may be reasonably sure that she does.

There are some obvious dangers to this approach, and maybe we at least ought to mention them. One is simply to avoid the issue. We need not do this anymore than Jesus did. In the long run He answered the lawyer's question—He defined "neighbor"—only He answered much more. I'm not suggesting that we run away from difficult questions. I am suggesting, though, that we may have to do more than answer the particular question raised. Another danger is judging. We must be careful not to see in every challenge to a familiar truth a love of heresy or in every vigorous defense of a commonly accepted truth a stubborn resistance to change. Our conclusions, our judgments, our long shots, if you please, will have to be charitably arrived at and evangelically broached. Should they prove wrong, they should be hastily withdrawn. After all, we lack the divine omniscience that Jesus had, who could look into the hearts of men. A final danger is being too subtle, of reading between the lines so much that we fail to read the lines. Maybe the student who says, "I'm tired," means just that, nothing more, nothing less. Perhaps the fellow Christian is in danger of committing the sin against the Holy Ghost, and we'd better talk to the point. It is even remotely possible that the lady doesn't like to gossip, that she is genuinely interested in the welfare of the person whose scandalous conduct she is about to describe.

Obviously these situations require considerable wisdom and sanctification. That's why we pastors spend so many years acquiring an education: in order to learn all the psychology and sociology and history and philosophy and what not that we need for effectively dealing with people. Most of all, that's why we pastors feed ourselves so richly and regularly on the same

Word that we dispense to our congregations. "The fear of the Lord is the beginning of wisdom." Only that Jesus who authored the pastoral approach suggested by our text, only that Jesus who died and rose for us can give us the wisdom to employ that approach wisely. The story of the Good Samaritan, which is sandwiched between our question and answer texts, abounds in the Gospel which we so desperately need to enable our effective ministering. Let us briefly look at a few of these Gospel aspects.

Problem and Solution

Another possible relationship in a multiple text arrangement is a problem-solution format. One of the question-answer examples cited earlier doubles as a problem-solution example. Problem: "If a man die, shall he live again?" (Job 14:14). Solution: "He that believeth in Me, though he were dead, yet shall he live" (John 11:25). The next example is one I have frequently encountered in homiletics textbooks. Problem: "Upon the earth distress of nations, with perplexity" (Luke 21:25). Solution: "Peace I leave with you, My peace I give unto you: not as the world giveth, give I unto you. Let not your heart be troubled, neither let it be afraid" (John 14:27).

The model below is a Christmas sermon preached by one of my students during his internship.[1]

> Job 3:1-4a—"After this opened Job his mouth, and cursed his day. And Job spake, and said, Let the day perish wherein I was born, and the night in which it was said, There is a man child conceived. Let that day be darkness."

> Luke 2:10-11—"And the angel said unto them, Fear not: for, behold, I bring you good tidings of great joy, which shall be to all people. For unto you is born this day in the city of David a Savior, which is Christ the Lord."

Back in the fifth century before Christ, the Greek city-state of Athens was in its golden age. This was the age of Pericles, the great leader under whom Athens reached its height in democracy and in the arts. This was the age of the great dramatists, Aeschylus, Sophocles, and Euripides, who left plays of such universal impact that they are still read and appreciated today. This was, in fact, the age in which Athens became the center for the expression of the human spirit. And therein lies the catch: because at the height of Athens' golden age, one of the dramatists wrote a play in which he expressed his conclusions about how worthwhile it was to live at such a time. Sophocles wrote: "Not to be born is, past all prizing, best; but, when a man hath seen the light, this is next best by far, that with all speed he should go thither, whence he hath come" (*Oedipus at Colonus,* 1225 f.). One of the most perceptive men of a great age wrote that it was best never to be born, and, if born, it was best to die quickly.

102

What a tragic attitude, we might say. Yet Sophocles is not alone in feeling this way. Great writers from Euripides to Nietzsche have said the same. It's even in the Bible, in our first text for today, from Job. Job was responding to the loss of all his property and of his children and, now, even of his health. Job had gone from riches to rags and worse; he had been stripped of everything but his life, and now he wondered how much even that was worth. Wouldn't it have been better never to have been born?

Few of us, thank God, will ever approach the situation of Job when he spoke these words. Yet each of us faces the stress both of personal problems and of the sheer impersonality of our age. We live in an age in which terrific pressures seek to make all things temporary, whether marriage, or friendship, or home life at any one place. We live in an age in which the cost of living seems to make living cost too much for too many. We live in an age of kilotons and megawatts, of kill ratios and million dollar projects, which make thinking of real people out there beyond our own circle of loved ones and friends most difficult. It seems we can have so little impact on what shapes our lives, especially when things go wrong. In fact, as one of Job's friends observes later in the book, it seems that "man is born unto trouble" just as surely as sparks go upward from a fire (5:7). In the final analysis, what difference does it really make whether or not you or I were ever born?

That's not even the worst part. The worst part is something which we don't like to think about much and which our age has done much to hide from us. The naked fact is, however, that each of us is going to die. From the moment of our birth that is the one thing of which we can be *absolutely* certain, Ben Franklin's taxes notwithstanding. That seems the final nail in the coffin of our reasons for living. If all we are and do will crumble into dust eventually and if "you can't take it with you," what's the use of living? Again this sort of thinking is not peculiar to our time. Already Shakespeare wrote of it in *Macbeth*:

> Out, out, brief candle!
> Life's but a walking shadow, a poor player
> That struts and frets his hour upon the stage,
> And then is heard no more. It is a tale
> Told by an idiot, full of sound and fury,
> Signifying nothing. (V, v. 23-28)

Again we may not like this sort of thinking, but unless there is something to give meaning to our life or to change the meaning of our death, then "that's all there is."

We're in this fix, of course, by our own fault. Even Job, whom God called "a perfect and an upright man" (1:8), could not rail at God for doing him an injustice. For Job and we have sinned. God, in creating all things good, said, "Let there be light" (Gen. 1:3); we say with Job, "Let that day be darkness" (3:4). Because we have chosen sin we have spoiled the perfection of creation, have brought trouble between one person and another, and have placed ourselves on the road to death from the day of our birth.

About this time what we really need is some good news. But the kind we usually get just doesn't work. "Eat, drink, and be merry, for tomorrow we die" is one way out, but it's a cop-out since there's such a limit to how much revelry can lead to lasting happiness. The other approach of finding some lasting value in our contributions is stared down firmly by the facts of history, which say that "this, too, shall pass."

What we need is some good news about something from outside the cycle of birth and death. And that's exactly what our second text for today gives us. This text, too, talks about birth, but this is not the birth of any mere man. The good news is that there is born to you this day a Savior, the Messiah, the Lord God Himself. God Himself breaks radically into history, choosing to be like us, so that He might heal us and the creation we spoiled from the inside out.

The results are clear from the angel's words. First of all, we need no longer fear. We need no longer fear the pressures and uncertainties of our age: we now have something solid and lasting. We need no longer fear the feeling that the world is rushing on by us as we play out our bit part in the cosmic drama: we are important ourselves, so important that God burst into history to save each and every one of us. Our lives *do* have meaning, meaning provided by the God who says, "I call *you*; I forgive *you*; I send *you*." Best of all, we need no longer fear even death since the death of God the Son on the cross turned death from the end of futile life into the beginning of full, eternal life.

Because we need no longer fear meaninglessness in life and finality in death, we are free to rejoice in both with the "great joy" of our text. This is not the sort of bubbly joy which the "eat, drink, and be merry" types are after; that sort just doesn't hold up. Rather, this joy is akin to that of really falling in love or of having a child. It seems to influence how we feel about everything else; it gives new meaning to the life we lead.

When good news comes to people in any tight situation in life, one thing we can be sure of is that there is no way to keep it a secret. In no time at all word gets around that the cavalry is on the way, or that Dad has pulled through the operation, or that it's a boy or a girl. So it is here. This good news is for all people. All people must hear that life and death "ain't what they used to be." And who can tell but those who know? Our second text was, of course, first addressed to the shepherds outside of Bethlehem on Christmas night. After going to see what this thing was which the Lord had done in the stable, what did they do? They told all who would listen what they had seen and heard. So it is with us who have seen, heard, and even tasted the goodness of the Lord in Jesus Christ. We, too, must share the good word that the day of His birth makes the day of our birth a matter of celebration instead of cursing.

Job, we know, grew in faith through his trials and finally was blessed richly by God, even double what he had lost. The last verse of the book reads: "So Job died, being old and full of days" (42:17). By the grace of God the man who once cursed the day of his birth died in the hands of the Lord "full of days." So by the grace of God it can be for us. On our birthdays we can praise God for our creation; on the day of our death we can rejoice with "great joy" in our new life. For ever since we got the good news, for us "to live is Christ, and to die is gain" (Phil. 1:21).

Multiple Aspects of a Given Truth

In this multiple text arrangement a number of Bible passages are pulled together in order to explore the various facets of a certain Biblical topic or concept. "Burden-bearing" is the common denominator in the three texts constituting the frequent textbook example cited below. Not only does the arrangement of the three passages shed light on the various facets of burden-bearing, but it also, in this instance, suggests an intriguing paradox.

1. "Every man shall bear his own burden" (Gal. 6:5).
2. "Bear ye one another's burdens" (Gal. 6:2).
3. "Cast thy burden upon the Lord" (Ps. 55:22).

In the next textbook example the arrangement of Bible passages not only demonstrates a variety of assessments of Christ but also suggests a progress from gross error to lesser error to improving degrees of correctness.

1. "He hath a devil, and is mad" (John 10:20).
2. "He is a good man" (John 7:12).
3. "Thou art the Christ, the Son of the living God" (Matt. 16:16).
4. "My Lord and my God" (John 20:28).

Early in my ministry I wrote a sermon based upon the following outline in which the word "mind" was the common denominator in the three Bible passages making up my text. The texts were arranged in a logical sequence, progressing from Law to Gospel, with God ultimately enabling what He commands.

1. "Be of the same mind one toward another" (Rom. 12:16).
2. "Let this mind be in you, which was also in Christ Jesus" (Phil. 2:5).
3. "But we have the mind of Christ" (1 Cor. 2:16).

The model below is a sermon written by one of my students.[2]

Psalm 122:1—"I was glad when they said to me, 'Let us go to the house of the Lord!' "

Luke 2:49—"Did you not know that I must be in My Father's house?"

Hebrews 3:6—"Christ was faithful over God's house as a son. And we are His house...."

"I was glad when they said to me, 'Let us go to the house of the Lord!'" So sang the devout psalmist.

When the church calendar announced to you this morning, "Service at St. John's Lutheran at 8:00 a.m.," how glad were you? With what eagerness did you awake to know, "Good! Today is church-going day!" How joyfully did your heart and body respond to that first call to worship shouted from the bottom of the stairwell, "Come on, everybody up! Out of bed! We leave in 45 minutes!"?

Maybe this morning happened to be one of those worship days when you really did long to come to the house of God, perhaps because of a real spiritual hunger, or personal sorrow, or because of the pain of wounds from the daily battle against sin. Or maybe you came because you really long for fellowship with God and other Christians. If so, well and good. Would that it were so for all of us every worship service.

But I more than suspect that this may have been one of those mornings when you came out of habit—although there is really nothing wrong with that; some habits are very good, and church-going is one of them.

Or you may have come out of a sense of duty, which is better than nothing.

Or perhaps you would much rather have stayed home and finished that weekend painting job; but you felt that you had to set a good example to the children—which isn't the best of motives.

Or you may have thought, "Well, let's get it over with so that I can have the rest of the day to myself."

Or maybe it was all rush and bustle, punctuated with such typical but rather unliturgical pre-church phrases as Dad's "I'm starting the car in three minutes! I want everyone there by then!" or teen-age son's "Aw! What's wrong with these shoes? And I haven't got time to change them now!" and daughter's "My hair looks terrible!" and various "Who's locking the house?" and "Have you got a comb?" and so on, with familial order being restored out of the chaos only at the very portals of the church. As I said, there was so much rush and bustle that there simply wasn't room for any feelings of gladness or duty or otherwise.

Whatever the pre-church scene was for you, we all have to admit that for most of the time the psalmist, with his deep sense of joy and prayerful preparation and anticipation, puts us to shame. I too must admit that I wince inwardly whenever I hear those words, "I was *glad* when they said to me...."

Let us leave for a while this uncomfortable word of the psalmist and move to our second text. Perhaps this one will be better news for us. After all, being from Luke 2, it is part of a gospel, and "Gospel" means "good news."

106

What do we find here? Ah! Here is someone who was in the house of

God and was *not* glad. Do we then have someone here who is more like us, someone with whom we can feel more comfortable?

But wait a moment! What was He not glad about? He was not glad about leaving! When the services were over—and He had been through a whole week of them—He did not want to go home. He could not drag Himself away, and He a 12-year-old lad! No wonder the parents could not find Him, for who would expect to find a 12-year-old boy sitting in the faculty lounge of the Jerusalem temple seminary discussing exegetical theology and Biblical hermeneutics, morning, noon, and night, for three days? So absorbed was He with the Word of God that time meant nothing.

And we? After 45 minutes in God's house, how do we feel? What about that casual refolding of the arms or readjustment of the shirt-sleeve just to be able to take a furtive glance at the watch face without letting our neighbor in the pew know that this is what we are really doing? Or that secret thought, "With a bit of luck and a short General Prayer, we should be finished within the hour."

Let's face it. How often do we have feelings of regret when the final "Amen" is sung? How often do we wish that the service could have been much, much longer?

Of course that surreptitious glance at the timepiece, that impatience at the long prayers or sermon, that wanting to get back to the project in the basement—all these are not serious maladies in themselves. Sometimes the sermon is too long anyhow. But mostly they are signs of a much, much deeper malaise. They are the surface indicators of a deep-seated malady, the lack of love for God—the kind of love which is supposed to come from our whole heart and mind, the kind of love which loves the Father above all things. After all, what would we say of the love of a lover who goes to meet his beloved only out of a sense of duty, or who hopes that the time spent together will be as short as possible, or who says, "Good! It's time to go."? What can we say about our kind of love for God which finds going to His house a chore and worshiping Him there tedium?

How different it was with the 12-year-old! So totally committed was He, already at that age, to His Father and His Father's work, so absorbed was He with the Scriptures, that all other ties and duties took second place.

So where does that leave us? If the devout man of the Psalms puts us to shame, the devout youth from Galilee by His example devastates us completely.

But wait! Is this Luke's reason for telling us the story of the boy Jesus in the temple? Is he saying to us, "Look at Jesus' love for God's house. Now follow His example."? Or is he only telling us this story because it is further proof that Jesus is the Son of God? That is part of the reason, no doubt. But there is more, much more. Luke is really telling good news here, and there is real sweetness in this good news.

What is this good news for us, the tardy worship-goers and impatient worship-stayers? This becomes clear when we add the third text for today to the story, "And we are His house." "So what?" you may ask. Well, from the Lukan story we have already seen that the place where Jesus really loves to be is in His Father's house. That is where He loves to go; that is what He hates to leave. And that house, YOU ARE. You are God's house; you are the temple of God made up of living stones, you, the congregation gathered here this morning. He loves to be here with you!

Your gladness at the sound of the call to worship may have been lacking, but not His.

You may have come here this morning dragging your feet, but not He.

Your motives may have been very mixed up and questionable, but not His.

Your concentration may have wandered all over the place, but not His.

It is to you that He says, "Do you not know that My top priority is to be here among you?" When He says that He means also what the old Authorized Version says, "I must be about My Father's business." What is this business? Precisely this: to answer our lack of love with His total love; to answer the coldness of our devotions with the enfolding warmth of His compassion; to answer our mixed motives with His single-minded motive of pronouncing forgiveness upon all our coldness and lack of love; to answer our impatience to leave His place of worship as soon as possible with the news that He is preparing an eternal mansion for us. In fact, one can even go so far as to say that there are two houses where Christ is joyously busy. He is joyously present here in this house busily preparing us for entrance to the mansion there; and He is joyously busy there getting that mansion ready for us who are still here.

So you can see that God's house here is not made special by *our* religious input, *our* joy and gladness, *our* devotional fervor, *our* eagerness. What a sorry place it would be it if were! But it is *His*. Who then says, "I was glad when they said to me, 'Let us go to the house of the Lord' "? It is Jesus Himself who says it, who says it every time His people scramble or bustle or dawdle or yawn their way to worship. It is His gladness that makes the worship—not ours.

And for that we can be really glad!

Literature

Of the general value of literature for the preacher I have already spoken in the introductory chapter. In this chapter I have in mind the homiletical use of the content and/or structure of a literary selection as a means for communicating the truth revealed in a given Biblical sermon text and, particularly, for communicating the Gospel that that text contains. However, more than a casual or brief illustration from literature is involved in the creative format we are presently considering. Rather, the illustration is *extensive,* not monopolizing the sermon or "running away" with it, but seasoning it from start to finish, providing a point of reference to which the sermon frequently returns. The preacher uses the content and/or structure of a literary selection as more than a springboard by which he plunges into the sermon and as more than an insert by which he recaptures waning audience attention. In the creative format currently being considered, the preacher uses the content and/or structure of a literary selection as a "motif," as a recurring element in the development of his sermon. Defining our format is easier done than said; the sermon models that follow should clarify the character of this particular creative format.

To be sure, there are potential dangers connected with the literature format. The preacher must be careful not to permit the literary selection employed in his sermon to upstage his Biblical text. While normally this kind of sermon will probably be more topical than textual by the very nature of the case, the preacher dare not allow his sermon text to become a mere pretext. Extensive as his use of the literary selection is, that usage should highlight the text, make it eminently memorable, put it into the very blood-stream of his listeners. In short, however prominent the role of the literary selection in the sermon may be, it should play a servant role in respect to the text and to the Gospel that the text contains. In my experience achieving this relationship is more a matter of quality than of quantity, more a matter of accent than of space.

Another danger that may arise is elevating extra-Biblical revelation to the level of Biblical revelation. This danger is present whenever the literary selection that the preacher uses for his sermon treats, intentionally or unintentionally, certain aspects of the Christian Gospel with varying degrees of accuracy. It is reassuring to the Christian to know that there are areas outside the Scriptures corroborating, in varying degrees, the presentation of the Gospel-event in the Scriptures. But however useful it may prove to be, such extra-Biblical revelation dare never be substituted for or made equivalent to the inspired, inerrant, wholly sufficient Biblical revelation of the Gospel. At all costs the uniqueness of the Scriptures must be preserved.

For that matter, there is danger in the opposite direction too: the literature sermon format, irresponsibly handled, can abuse literature as well as the Scriptures. The preacher may "insult" this area of the arts by treating literature as little more than a source for sermon materials—especially illustrations—and by determining the aesthetic merit of specific literary selections according to the degree to which they supply such materials. He must not regard literary works as a mere mine from which he extracts its homiletical ore and then treat the rest as dross. Literature stands on its own merits and warrants his attention whether or not it meets the exigencies of the impending Sunday sermon.

Further, too frequent a use of the literature sermon format poses a danger for the preacher's image. However good his intentions may be, he may become in the opinion of his congregation a "culture-vulture," a dilettante, a book reviewer, a mere lover of the arts, a practitioner of cultural one-upmanship, rather than a pastor. Too continuous a fare of literature sermon formats may cause listeners to say, "Oh, Pastor's been reading again," or "Here comes another book review."

Finally, the use of the format, especially if it deals with an unfamiliar literary selection, may pose a danger for the audience. If insufficiently explained, the unfamiliar selection may confuse the audience rather than clarify matters for them. On the other hand, to provide sufficient explanation may preempt too much of the sermon, leading to the danger of upstaging the sermon text. In his use of an unfamiliar literary selection, the preacher may end up in a no-win situation.

These dangers aside, the literature sermon format can be an effective preaching vehicle in the hands of a skilled and responsible pastor. In addition to the format's obvious potential for capturing and retaining listener interest ("Everybody loves a story"), the literature sermon format is one more way of bridging the gap, the false dichotomy, between the secular and the spiritual that permeates too much of our everyday thinking and living. Like our Lord's parables the literary selections we employ can become, to a degree, "earthly stories with heavenly meaning," thereby reducing the distance between the earthly and the heavenly. Without saying so in so many words, they can suggest that the two areas, secular and spiritual, are not really two different entities but rather two aspects of a unity, two sides of a coin, as it were.

Novels, Plays, Poems, and Short Stories

In this subdivision of our presentation of literature sermon formats, it is suggested that the literary selection providing the content and/or structure for the development of a sermon text and the Gospel it contains could be a novel, a play, a poem, or a short story. The sermon model below, making use of a novel, *The Picture of Dorian Gray*, was delivered to a college community.

2 Corinthians 5:21—"He hath made Him to be sin for us, who knew no sin."

Galatians 3:13—"Christ hath redeemed us from the curse of the law, being made a curse for us."

Some believe that the prominent themes of the Bible, such as the Creator sacrificing Himself for the creature, the Son of God becoming incarnate, the God-Man dying and rising again, are foreshadowed or reflected in many different ways in our universe: in the arts, in mythology, in pagan religious beliefs and practices, in legends, in fairy tales, and so on. For example, the burial of a seed in the ground and the new plant life that results testify to the death and resurrection principle. The peculiar manner of birth, via the womb, suggests the peculiar manner of birth into the life of heaven, via the tomb. Accounts of fairies, elves, sprites, and demons hint at the doctrine of angels, both good and bad. However varied and fantastic and untrue the numerators, there seem to be these common Biblical denominators. Most of this foreshadowing or reflecting, to be sure, is unconscious and unintended.

With apologies to Oscar Wilde, who I am sure would not approve of my treatment of his work of art this morning, I would like to reinforce the belief described above with material from the masterpiece *The Picture of Dorian Gray*, a fantasy that many of you have read and that all of you know something about. Unwittingly, this novel in many respects reflects the Christian Gospel.

You recall the story. Basil Hallward paints a portrait of the handsome young Dorian Gray and gives it to him. One day Dorian rather casually expresses the wish that his picture could grow old and wrinkled and careworn while he himself might retain his vigor and youth and good looks. Lo and behold, that is exactly what happens! Dorian had forgotten about his careless wish until one night he looked at the portrait right after he had cruelly and snobbishly jilted Miss Sibyl Vane, causing her to commit suicide. To his surprise he noted a cruel sneer on the portrait that wasn't there initially. From there on it snowballed. Whatever crime Dorian committed, the ugly consequences were reflected in the portrait rather than in himself. When he finally committed murder, there was even blood on the picture. Eventually, the portrait became a hideous monstrosity, but Dorian himself remained young and handsome.

Fantastic and incredible? Yes. But there is a profound grain of truth in it. You see, Christ is to us as the portrait was to Dorian Gray. He grows old with our sins, so to speak, while we remain young and innocent; that is, Christ has been made our sin and our curse for sin. Whatever wrong we have done, still do, and will do, He has suffered the ugly consequences of it on the cross, while we get off scot-free. He became vile, a worm and no man, a reproach unto people and an abhorring unto God, while we are regarded as children of the kingdom. Fantastic, yet gloriously true! Incredible, humanly speaking, yet credible when the Holy Spirit takes over our heart and mind.

Like all analogies this one breaks down. None of us of course will do what Dorian did: take advantage of the situation and live it up and crucify Christ anew. And unlike the portrait, Christ can do something to change our way of life for the better. But there is one more similarity between the novel and the Gospel, and I feel constrained to unload it on you today. Dorian, you will recall, finally stabbed the portrait in a fit of rage. There was a loud cry of pain and terror, and when his domestics entered the room, they found the portrait of a handsome youth and the body of an old, wrinkled, withered man lying on the floor with a knife in his heart. You see, in rejecting Christ you become your old, hideous, sinful self again, destined for that abode technically prepared for the devil and his angels. In a sense it is hard to appreciate the Gospel. Like all true things it is so devastatingly simple, and like always we are so devastatingly sophisticated. We lay our sins on Jesus. That's it. That's all there is to it. We can either take it or leave it—preferably take it. That's why chapels are built and services are conducted every morning, so that we might take it and enjoy the eternal life that goes with accepting Christ as our substitute, as our sin and our curse for sin. May God the Holy Spirit help each of us to regard the innocent but accursed Jesus on the cross as the portrait, so to speak, of our sinful nature and of its inevitable consequence.

Fairy Tales

Beginning with this sermon format we are definitely making a transition from mild creativity to "wild" creativity. Even the most ardent supporter of creativity may experience some qualms at the use of this format for preaching. On the other hand, even the most hostile critic of creativity will feel that for once at least the word "creative" is not being strained when applied to the fairy tale format, that the usage of the word in this instance is not hyperbolic. However negative his feelings toward creativity may be, he recognizes that he is at last in the very presence of the real thing.

Offhand, it would appear that if ever negative feelings toward creativity in sermon construction are justified, they are in this particular case. Obviously, a sermon making extensive use of the content and/or structure of a fairy tale will seldom be a textual sermon—at least "textual" as traditionally defined, in which the sermon derives both its material and its form from the text. (It can still be a textual sermon in the amended sense that it can make the text graphic, vital, memorable.) Even more serious will be the impact of the format on the average listener. It will probably jar him, wave a sort of theological red flag before his face. "Are you trying to suggest, Preacher, that the Bible is a fairy tale?" may be the audience reaction even when such an outcome is farthest from the preacher's intention. In the use of this particular format the preacher must not only be utterly responsible but also highly sensitive, sensitive enough to anticipate the sort of reaction just described and sensitive enough to deal with it kindly rather than write off such critics, erroneous as their reaction is, as theologically unsophisticated. At any rate, it may seem initially that the fairy tale format has so much going against it that its usage is off limits not only to the novice but even to the veteran.

Let me hasten to the defense of this sermon format. Needless to say, such a format will be eminently "listenable"; it will attract and retain attention. But more importantly, there seems to be precedent for the format in our Lord's parables. Our Lord used stories, fictional ones at that and surprisingly earthly, as vehicles for divine truth. Why, then, may we not also use fictional stories—among them fairy tales—as conveyors for His truth? There seems to be but a whisker's difference between the two genres, parables and fairy tales. Finally, bizarre as use of the format may initially seem, it is actually surprisingly conservative. It reverses the current trend: instead of finding myth in the Gospel, it finds the Gospel in myth. Instead of demythologizing the Gospel, it "de-Gospelizes" the myth!

The fairy tales, in my opinion, are the principal evidence for my belief that the central event of history—the Gospel-event of the Son of God's incarnation, life, death, damnation, and resurrection for our salvation —has had so profound an impact in our world that it has spilled beyond the bounds specifically chosen by God to contain it and convey it, namely, divine revelation, the Holy Scriptures. Many aspects of the Gospel, such as the Son of God becoming man, the Creator sacrificing Himself for the creature, the God-Man dying and rising again, are in varying degrees of accuracy and completeness foreshadowed or reflected in nature, in pagan religious beliefs and practices, in mythology, in music, in art, and in literature.[3] When I read fairy tales to my children some years ago, I began to notice certain common denominators in them that were—or could be considered—reflections of, more often distortions of, familiar Christian truths, particularly that greatest of all Christian truths, the Gospel. For example, so many of the fairy tales depicted the struggle between good and evil on a sub- or supra-human level. Could this, I wondered, reflect the classic conflict between God and Satan, between the kingdom of light and the kingdom of darkness? The frequent imposition in these tales of impossible tasks on ordinary mortals, tasks that could be accomplished only by supernatural aid, could this reflect that we can do all things only through Jesus Christ, who strengthens us? Over and over in the fairy tales, prince courts and marries princess, often elevating her in rank, beauty, and character in the process. Might this not remind us of the marriage of Christ, the Bridegroom, and His church, the bride—as well as all the glorious consequences for the bride of that marriage? Above all, there was that frequent refrain "and they lived happily ever after." Wasn't this perhaps a reminder of our blessed hope that we shall live happily ever after in heaven with God, a hope that is not a fairy tale but solid truth itself?

However varied or fantastic or even untrue the numerators in the fairy tales, there seemed to be these common Biblical denominators. Admittedly, any one of these aspects of the fairy tales by itself was not particularly impressive. But it was their totality and their frequency that made me suspicious of the probability that the fairy tales were reflections of, or distortions of, certain facets of the Gospel-event. The discovery excited me. I began to use the fairy tale more and more as a sermon format. Of course there are dangers. But can not the practice also be to the glory of God and His Gospel? In view of the "whatsoever ye do" the passage contains, is it too **113** irreverent to amend Paul's words to read: "Whether therefore ye eat, or drink [or read, or preach], or whatsoever ye do, do all to the glory of God" (1 Cor. 10:31)?

The model below is just one of many in my files. I have selected this particular one because it was preached in a parish rather than in an academic setting and because it seems to be surprisingly textual even in the traditional sense of the word.

> 1 Corinthians 3:11-15—"For other foundation can no man lay than that is laid, which is Jesus Christ. Now if any man build upon this foundation gold, silver, precious stones, wood, hay, stubble; Every man's work shall be made manifest; for the day shall declare it, because it shall be revealed by fire; and the fire shall try every man's work of what sort it is. If any man's work abide which he hath built thereupon, he shall receive a reward. If any man's work shall be burned, he shall suffer loss: but he himself shall be saved; yet so as by fire."

Again and again, as you know, the Bible exhorts us to build Christ's church. It aims this appeal not just at people who go to seminaries and wear special vestments, but also at people who work on assembly lines and punch keyboards and take dictation. All of us, in other words, clergy and laity, audience and speaker, have been exhorted by God to build His church. What kind of structure are we erecting?

Actually, we've got a lot going for us, for God with His customary goodness has already supplied us with the foundation for our structure. "Other foundation can no man lay than that is laid, which is Jesus Christ," our text assures us. We know that foundation so well, don't we? Yet we can never know it too well. Out of love for us sinners God sent Jesus, His Son, as a man to our world to spend 33 years on our planet living the perfect life that we had failed to live and to spend a few excruciating hours on a cross undergoing the damnation and dying the death that we deserved to experience. In raising His Son from the grave three days later, God assured us that all this had indeed been accomplished, that we were now in fact His people, secure in the love and companionship of God here on earth and hereafter in eternity.

But given this glorious given, granted this foundation, what kind of church are you and I building on it? Our text goes on to say that it is possible to continue construction on this foundation with a variety of materials, superior materials like gold or inferior materials like stubble. Although the text details six different building materials, they actually fall into basically three different groups. The gold, silver, and precious stones are all jewelry and constitute the first group, the best group. Wood, in a class by itself, a more dubious building material, constitutes the second group.

Flimsiest of all the building materials is straw, specifically, the hay and stubble, which constitute the third group.

Every time I read this text I can't help associating it with a children's story we are all familiar with, *The Three Little Pigs*. In the earlier versions of this fairy tale the wolf not only destroys the house of straw and the house of sticks but also eats up the occupants thereof. In Walt Disney's arrangement, however, the first two little pigs survive by taking refuge in the brick house of the third little pig. Traditionalist though I am, I find this later rendition more suitable to the development of our text this morning, which also speaks of flimsy dwellings that perish but of builders who survive.

Did you hear that (for that is our topic today): Flimsy dwellings that perish but builders who survive? And I hope you will not think it irreverent of me to use *The Three Little Pigs* as an outline for our treatment of the sacred text today, as each of us considers the structure he builds on the foundation of Jesus Christ that God has supplied.

Some of us may be tempted to build a house of straw. Let's call it what Sinclair Lewis might have called it: a Babbitt church. Or maybe it's simpler to call it an over-organized church, an organization that exists for the sake of organization. You know the kind I mean. Structured flawlessly from top to bottom, from elder to custodian, not a hitch in the administrative flow chart. Supper-serving societies that supplement, even supplant, stewardship, that attract not only the outsider but also his dollar. Organizations that give you a sense of identity and a feeling of belonging, something for everybody from diaper to dotage. A friendly, back-slapping parson buttressed by a team of unctuous ushers quick to get your name on the guest register and, a few weeks later, on the church roster—after six easy lessons. Inspiring, uplifting sermons that brighten your day and supply you with a comfortable ethic to live by. But along comes Satan, that eminent wolf, who huffs and puffs and blows our house down. For it was superficial, made of straw. It was never a church in the first place, just a glorified club, a variety of Kiwanis or Rotary in disguise.

Some of us may be doing better. We are building a house of wood, contemporary, relevant, "mod." Let's call it an "issues-church." We get out the vote. We reform the city council. We erect a community center or a fine arts building. We clean up the ghetto. We provide free coffee and doughnuts every Wednesday morning at the corner of Ninth and Lapeer. We protest whatever it is in the area of political and social concern that's fashionable to protest at the time. We liberalize the church's theology or we hold firm to the traditions of the fathers—whichever we view as our particular messianic mission. We push for improved liturgical practice or we foster rock services—whatever the current fad dictates. We involve ourselves in this, we involve ourselves in that, but—we get involved, for that is the important thing. But along comes Satan and huffs and puffs and huffs and puffs and blows that house down too. The material may have been **115** better, better as wood is better than straw, but it was not good enough.

Be it far from me to dictate what constitutes the third house, the one built of more substantial stuff, be it gold, silver, precious stone, or brick, the house that Satan's huffing and puffing cannot blow down. It's always easier to say what a church shouldn't be than to say what it should be. But I dare say it will be a church in which both Law and Gospel are regularly and effectively proclaimed, where sin is quietly and honestly labeled as sin and where Christ crucified and risen is unabashedly offered as Savior and solution. I dare say it will be a both/and church, stressing both truth and love, both people and doctrine, not a divisive either/or church. I dare say it will be a church in which there is enthusiasm for worship and hunger for the Word, where people, like the psalmist, would rather spend a day in God's court than a thousand elsewhere, and where people, like St. John in one of his visions, will eat the little book up. I dare say it will be a church in which the people love one another, not just in badge or in banner or in ballad, but in deed and in truth. Certainly it will be a church that moves out into its community and its world to eliminate human evil and to alleviate human suffering, but it will always do so from the perspective of eternity, viewing the objects of its help not as creatures of a day but as beings destined for immortality, people therefore in need of heaven as well as of a shirt on their back.

During our childhood that foundation was laid other than which no man can lay, namely, Jesus Christ. It was laid at our mother's knee, in Sunday School, in parochial school, in catechetical instruction. Now that we are grown up (or growing up), we are learning the art of building upon that foundation. This is the main purpose—or should be the main purpose—of all our education and training: to develop in us the art of building, to so improve our wisdom and our sanctification that in our everyday life we erect solid structures of gold, silver, and precious stone rather than flimsy ones of wood, hay, and stubble. "Every man's work shall be made manifest," our text says, "for the day [Judgment Day, no doubt] shall declare it, because it shall be revealed by fire: and the fire shall try every man's work of what sort it is. If any man's work abide which he hath built thereupon, he shall receive a reward." To prepare us for and to help us pass that test is the goal of our education and training.

If this sounds challenging and disturbing, it is; it only reflects the challenge of our text. But there is more than a challenge in our text. There is comfort too. And not only the customary comfort that we have God's help in Christ to enable us to meet the challenge. There is comfort plus, Gospel extra! Just listen: "If any man's work shall be burned, he shall suffer loss: but he himself shall be saved; yet so as by fire." Of course we want ours to be a productive life, a fruitful ministry. But even if we blow it, *even if we blow it,* God's mercy is big enough to incorporate that failure into His eternal plan. We, at any rate, will be saved. We, bumbling, stammering, shallow, cloddish, ignorant, error-prone creatures that we are, we will be saved—so long as we have the glorious given, the foundation of Jesus Christ. Once again we are assured that salvation is by grace, not by works. Don't we have a wonderful God?

Nursery Rhymes

Most of the advantages and disadvantages of the fairy tale format for preaching, previously itemized, apply to the use of a nursery rhyme format for preaching, except that the connotations of "nursery rhyme" are probably more favorable than those of "fairy tale." In respect to nursery rhyme usage the pastor runs less risk of the audience suspecting him of casting doubt upon the veracity of Scripture.

The model below is a New Year's Eve sermon delivered in a parish setting.

> Psalm 127:1—"Except the Lord build the house, they labour in vain that build it."

The nursery rhyme "This Is the House That Jack Built" could well serve as a parable of our era—or at least of an era now in the process of vanishing. Take "jack" in either sense: with a capital "J" denoting the name of a man or boy, or with a small "j" functioning as a slang word for money. In the first instance "This is the house that Jack built" would be a boast about what a person can do; it would be an assertion of rugged individualism. In the second instance "This is the house that jack built" would be a boast about what money can do; it would be a tribute to materialism. Both of these, individualism and materialism, are—or at least have been—characteristic of our American way of life.

From the first log cabins hewed out in the Indian-populated wilderness to the modern ranch style homes erected, often with a considerable degree of owner participation, in our present-day fashionable suburbs, the average American has taken a fierce pride in his rugged individualism. "This is the house that Jack built"—or maybe it was Bill or Paul or Sam. But we need not be so literal. Let the word "house" stand for any kind of individual achievement. Do-it-yourself kits enjoy immense popularity and sales not only because they supposedly save the buyer money but also because they provide an outlet for his individualism, giving him a sense of personal achievement. The story of the self-made millionaire who has risen from rags to riches, from grocery store to executive suite, is a common pitch used by politicians in their appeal for votes as a means to ever higher offices. Even the Christian religion has felt the impact of the phenomenon of individualism. It is difficult to preach God's grace to a society so bent on saving itself; people want their heaven to be, not a gift from God, but a reward for individual accomplishment. Among the obstacles to the current efforts of the various church denominations to iron out their differences **117** and unite as one is the desire of many an American to have his own personal, unique, individual brand of religion. Jack not only wants to build his own house but also wishes to be the captain of his own soul.

Materialism is the other ingredient in the American dream, although one we're not quite so proud of as individualism, and so we try to find kinder words for it, like "prosperity" or "a high standard of living." But ours is, even after taxes and in spite of inflation and recession, an affluent society. A house no longer is a mere shelter; today it is a status symbol, a concrete reminder to every passer-by or guest of the amount of money, of jack, possessed by its owner. "This is the house that jack built"—and goodness knows, as every would-be home owner soon learns to his dismay, it takes plenty of jack to build one or buy one, even to rent one or maintain one. But again we need not restrict ourselves to actual houses. It may also be a car in the garage, a freezer in the utility room, or a colored television set in the family room that testifies to the presence and power of jack.

Individualism and materialism are of course still values in our society, but there are signs of a breakdown. Cracks have appeared in the structure, and many of them surfaced during the 60s and the 70s, a product of the youth movement a decade or two ago. Some of you may recall a much publicized analysis of the Viet Nam War by *Time* magazine in which the editors pointed out that many American soldiers were no longer strongly motivated toward individual heroics in battle, nor were the people back home interested in a recital of the individual accomplishments symbolized by the Bronze Star or the Purple Heart that the returning soldier wore. Some of you may remember also the phenomenon of distinguished graduates of distinguished colleges turning down distinguished positions that paid well besides, the graduates instead seeking out positions of nameless service in the nameless ghettos. Many parents at that time were appalled at the dissatisfaction of their children and occasionally referred to them as "the spoiled generation." How could they be so unhappy, they wondered, when they had positively everything? Even our language eventually betrayed the change in values that was initiated; people used to have things, but now they do their thing—an obviously less materialistic idiom.

Many middle-class, middle-aged Americans are uneasy over this shift in values. Not only do they decry it but they also sometimes attribute it to causes as oversimplified and as illogical as those described in the nursery rhyme "This Is the House That Jack Built." This is the hippy, they say, who tore down the house that Jack built. And this is the professor who taught the hippy who tore down the house that Jack built. And this is the communist who brainwashed the professor who taught the hippy who tore down the house that Jack built. And so on. As a member of the middle-class, middle-aged American group, I frankly sometimes share its uneasiness over the shenanigans of our youth. But I must concede that the slippage in individualism in part and in materialism for most of its parts is not something to grieve over. "Good riddance," I am tempted to say. "If this is the structure that is cracking, speedy be its fall!"

But there is one aspect in the current shift in values over which middle-class, middle-aged Americans—and, for that matter, over which all people of all classes and all ages—have a right to be uneasy. That is the slippage in the Ultimate Value. I mean God Himself. If the youth, to their credit, have triggered the decline of individualism and materialism, they have also, to their shame, participated in the death of God. Rather I should say "the so-called death of God." For of course God cannot die (a fact of which we need to remind ourselves especially this evening, a New Year's Eve, that marks the death, the passing, of another calendar year). God is not a perishable value. He is more unalterable than the proverbial laws of the Medes and Persians. Of His years there is no end. He is the same yesterday, today, and forever. In Him is life, and His life is the light of men. No society can endure, no structure can stand, without God, a fact of which our text reminds us when it says, "Except the Lord build the house, they labour in vain that build it."

Oh, there is one respect in which the current phrase "the death of God" is not entirely inappropriate. It is true in a sense, a sense not intended by its users. God did die! It happened on a cross. That is the central message of God's unique revelation, the Holy Scriptures. That is the foundation on which everything in our world depends. The death of the Son of God is the difference for us between life and death. But God didn't stay dead. His flesh did not see corruption. He rose again. If Christianity proclaims the death of God—and it does—it also proclaims the resurrection of God. Christ crucified *and risen* is the complete formula that we apply to society's ills. When we proclaim that twin fact, Christ crucified and risen, then God, not Jack (be it money or be it the person of that name)—then God, not Jack, is building the house. And when the Lord builds the house, our labor is not in vain. May that unshakeable truth give us courage and hope for the new year ahead.

Legends

Unlike the word "nursery rhyme," the word "legend" has unsavory connotations—at least for the area of preaching. In conceding this fact I do not at all mean to imply that the use of this format is therefore off limits to the preacher. But I am suggesting that when he uses the content and/or structure of a legend to develop a Biblical sermon text, the preacher exercise care that he not be misunderstood as suggesting that the Biblical material itself is legend. People may infer this conclusion even when the preacher does not imply it, so without being unduly and overtly defensive, the preacher in his legitimate use of this particular creative format needs to employ the kind of language in his sermon that makes crystal clear his conviction that Biblical truth is indeed truth, very truth of very truth.

119

The brief devotion below was given in a dormitory setting.

Ephesians 2:1—"And you hath He quickened, who were dead in trespasses and sins."

Ezekiel 36:26—"I will take away the stony heart out of your flesh, and I will give you an heart of flesh."

Isaiah 62:5—"As the bridegroom rejoiceth over the bride, so shall thy God rejoice over thee."

According to a well-known Greek legend there was once a king in Cyprus named Pygmalion, who fell in love with a statue he had made. He took his peculiar problem to Aphrodite in prayer, and the goddess answered his request by making the statue come alive, converting it into a beautiful young woman traditionally referred to as Galatea. Of course Pygmalion married her.

For many centuries there has been a theory—a rather reasonable one to my way of thinking—to the effect that many pagan legends are reflections of or, at worst, distortions of Christian truth. Might not the legend of Pygmalion and Galatea bolster this theory? If it doesn't, perhaps like Shakespeare's Malvolio we can crush it a little and make it bow to us. Perhaps we can make this legend resemble something in Christian theology.

The analogy this legend suggests is strikingly apt. Like the statue, you and I were dead, dead in trespasses and sins according to one of our texts. Like the statue we were stony, stony-hearted according to another of our texts. Put the two together and what have you got? That's right, stone-dead! And like Pygmalion God was in love with us, stone-dead as we were, a love every bit as unreasonable and irrational as the love of Pygamalion for his statue. As in the legend, the impossible has happened: the statue has come to life! "And you hath He quickened, who were dead in trespasses and sins." "I will take away the stony heart out of your flesh, and I will give you an heart of flesh." Crush it still farther. Make it bow a little more. Yes, like Pygmalion God has married the one-time statue. We are His bride. "As the bridegroom rejoiceth over the bride, so shall thy God rejoice over thee."

In changing the statue into a person, Aphrodite worked directly, independently. But in changing us God worked through His Son, Jesus. It is He who quickened us. It is He who gave us a heart of flesh. It is He who married us to God His Father. By His death on the cross in trespasses and sins—our trespasses and sins that is—Christ has achieved the impossible: He has brought us to spiritual life and has rendered us marriageable to God.

But the miracle isn't finished yet. True, we've emerged from one death, spiritual death. But we're headed for another, physical death. When and how we don't know, but it's as sure as taxes. Give us a couple of centuries and we'll be reduced to the dry bones described in our Scripture reading this evening (Ezek. 37:1-14). But God will assemble these bones. He will clothe them with flesh and skin and sinew. He will endow this assemblage with breath, His breath. We will be alive again, fully alive and eternally alive. The marriage will be complete. And as in the fairy tales, we will live happily ever after. There's only one difference, though: this is no fairy tale!

Fables

In the preaching context the word "fable" has a pejorative sense equal to that of the words "fairy tale" and "legend." But in another respect, fable enjoys an advantage over the other two genres. People familiar with Aesop's fables are at least accustomed to fables being vehicles for moral truth. Hence, the use of a fable as a sermon format will not seem as bizarre or contrived as the use, for example, of a fairy tale or a legend. Conveying a moral or lesson is the very essence of fable, whereas such is not the case with the other two genres. Yet that very strength can be its weakness. If the fable sermon format *merely* moralizes, it may constitute good fable but certainly not good preaching. The challenge, ultimately, is to make the fable a vehicle for Gospel, not just for moral truth.

The student sermon excerpted below exemplifies what I believe is the appropriate use of fable for Christian preaching.[4] Notice how skillfully the author uses the fable first for Law and then, via some modifications (making extensive use, incidentally, of Biblical imagery), for Gospel.

Psalm 124:7—"Our soul is escaped as a bird out of snare of the fowlers: the snare is broken, and we are escaped."

Today I want to share with you the fable of *The Crane and the Stork*. Once there was a farmer who planted a cornfield near a marsh. As the corn was ripening, flocks of cranes began to fly in from the marsh and to plunder the grain. The farmer, becoming angry, set a trap in the field. The next day he found that he had indeed caught a large flock of cranes and, among them, a stork. When he came to the stork to kill it, it protested vehemently. "You cannot kill me! Can you not see that I am not a crane but a stork, the most devout of all birds?" (The ancient Greeks considered the stork to be partly sacred.) The farmer simply replied, "You may be a stork, the most devout of all birds; but if you fly with cranes, you die with cranes!" And that was the end of that.

Now what does this fable tell us about human nature? Simply this: when human beings get caught doing something wrong, they are very quick to protest that the action is not a true indication of what they are really like, namely, decent, upright, yes, even devout people by nature. The fact that they were caught stealing, or in the wrong bed, or fiddling with the books—well—that was just a momentary aberration, a thing which could easily be explained by the circumstances. "I may have stolen something, but I am not a thief by nature. I may have spread my affections a little too widely, but I am not immoral. Actually, I am all for integrity in business and the strength of family ties at home. I am really a stork who just happened at this particular moment in time—would you believe it?—to be in the corn-field with these cranes. Well, not really in it—just at the edge, and I took only a few morsels of grain—nothing of any consequence. So, please, please do not make the mistake of confusing me with these low-class, swamp-bred, thieving cranes!"…

The New Testament also knows of those who claim exemption or favored treatment on the grounds of piety. Listen to these words of Christ:

> Many will say to Me in that day, Lord, Lord, have we not prophesied in Thy name? and in Thy name have cast out devils? and in Thy name done many wonderful works? And then will I profess unto them, I never knew you: depart from Me, ye that work iniquity. (Matt. 7:22-23)

To put it in other words: "You may, like storks, have built your nests in church steeples; but if you rob in cornfields, you die!"

Again, another word from our Lord:

> Then shall they also answer Him, saying, Lord, when saw we Thee an hungred, or athirst, or a stranger, or naked, or sick, or in prison, and did not minister unto Thee? Then shall He answer them, saying, Verily I say unto you, Inasmuch as ye did it not to one of the least of these, ye did it not to Me. And these shall go away into everlasting punishment. (Matt. 25:44-46)

Suddenly something has happened to our simple fable in the light of the Word of God. The cornfield is now as large as life itself. Suddenly we realize that to fly with cranes means not only to do things we should not, but not to do the things we should. We are now no longer an audience listening to an amusing tale. We are no longer sideline spectators of the pious foibles of certain individuals who have been caught with their fingers in the till. Suddenly we find that the trap has snapped shut, not in front of us, but behind us, and we too are caught.

But we dare not leave our story there. If the ancient Greeks could invent fables based on careful observation of human behavior, we too may reconstruct our story based this time, not on the observation of human nature, but on that of God's nature. So let us return to our story, changing it somewhat and adding to it.

Early one morning the farmer placed a large trap made of steel mesh in his cornfield. At noon he returned to find that he had indeed caught a great flock of cranes. He said to the cranes, "At sunset, when my day's work is done, I will return to cut off your heads and to hang you from the limbs of yonder tree as a lesson to all thieves." He then left to work in his fields.

As for the cranes, it was pitiful to see their misery. Some huddled in a corner, trembling and paralyzed by fear. Some paced endlessly round and round looking for an opening. But most, in mad panic and frenzy, hurled themselves against the mesh again and again until, bruised and bleeding, they collapsed from exhaustion. As the sun sank lower and lower, so did their spirits.

Suddenly a shadow fell across them. Instinctively they were galvanized by a new terror. They knew the meaning of that cross-like shape. An eagle, feared predator of the skies, had circled overhead and was now settling on the roof of their prison—but such an eagle as they had never seen before—his wingspan broader, his colors richer, his eyes more piercing, his mien more regal than anything they had ever seen. They cowered with new fear. But then the eagle spoke. "Do not be afraid! I have come from the Mountain of the Far North. I am here to set you free!"

With that he began to tear and strain at the steel mesh with his powerful beak and talons, twisting and straining and bending. His beak became broken, his mouth bloody, his flesh torn; but still he worked feverishly, for there was little of the day left.

At last a jagged hole was opened. Through this he squeezed his body, the jagged edges cutting deep into his flesh. Then began the rescue operation. Those who were able flew through the breach to the safety of the reeds. Those cranes that were too weak he carried to safety, one by one. Just as the last crane had been helped through the hole, the farmer suddenly appeared, axe in hand. From their covert in the reeds the rescued watched, expecting to see the eagle soar through the gap and away into the skies. But no! He just lay there, a crumpled mass of feathers, on the floor of the cage.... The farmer seized the eagle by its feet, dragged it to the root of the tree, and there struck off its head. He then hung the body from a limb as a spectacle to all.

The cranes watched all this, shocked, bewildered, and with heavy hearts, until the darkness deepened and the swinging body was no more than a black cross against the moonlit sky.

That night they slept fitfully. In the morning they crept again to the edge of the reeds to look once more at the tragic figure. But the body was not there! Could wild dogs have stolen it overnight?

Then they saw him! But surely it could not be he? Yet there was the same magnificent body, the same brilliant colors of gold and bronze and black, the same majestic head, the same piercing eyes. He was alive and circling gracefully above them. Then he settled down among them saying, "Yes, it is I. If you doubt me look here at the throat. See the darkened stains of blood still upon it. I am no ordinary eagle. I come from the Mountain of the Far North, also called Mount of Swallowed Death. My name is Lord of Life. I have come to take you to the great mountain. That is your real home, not this swamp of reed and tadpole and mudworm. You were made to live with me high above the clouds, in the mountains higher than the eye can see. Come! I have prepared a great banquet for you, and a great company awaits you."

"But how are we to get there?" asked the cranes, still weak from their ordeal. "We have never ventured much beyond the treetops, and our wings are not strong enough to carry us."

"The thermals!" he said. "It is not by your own strength, but by the power of the thermals, the air currents. I will take you where they rise and they will bear you up and up."

What happened then was remarkable to behold. It seemed the great eagle was everywhere at once, lifting them in turn and teaching them to soar. If they tired and faltered, he was there beneath them. If they became overconfident and drifted out of the thermals, he would rebuke them. If they did not listen, he would buffet them and cause them to plummet back to earth. But at the last moment he would swoop below them and turn their fall into a swift, graceful arc back to the heights. If they were tempted to return to the swamp and cornfield, he reminded them of the axe laid at the root of the tree. When they became hungry he sped away to return swiftly with morsels from the banquet table.

So the flock circled higher and higher. At last they saw the mountain, and then they knew instinctively that this had always been their true home, and not the marsh. When they heard the jocund sounds of company, of feasting, of song and music, they marveled that their misery and despair of so short a time ago could be changed to such ecstasy. They could think of nothing more desirable than to be forever at this banquet on the Mountain of the Far North with their Rescuer.

So ends our tale. Do I need to add an interpretation? This is the story of our God, who says of us, as He said of Israel, "I bare you on eagles' wings, and brought you unto Myself." This is our rescuer God, who, as the psalmist says, renews our strength like the eagles. This is our Lord, who promises through Isaiah that those who trust in Him "shall mount up with wings as eagles." What a promise for ignorant, guilty cranes and pompous, deluded storks like us, who deserve to die but who can sing with the psalmist: "Our soul is escaped as a bird out of the snare of the fowlers: the snare is broken, and we are escaped."

We have escaped and the feast awaits us!

Extended Analogy

In an extended analogy, as the name implies, an illustration simply occupies more space in a sermon that it customarily does. Ordinarily, a preacher employs an illustration either as a springboard at the start of his sermon or as an insert in the body of his sermon. In the extended analogy format the illustration permeates the sermon from beginning to end, not "taking over" the sermon in its entirety but surfacing periodically. As was the case with the various literary genres previously discussed, the extended analogy is a point of reference, a "motif," a recurring element in the development of the sermon. Hence, the analogy plays a qualitative as well as a quantitative role. While the use of the analogy must be extensive in order for the sermon to qualify as an instance of extended analogy, the preacher must be careful not to overdo it, not to squeeze every detail of his analogy, not to carry his illustration too far. A skillful writer knows when to quit as well as when to forge ahead. Above all, the preacher must avoid using the analogy to prove his point (a logical fallacy called "misuse of analogy"). The preacher of course may use an analogy to illustrate, clarify, or dramatize his point.

Because overuse of analogy is as hazardous as underuse, this creative format is normally more successful when employed in a brief sermon than in a regular length sermon. The model below is a sermon addressed to a college audience in a setting in which short sermons were the rule.

1 Corinthians 15:58—"Therefore, my beloved brethren, be ye stedfast, unmoveable, always abounding in the work of the Lord."

Although I spent a childhood constantly confusing the two, I believe I can safely assume that all of you know the difference between deciduous and coniferous trees. Deciduous trees lose their leaves when winter comes, but coniferous trees retain them—at least most coniferous trees do. Strictly speaking, I guess the kind of tree I have in mind is more accurately called evergreen than coniferous. The proper antonyms are deciduous and evergreen rather than deciduous and coniferous, but to say "deciduous and coniferous" sounds better. They rhyme, both have four syllables, and both offer some of the advantages of scientific, prestige jargon. Against the background of all these similarities, their difference in respect to leaves will stand out all the more sharply. Which is a difference I want standing out this morning. Evergreen might spoil my parable.

And the parable is this. There are also two kinds of Christians: deciduous and coniferous. There are those who drop their leaves when the temperature cools, and there are those who stay green no matter what happens. Every year we witness this phenomenon on our campus. At the start of the school year the chapel is regularly packed with students. Enthusiasm runs high. Morale is good. Students do favors for one another. They exchange friendly greetings. Then come the first icy blasts. There are tests. There are term papers. There are grades. There are failures. There are unprepared profs. There are rigid profs. There are permissive profs. There are disappointing chapel services. There are "Dear John" letters. There are institutional meals. There are rules—even in this citadel of freedom. And . . . there aren't girls. Worst of all—and here our analogy becomes strikingly apt—there are severe winters. And what happens? We get deciduous. Leaves start dropping. Our sap dries up. We become stark, barren, naked, gaunt. Depression rolls over the campus. Chapel attendance dwindles. Greetings become grunts. The social amenities are forgotten. Comes Lent, however, comes spring, comes the end of the year, and things start picking up again. Campus people begin to bud, things turn green once more, and we end the year in a style approximating that of the start of the year.

One part of the remedy, of course, is to remove, or at least reduce, the icy blasts. While tests, term papers, and grades can hardly be eliminated from an academic setting, still it seems that we on the faculty should do our best to make them meaningful. And certainly it is within our power to do something about unpreparedness, excessive rigidity, or excessive permissiveness.

The other part of the remedy, however, is the more crucial, and that is that all of us quit being deciduous. No life—not even life on this architectural masterpiece—can be without trial and fiery affliction. Nor is it meant to be. God intends that our Christian faith be tried and that our Christian life be put to the test. Anybody can hang on to his leaves when he is wafted by balmy spring breezes. But how about when the gales and storms and frosts start coming? What then? Can we then be coniferous? Can our spirituality survive a low grade, a cheap prof, a confining blizzard, an unanswered letter, or a limited serving of roast beef? Certainly it had better if it hopes later on to survive the fiery darts of the wicked that will be leveled at us in our ministry. What is needed on this campus, what is needed in the ministry, is a man for all seasons, one who in the language of our text is "stedfast, unmoveable, always abounding in the work of the Lord." What is needed, in short, is a coniferous Christian.

Merely wishing it will not make it so, not even wishing it from a pulpit. Only Christ can make it so, that Jesus Christ who is the same yesterday, today, and forever, whose love is coniferous, evergreen. What He achieved for us on Good Friday and Easter has opened up a whole new world for us, a world of heaven and world of new creaturehood. If you'll pardon my getting all the mileage I can out of my analogy this morning, "if any man be in Christ, he is a new tree. He puts off deciduous and puts on coniferous."

Role Playing

Role playing (also called monolog), in which a pastor assumes the role of some Biblical character and preaches the sermon from that perspective, is perhaps the most familiar of all the creative sermon formats discussed in this book. For that reason it is also one of the formats most acceptable to Christian audiences. Unlike fairy tale or letter formats, role playing lacks the disadvantage of novelty. Accustomed to the approach, traditionally oriented audiences will not be offended by its use. Accosted by this particular sermon format, listeners are less likely to say of their pastor, "What's he up to now?" or "Who does he think he is?"

Yet familiar as the format is, role playing, unlike so many other familiar things, has never lost its capacity for creativity. To this day I am tricked into listening whenever a pastor assumes the role of a Judas or a Peter or a Caiaphas and preaches a sermon from that perspective. There seems to be something inherently creative about first person preaching. I am tempted to conclude that the advent of the first person point of view was as revolutionary in the area of homiletics as it was in the history of literature. Besides its ability to attract attention and put familiar truths into new perspective, role playing has the advantage of allowing the preacher to say things to his audience that he might not otherwise be able to say. That is, as a Judas or Peter or Caiaphas he can point out certain failings in his listeners that, speaking in his own person, he could not do without hurting their feelings. So successful is the role transference that the audience will attribute the sensitive observation to a Judas, for example, rather than to their pastor. Because the preaching of the Law does not come on strong, does not confront them directly, the listeners are more receptive to it. People hear the Law precisely because they overhear it, eavesdrop on it, so to speak.

Books exemplifying role playing or monolog sermons, especially involving Lenten characters, are plentiful.[5] However, role playing need not be restricted to participants in the passion narrative. Other Biblical characters qualify too. I have read, for example, monolog sermons involving Cain, Job, and the widow of Nain. For that matter, the character need not be a Biblical one. Why couldn't it be a Nero or a Darwin or a Nietzsche who delivers the monolog—so long as a Biblical sermon text is seriously used and so long as basic Law and Gospel are presented?

The following student sermon not only models the monolog format but also constitutes a penetrating presentation of Law and an incisive proclamation of Gospel.[6]

Genesis 4:1-16: The story of Cain

I am Cain, murderer of my brother Abel. You know my story well—all too well. But there are some things about me that some of you of the 20th century have misunderstood. It is of these that I wish to speak. Most of all, I want to share with you something that I have not been able to understand. Something is a baffling mystery to me even after all these ages. In fact, the longer time continues, the more baffling this mystery becomes. Perhaps you will be able to help me understand it.

First, let me tell you some things about myself that some of you moderns have misunderstood.

I was a cultured man. This may surprise you. Most of your artists have portrayed me as a rough man, a violent man by nature, almost sub-human, driven by wild passions. Abel, on the other hand, is seen as a more gentle and refined and devout person. In fact, the opposite is the case. I turned to agriculture while Abel remained the rough nomadic shepherd. I

127

was the one who stood for the progress of civilization. You may remember that it was I who became the founder of the first city, and therefore the father of all that urbanized society means in terms of art, culture, and refinement of life.

Why do I mention this? To warn you that the natural habitat of that crouching beast of sin (for so God called it) is not the open veldt or the lonely wilderness, but the world of plush carpets and stereos, of theater and library. It is not where the wind howls in wild mountain regions, but where the air is filled with the strains of Mozart and Wagner. Let my fate warn you that cultured sophistication is no stranger to brother-murder. Need I remind you of what your cultured brothers did to their brothers in the concentration camps? Remember too that the crimes of defeated nations are exposed immediately; those of the victors only half a century later.

Yes, I was the cultured one. Yet it was at my door that sin was crouching ready to destroy me.

It may also come as a surprise to you that I was a very pious man. Again some of you seem to have assumed that I had no time for God—not like my brother Abel. How wrong! Did I not bring my sacrifices? Was it not important to me to be accepted by God? I needed—I wanted God's approval. When I did not get it I was deeply disturbed. Is that the sign of an unreligious person? So anxious was I to gain the favor of God that I was prepared to kill for it, insanely assuming that with Abel out of the way God would have no choice but to accept me.

Why do I tell you this also? Again as a warning that piety toward God and hatred toward the brother are no strangers to each other. The tragedy is that piety can be so blind as not to recognize its companion for the beast that it is. The history of human brotherhood is scattered with the bodies of brothers slain to gain the approval of God. Need I remind you of Saul of Tarsus, or of the Crusades, or of some events in your own century? Be warned then that piety or religious zeal is no guarantee that the crouching beast is not at the door. In fact, where he sees or smells the signs of religiosity, his muscles tense and his nostrils dilate in eager anticipation. One of your own writers has said that the devil tempts no more successfully than at the very sanctuary itself.

There is one more thing I want to share with you before I come to the big mystery. Some of you have wondered why God did not accept my offerings. This much the sacred writer has let you know, that it was because of some particular sin on my part. When God said, "If thou doest well, shalt thou not be accepted?" I knew what He meant. But I wanted to be accepted by God and still be able to hold on to my secret sin as well. What was that sin? The sacred storyteller does not say, not to protect my reputation, but to make you see that it is not the *kind* of sin that matters, but the fact that I wanted to hold on to it, even at the very altar of God. Were you to know my secret sin, you might say, "I am not guilty of that sin. Therefore, I am in no danger." So do not make inquiry about my sins, but about your own personal, secret sins.

Most of all, do not assume that this secret sin of mine was hatred for my brother. No, it was nothing so serious to begin with. I never dreamed it could explode with such monstrous force. I meant no harm to anyone, least of all my brother. How often have I not heard countless brothers of mine, also in your 20th century, say, "But I'm not hurting anyone!" How ironical that was to be in my own case! Before we know it the crouching beast springs, we are overpowered, and our brother's blood stains the earth. Before we know it the happiness of our homes, our families, our children, our friends lies shattered in the dust—and all because of that so-called innocent affair or petty graft for which there were a dozen pious justifications at the time, not least of all that it was not hurting anyone.

The rest of the story you know well—the deception, the slaying, the foolish attempt to cover up, the denial of responsibility, the judgment of God, and the collapse of my world.

And now at last I come to the mystery.

You will remember the hammerblows of God's judgment—cursed from the ground and destined to be a fugitive and a wanderer on earth. A fugitive and a wanderer! You of the 20th century, who no longer live in close tribal communities, may not understand what it means to be expelled from the tribe. Those to whom my story was first told—they knew. They knew what it meant to lose not only the fellowship of kinsmen, but, far worse, their protection. Nor could I as murderer now expect the rights of hospitality and sanctuary owed to strangers—a precious right to travellers in the ancient world. I could hope for no protection from kinsmen or from host. Henceforth, every living moment would be haunted by the fear and terror of the avenger.

In anguish I cried out, "My punishment is greater than I can bear."

Then it happened—this baffling mystery! At that very moment there sounded from the heavens an oracle from God: "Whosoever slayeth Cain, vengeance shall be taken on him sevenfold."

Vengeance! Sevenfold! Can you of the 20th century now grasp the incredible implications of these words? Suddenly I had a protector. God Himself was stepping forward as my kinsman—my brother. God was declaring to the world, "If anyone lays a hand on Cain, he will have Me to contend with, and the consequences will be dire." God was acting as my brother—a brother to a brother-murderer! This is what I have never been able to understand. What strange love was this? What strange God was this?

Nor was this to be a wild, impetuous action, never to be done again. Far from it. What He did to me was but a sign of something far, far greater still to come—and far, far more mysterious. I speak, as you can guess, of His coming to the earth as brother in the flesh to all mankind. We, His brothers, murdered Him—murdered God Himself. If the blood of Abel cried to the heavens for vengeance, what vengeance befits the shedding of God's blood? Yet in that shed blood God offers pardon and the hand of brotherhood to all—to all who have the blood of brothers on their hands.

To all, I say. For your hands too are not unstained. You know that you need not kill as I did to be guilty of your brother's or your sister's blood. You need only to have hated, to have hurt, to have spat out barbed or cutting words in anger, spite, revenge—words which sink deeply into the hearts of brothers and of sisters and make them bleed.

Yet I see that God has marked you too with a special sign of kinship —the sign of the cross on the forehead and on the breast. Strange, is it not, that the very weapon used to slay the Son of God is now, for you, the sign of special kinship with the Son of God?

I will never understand my mark. Hold on to it? Yes! Love it, celebrate it, live and die by it? Yes! But understand it I never will. God's strange kind of love is too deep for me. Perhaps you, the bearers of that special sign on forehead and on breast, in silver and in gold, on altar and on steeple— perhaps you can understand more clearly this mystery of love, that God makes Himself a blood-brother to brother-murderers. Or is it for you as well a love that surpasses all understanding?

Dialog

Although not quite so familiar as the role playing format (and therefore, perhaps, not quite so palatable to the average audience), the dialog sermon, nonetheless, can be every bit as effective. There is intrinsic in the dialog format an interaction, a dialectic, a give-and-take, that not only interests the listener but also invites considerable audience involvement. Compared with conventional sermon approaches, the dialog format, I suspect, has the same things going for it that conversation has on the printed page of a novel in contrast to its longer narrative sections. The dialog format is most effective obviously when there is a genuine dialog going on, for example, between two pastors or between a pastor and a lay assistant. But if carefully planned, the dialog format will work even if there is only one speaker to deliver the sermon. He simply plays two roles, and a carefully programmed change of position or of voice—or even carefully chosen words—can mark the transition from one role to the other.

The following Advent dialog, written by one of my students, is perhaps more suitable for a youth group or a small group devotion than for a public worship service.[7]

1: Excuse me, sir! Can you tell me where...

2: (INTERRUPTING) Sir? I haven't heard that one in a while! (PAUSE) Well! Whadya want?

1: I was wondering if you could direct me to the record department?

2: Look at the sign, buddy! This is the complaint department. Information is on the first floor. Just hop on the escalator and take a quick right when you get there.

1: Thank you! (POLITELY)

2: Hey! Wait a minute! I'm sorry—I'm just a bit edgy today. I guess I've had to listen to too many grouches these last few weeks. It seems like every weirdo and crackpot in the city comes in here at least twice a week during the holidays. If it's not some old biddy griping about the poor selection of crockpots, it's some hot-shot kid screaming because they won't accept his check for a color TV. I'll tell you, if one more...

1: (INTERRUPTING) Sounds like you haven't gotten into the spirit of Christmas yet.

2: Christmas spirit—garbage!

1: You sound bitter.

2: My, aren't you the perceptive one!

1: I'm sorry—I didn't mean to sound sarcastic.

2: Oh, that's all right. I'm always like this when it gets close to five o'clock. I guess that comes with the job. Sometimes I think I'd give a week's paycheck if I could haul off and slug some of the characters who come around here.

1: I guess it does get kind of discouraging just hearing people tell you about their problems all of the time. But, you know, your job serves a very useful...

2: (INTERRUPTING) Ah, that's not half of it! As soon as I finish here I just go home and listen to my wife gripe about how I'm "just not the same man she married." Gripe, gripe, gripe! She thinks I come home every evening just dying to hear her complain about the kids and about how little help I give her around the house! I mean, after a guy's worked all day, he oughta be able to go home and relax without having to listen to a sermon from the old lady. Don't you think so?

1: (UNCOMFORTABLY) Well, it's not that...

2: (INTERRUPTING) I mean a guy should be able to sit down, prop his feet up, turn on the TV, and drink his beer in peace! Now that Christmas is almost here, I can't even watch TV. Heck, I turn on *Charlie's Angels* and instead I get Burl Ives as Frosty the Snowman!

1: You know, I think you're missing the meaning of Christmas.

2: So now I'm missing the meaning of Christmas, huh? First I didn't have the Christmas spirit; now I don't know what it means. Let me tell you—I know the *real* meaning of Christmas. It's when you give things to people because they gave you something last year. It's just one big racket. You end up spending your hard-earned money on people who don't deserve it.

1: Well, I agree with you on one point, anyway.

2: Yeah? What's that?

1: Oh, that Christmas means giving something to people who don't de-

131

serve it. In fact, that's why we celebrate Christmas. It's because God gave His Son for you and me, even though we don't deserve it. That's the…

2: (INTERRUPTING) Don't tell me you're one of those religious fanatics! I just can't buy that stuff! I mean, I've seen too many religious people who aren't any better off than I am. Besides—now I don't mean to offend you—but I'm just not the type of person who gets all excited about singing songs and reading prayers. I figure that's the way the good Lord made me, so I'll just have to plan on getting to heaven some other way.

1: Well, once again I have to agree with you.

2: You do?

1: That's right. The Bible makes it quite plain that nobody is going to sing or pray or work his way to heaven.

2: Whadya mean?

1: I mean that no matter how good we try to be, no matter how well we treat people—God still says it's not enough.

2: Hey, wait a minute! Are you trying to tell me that there's *nothing* I can do to get to that great department store in the sky? (CHUCKLING NERVOUSLY)

1: That's right!

2: What are you—some sort of bad joke? What does God want, anyway?

1: Nothing short of perfection.

2: Look, buddy, I don't know what you're trying to do, but I'll tell you one thing, you're sure not improving my outlook on life. Let's face it, I don't know anyone who's perfect; even good people mess up now and then.

1: That's very true. In fact, God says that even "good" people sin constantly. Not only does God look at our actions, but He also looks at our thoughts. Did you know that Jesus even said that if you so much as get mad at another person you're guilty of committing murder?

2: Thanks a lot, friend—you've just convinced me that I'm going to rot in hell. Merry Christmas to you, too!

1: Believe me, that's not my intention.

2: Well, what *is* it?

1: I want to tell you about the joy of Christmas.

2: And just what might that be? Enjoy your turkey today because tomorrow you roast?

1: Not at all. The joy of Christmas is that God hasn't abandoned us to die. Even though we deserve nothing less than hell itself, even though we've abandoned Him, God hasn't run away from us. (PAUSE)

2: Well, go on! (SOMEWHAT IMPATIENTLY)

1: That's what Christmas is all about: God loved us so much that He sent Jesus.

2: Look, I like babies, too, but frankly I can't get terribly excited about any baby born 2,000 years ago.

1: Not just *any* baby. Jesus was more than just a little boy. He is God in the flesh. That's the miracle of Christmas. God loved us so much that He sent His Son.

2: Well and good, but what does that mean to me?

1: It means that God knows that there is no way that you can reach His standards. That's why He sent Jesus. You see, Jesus lived the perfect life that neither you nor I nor anyone else can live. Christ lived a life of perfect obedience.

2: I'll agree with you there—but look where it got Him.

1: That's precisely the point!

2: Huh?

1: God made Christ to be sin for us.

2: I'm afraid I don't follow you.

1: Well, it's like this. Jesus *always* obeyed God's will, and because of that fact, He is the only person in history who did not deserve to die. In spite of that, though, He chose to die. When Jesus was hanging on the cross, He was not only suffering physical pain, He was voluntarily suffering the agonies of the damned. God took all of our sins and guilt and placed them upon Christ.

2: Are you trying to tell me that God damned Jesus?

1: Exactly! When Jesus cried from the cross that God had forsaken Him, He was saying exactly that.

2: Wow! I'd never thought about it that way before. It's rather ironic.

1: What do you mean?

2: Oh, it seems so unfair.

1: You're right. But think how wonderful it is. God loves us so much that He was willing to suffer hell for us. The punishment we so richly deserve has already been carried out. In effect, Christ has wiped our slate clean. In God's eyes we are now perfect.

2: Well, what do I have to do to get this perfection?

1: Nothing! That's the beauty of it. Jesus has already earned it for you.

2: Hey, that's great!

1: It sure is great. God has said that we can do *nothing* to save ourselves. But He has *promised* to save everyone who trusts that Christ has saved him. Because of Christ, God has forgiven every one of our sins. We are free to serve God. There's no longer any reason to worry whether or not we're good enough to be saved. We can be *absolutely* certain of our salvation because Jesus has earned it for us. ... That's the true meaning of Christmas. God gave us the greatest Christmas present of all time—He gave us eternal life through His Son. Not only life for the future, but life for right now. You see, God's love for us in Christ causes us to respond in love. It affects every aspect of our lives. (PAUSE) Well, I've got to be going. Have a Merry Christmas!

2: Yeah—Yes, you too! Have a really Merry Christmas. By the way, the record department is on the fifth floor.

Letter Format

The creative potential of the letter format for communicating spiritual truth was dramatically demonstrated a few decades ago by the popularity and sales of C. S. Lewis' *Screwtape Letters*, a collection of letters allegedly intercepted by Lewis and allegedly written by a senior devil advising a junior devil how to achieve the damnation of a recent convert to Christianity. To "do theology" from a satanic perspective, to see the Gospel as devils see it—somehow this novel approach freshened Christianity for theologians and laypeople alike. Since the publication of this best-seller, journalists and pastors have repeatedly aped the Lewis method and, in my experience, always with success. While it is seldom that even the best imitators of Lewis match his unparalleled style, their efforts, nevertheless, are eminently successful in interesting and edifying their readers or listeners.

Because the approach is so familiar, however, and because no disciple can be above his master in the utilization of this creative format (in other words, there's nothing better in this area than the original *Screwtape Letters*), I have decided to present as a model below a different kind of letter format. What follows was not originally intended as a sermon at all. It was rather meant to be a chapter in a book that was never completed, one of a collection of letters supposedly written by people just arrived in heaven to friends or relatives still on earth, detailing for them that chain of circumstances by which a gracious God brought them to saving faith. The particular letter that follows is from a mother to her daughter explaining how God overcame her snobbery to bring her to eternal life. For reasons that will become obvious the text does not appear until the end of the "sermon."[8]

> Frankincense Room
> Heaven
> n. d.

Dear Jennifer,

Perhaps the very fact that this letter is not on proper stationery is indicative of the change that you—or rather, God through you—brought about during my late middle age when I was at the height of my snobbery. Before that time, you may remember, I was careful that every letter that went out from my secretaire (Oops! A relapse! I mean desk) was in proper form on proper paper in a proper envelope properly scented and mailed at the proper time. Oh, I was proper all right. I wasn't good, of course, or kind or likable. I was respected (I "had my reward"), but I wasn't loved: I lacked "the milk of human kindness." It is you, Jennifer, who changed all that. You're probably aware of your role, at least in part, but I want to tell you the whole story. There may be some things you don't know.

You, of course, were our only child. And it may shock you to learn that even you were not wanted. Chris and I had pretty well decided that we didn't want to be bothered with children, although I was more adamant about it than he was. I just couldn't see where I'd have the time. You remember my heavy schedule: bridge club on Tuesday evening and Thursday afternoon, Ladies Day at Pine Ridge every Wednesday, bowling on Monday evening right after the lodge meeting. And for many years I was chairman of Women for Progress. I was frightfully busy, and who would there be to take care of any children? Besides, so I thought then, children are so vulgar. I wasn't about to spend my life changing dirty diapers and wiping runny noses. Somehow this all seemed to be beneath me. But I wasn't as careful as I should have been after one of our frequent cocktail parties. Anyhow, we named you Jennifer, thinking that a distinguished sounding name was one way of making the best of a bad situation.

In retrospect, I guess we accepted the situation quite gracefully all around, once I got over the embarrassment of pregnancy and the inconvenience of childbirth. We saw to it that you got the best of care. The nurses and maids we hired all had the appropriate credentials and recommendations. You had your own room, properly decorated, with a regular menagerie of stuffed animals and a closet full of dresses and shoes for all occasions. You had your own record player, your own television, and whole set of a highly recommended children's encyclopedia. When it came time to send you to school, we chose carefully, finally settling on a private school where we could be sure that the teaching was of the highest quality and where we could be sure that you would not be exposed to any undesirable minority element. You were a good student, too, Jennifer; we even became proud of you. You lacked for nothing—Chris had a good position at the plant. You had everything, I guess, but genuine love and affection. When I look back now it's a wonder you weren't hopelessly spoiled. By rights you should have turned out to be even more of a snob than I was.

I guess it was Jane, Jane Foster, who saved you (more about that word later). You remember how carefully we chose the company you kept. Jane met all our standards. She was polite, well-bred, intelligent, came from a good part of town, and had respectable parents. It nettled us a little that she belonged to a church—religion always seemed so trite and vulgar to us—but when we looked into it more we discovered that it was a progressive church in a high-class neighborhood, and so we thought it would be all right. Well, you and Jane got to be real friends, and we actually didn't discourage it. We were impressed by her combination of good breeding and lack of affectation. She seemed to be every bit as proper as the other girls we selected as your playmates and yet seemed to be more genuine, less "tony" than they were. Her goodness seemed to come from the inside out. It wasn't just a veneer gradually acquired through careful and regulated training. She seemed to be giving you something that Chris and I couldn't, and so the more you got together the happier we were.

Then came the day you burst into my room (I believe you even forgot to knock, you were so excited) and said, "Mama, Mama, Jane has asked me to go to Vacation Bible School at her church. May I? May I?" I said I'd talk it over with your father. Which I did that night. I wasn't too keen on the idea, but Chris couldn't see any particular harm in it. "After all, it'll be over in two weeks," he said. Anyhow, we weren't in the habit of refusing you. So the next day I said, "O. K."

Well, one thing led to another. Pretty soon you started going to church with her and to Sunday School. Next thing I knew you were asking us to go with you. Once again I said I'd talk it over with your father. This time I put up an argument. "Look, Chris," I said, "we're going to get too involved. We've got all we can handle right now. Eventually, they'll probably find out we have money and then ask us to join so we can finance all their projects. They might even ask me to help out at a sauerkraut supper or bazaar or something. And, after all, we don't know about *all* the people over there; they aren't all like Jane's folks." But Chris never could refuse you anything. He shrugged his shoulders and murmured, "Why not try it? We can always pull out."

The rest you know. We enjoyed our first few visits at Jane's church. The people were friendly. The liturgy and music were impressive. The pastor's sermons were good. He said a number of things that got me thinking. He talked about another dimension to life, a spiritual and eternal one, one I had never thought about. I'll never forget his sermon on "For what is a man profited, if he shall gain the whole world, and lose his own soul?" Most surprising was the new slant he gave me on Jesus. I had always thought He was just a teacher and humanitarian. But the pastor insisted that He was the Son of God and the giver of this spiritual and eternal life he kept talking about. One day he visited us, asked us to take membership instruction, tacking on the usual "no obligation to join" clause. This time it was I who talked Chris into consent. (That was a switch!) I felt myself getting drawn in, but I didn't want to stop. Of course we joined. And to my utter surprise I *did* help out at a church supper—only it was a pancake supper. I never thought I'd see the day!

Outwardly things didn't change too much. Oh, I reduced some of my club activities—or rather I replaced them with church activities. But we made just as much money as before. And I can't truthfully say that I got off the cocktail merry-go-round. About the only change was in my attitude toward people. I widened my circle of acquaintances. I wasn't so selective anymore. I realized that the religion I professed cut across all social, economic, cultural, and racial lines. Some of my friends were disappointed at my new permissiveness in respect to friends—one even called me "culturally promiscuous"—but most of my set still tolerated me. In fact, a few of them even joined our church.

But here's the thing, Jennifer. It all started with you. You were our salvation. Or, to be exact, you were the instrument through which God brought us to Christ. *He* did the saving, of course. A careless moment after a cocktail party, a casual acquaintance between you and Jane Foster, a routine Vacation Bible School—up here it looks very much like a pattern, almost like a divine scheme. God, it appears, was out to get me—in the best sense of that word. Nothing on earth is "by chance"; I guess that's the first insight I gained here. Anyhow, I wish to thank you for your part in my salvation. And may I add that I now have a new appreciation for a passage I never understood before, not even when I joined the Tuesday evening Bible class, and that is 1 Timothy 2:15: "She shall be saved in childbearing." How true!—Although I'm not sure that's the right (what is the word?) "exegesis." I'll have to ask Pastor when he arrives.

Love,
Mother

Inversion

This creative approach to preaching differs from all the previous ones discussed in that it refers exclusively to the content or subject matter of a sermon rather than also or primarily to the structure or arrangement of a sermon. What we have in the inversion approach is a sermon topic rather than a sermon format. "Inversion" means just what it says: turning things around, reversing the traditional order, altering the normal and expected sequence, standing things on their head, putting the cart before the horse. (For example, to say "putting the horse before the cart" would constitute an inversion.) I remember beginning a sermon once with the statement, "Where two or three are gathered together, there is Satan in the midst of them." That was an inversion. *Time* magazine a few years ago contained an essay entitled "Thought for Food" and in another issue quipped concerning a husband and wife opposing each other politically, "Bedfellows make strange politicians." Those were inversions: the former of a cliché, "food for thought"; the latter of a Shakespearean line, "Misery acquaints a man with strange bedfellows." When the listener or reader confronts such an inversion, he is halted in his tracks. "What's going on here?" may be his reaction. Or, "That's not the way I've always heard it." When such an inversion is not merely an attention-getting device but becomes (as in the *Time* essay alluded to) the subject matter of the entire presentation, then we have a genuine inversion presentation.

Obviously, there are hazards to the approach. At the very least the inversion may be merely a bizarre gimmick to elicit attention, which, if not sustained, leads the reader or listener to feel let down or tricked or "had." At worst the inversion may provide an outlet for a person of a rebellious nature or of an ornery disposition. Mere perversity may prompt his topic, and he may dig himself into a hole so deep that he can extricate neither himself nor his listeners from it. Or his inversion may be so topsy-turvy that it constitutes bad theology.

But responsibly handled, the inversion approach can capture the tone and content of the Scriptures. For the Scriptures often present a topsy-turvy world: the last being first and the first last; publicans and harlots entering the kingdom before scribes and Pharisees; the least in the kingdom of heaven being greater than John the Baptist; people finding their life by losing it; Jesus saying, "I came not to send peace, but a sword." Above all, the Scriptures stagger us with that most delightfully upsetting inversion of all, salvation by grace. It is to highlight such Biblical inversions as these that the inversion sermonic approach is uniquely designed.

The Biblical inversion explored in the sermon below, addressed to a college audience, is "Living affects hearing."

> Luke 8:14, 18—"And that which fell among thorns are they, which, when they have heard, go forth, and are choked with cares and riches and pleasures of this life, and bring no fruit to perfection.... Take heed therefore how ye hear: for whosoever hath, to him shall be given; and whosoever hath not, from him shall be taken even that which he seemeth to have."

Let me start out by describing a problem I have. Maybe some of you have it too. The problem is this. Ever since childhood I've known from the Bible that there is a direct correlation between hearing and living. The more often I hear God's Word, the stronger my faith becomes and the better my life becomes. Actually, my awareness of this truth was one of the factors that impelled me to accept a teaching position here. "Look at the additional opportunities I will have to hear God's Word in the daily chapel services," I reasoned. "Why, in no time at all I should be moving mountains." Well, the mountains are still there. And like St. Paul I am more painfully aware than ever of "another law in my members warring against the law of my mind and bringing me into captivitiy to the law of sin." "O wretched man that I am! who shall deliver me from the body of this death?" Worse yet, I find myself on occasion becoming less attentive and less enthusiastic in my reception of the Word than ever before. How devastatingly applicable have the words of the Offertory been right after another unlistened-to Sunday sermon and how fervently have I prayed them: ". . . renew a right spirit within me. Cast me not away from Thy presence; and take not Thy Holy Spirit from me. Restore unto me the joy of Thy salvation...."

Well, there's the problem: All this hearing and things seem to be getting worse, not better as the Scriptures promise. What's the cause?

Part of the cause, I suspect, is natural. Anything frequent can easily become common. *Daily* chapel services—one can gradually assume a take-it-or-leave-it attitude toward them, I suppose, even when he attends them. What's more, the services become part of the routine. Sandwiched between the third and fourth classes of the day, these services can all too easily be reduced to the level of a class, a thing not only to skip but also in which to

138

be inattentive. Furthermore, going from class to chapel requires a shifting of gears, and sometimes our transmissions aren't up to it. The test you just blew or the one you still have to cram for after chapel, the question you didn't get to ask in class, the question you shouldn't have asked in class, the blunder you made, the annoying habit that the instructor has of smacking his lips—thoughts of all these accompany us to chapel and interfere with our receptivity. And let's face it: Sometimes the officiant in chapel hasn't done his duty. He's dull, unprepared, or long-winded, and it requires a herculean effort as well as a heap of faith and charity to tune in on him. It's not always our fault!

Another part of the cause, I am sure, is supernatural. I mean the devil. We don't always give him his due. But the parable of the sower and the seed, from which our text is taken, surely does. It says quite flatly, "Then cometh the devil, and taketh away the word out of their hearts, lest they should believe and be saved." I think many of us have experienced this. We can listen to a dull, jargon-laden lecture on Shakespeare or Kant, we can tune in to a political speech riddled with clichés and abstractions and delivered in an asinine manner, but comes a sermon, a message of life and death, and we're not listening. What but a devil can account for such perversity? And have you ever noticed what it is you're thinking about when you're being inattentive during the service? Planning your next chapel address? Uh, uh. The term paper due next week? Perhaps. But what is it? Shapely blondes and shiny cars! No question about where those thoughts come from. Nothing has more convinced me—and I am not being facetious now—nothing has more convinced me of the existence of a devil than the utter depravity of the things I can think about during a sermon, and only during a sermon.

But the part of the cause I wish to call your attention to today is the thing our text makes clear, and that is that living affects hearing. You see, there are two sides to this coin. Not only hearing affects living but also living affects hearing. As our text suggests, if we're choked with cares and riches and pleasures of this life, we bring no fruit to perfection. How come our faith and sanctification are worse even though we're attending more services than ever before? How come we're hearing God's Word more but enjoying it less? These situations don't prove that the Bible is lying when it says that the more we feed on God's Word, the better we get. They only remind us of another truth the Bible tells us: that if we have too many thorns in our life, God can't get a Word in edgewise. If our house is filled with unclean spirits, the Holy Spirit simply can't crowd in; there's no room for Him.

So the next time you're perturbed at the lack of correlation between your hearing and your living, don't right away blame the preacher, fault the system, or put your hope in a liturgical reform. Just check your thorns, that's all. Maybe this life of easy dates and frequent cocktails and off-color stories and monthly payments and trivial gossip isn't so innocuous as it appears. It is just possible that these things are choking the Word of God in our life or, to mix the metaphor, causing our antennae to cake over and lose their receptivity.

"Take heed therefore how ye hear." Bad living makes for poor hearing—which, in turn, makes for bad living. The thing snowballs. One gets caught in a vicious circle, and the mystery of our text suddenly dissolves, "Whoever hath not, from him shall be taken even that which he seemeth to have."

But, thank God, there is the other circle too: Careful hearing makes for good living—which, in turn again, makes for careful hearing. Let's give God's Word every chance we can. After all, it is "the power of God unto salvation." It does not return void. Its account of God redeeming us through His Son crucified and risen works wonders on us. This thing snowballs too. Caught up in this circle, we discover it to be a glorious circle, the circle described by our text when it says, "For whosoever hath, to him shall be given."

Cliché Redemption

The inclusion of this classification in our catalog of creative sermon formats may come as a surprise, for nothing ordinarily is more inimical to creativity than clichés. More often than not it is the overuse of clichés that accounts for the dullness of dull preaching. But what I have in mind in this creative format is the *redemption* of a cliché, making a familiar cliché the topic of a sermon and giving it a twist, putting it into a new context, looking at it from a fresh perspective.

For example, we have all shuddered at the nth hearing of the cliché "making a mountain out of a molehill." But consider how that platitude could be redeemed if it were applied to Calvary. There indeed, by His atoning death, our Lord Jesus has made a mountain out of a molehill; He has converted a relatively small knoll (the place of skulls) into a majestic peak in Christian experience. Many of us have recoiled not only at the triteness but also at the rudeness of the expression "born in a barn." Yet applied to our Savior's birth, the tired phrase comes alive. All the rudeness remains, to be sure, but the dullness disappears. Our Savior was indeed "born in a barn"—whether in a stable or in a cave, we're not sure, but certainly in the company of animals. The platitude in this context captures both the wonder and the humiliation of our Savior's birth, and suddenly the cliché has been redeemed. "Over my dead body" is another all too familiar saying. Usually, it is said as a threat or a challenge, like "You'll get that promotion over my dead body." But think how the cliché would be redeemed if it were put on the lips of Jesus, if He were represented as saying, in effect, "You'll get to heaven over My dead body"—which is precisely the

140

way we do get there, via His death on the cross! What is ordinarily a threat becomes a promise, and once again a cliché has been salvaged for the furtherance of the Gospel.

The excerpt of a student sermon that follows redeems a cliché in a slightly different manner: by exploding it, detonating its folk wisdom. Both the cliché and the "pop" religion it encapsulates are deservedly crushed, but the cliché is redeemed in so far as it is put into the service of the Gospel.[9]

John 14:6b—"No man cometh unto the Father, but by Me."

John 15:5b—"For without Me ye can do nothing."

The man was clearly upset. His hands were restlessly stirring one minute and jingling pocket change the next. His lips hardly moved as he silently conversed with himself. Pacing about in his office—not unlike an anxious father-to-be in a maternity ward lounge—he could be seen exchanging glances between his watch and his office door. A moment later his business associate arrived. No sooner had his friend closed the door behind him than the man sprang forward, breathed a short sigh of relief, and offered his private confession.

"I'm miserable, Ted," he blurted. "I just can't seem to get a handle on things lately. I'm on edge with my wife and kids, and my sales quotas are down by six percent." Gazing out his office window, he continued: "I'm bucking for that management position in the regional office, you know. I can't afford to blow it now!" Turning again to his friend, he inquired: "You are a religious man, Ted. What should I do?"

With an air of authority and conviction, Ted responded. "C'mon, Bob, you're a capable guy with a good head on your shoulders. Get a hold of yourself. Don't you know that God helps those who help themselves?" The man caught the words like a hungry dog catching a bone: giving more thought to his appetite than to the quality of the food being offered. "You're right, Ted," said Bob with a glimmer of hope in his eyes. "I guess I'll just have to work harder at things..."

"God helps those who help themselves"—do you *really* believe that? Perhaps you can recall a time when you were down and unsure of yourself and someone tried to reassure you with these words. How did you respond? If there is still a question in your mind, it may be that you have heard other common variations that fall under the umbrella of this theme. For instance: "You've got to pull yourself up by the bootstraps, man!" Have you ever tried pulling yourself up by the bootstraps without falling flat on your face? Or maybe you have been consoled with this more palatable, but still misleading, version: "Pray as though it all depended upon God; work as though it all depended upon you."

Whatever the case, Christ, our Lord, has a sobering reminder for those who nibble at these pious sounding clichés. He declares to those who have ears to hear: "No man cometh unto the Father, but by Me. For without Me ye can do nothing." Apart from Jesus Christ we are helpless and in no position to expect God's intervention after we have initiated our own self-help programs. God, rather, helps those who *cannot* help themselves...

What is in us that men have found it necessary to devise such pious platitudes? What is with us that we bite at this questionable wisdom in such an unquestioning fashion? Why is it that Christians, perhaps more than any other "religious" people (at least in my experience), seem to identify so haphazardly with the trappings of this worldly advice? Much of it has to do with our lack of adequate information—we are not reading the Word of God. Most of it has to do with our almost universal hunger for facile wisdom—we are not believing the Word of God. It is part of our sinful desire for easy answers to difficult questions in life, couched as they so frequently are in language that tickles our ears and dazzles our minds. It is evidence of our haste to believe, and the waste that accrues to human life when we believe almost anything. It is a confirmation of our deluded belief that we, as modern men and women, have the resources, the knowledge, and the ability to accomplish just about anything if we just try hard enough.

One question remains, however. How, after all, will we know for sure that we have worked hard enough to merit God's intervention? The answer comes easily for those enlightened by the Spirit of God through the power of the Word of the Gospel. Those who spiritually discern God's ways among men know that we can try to do, say, and think the best things, and give it our best effort, yet best, from a human standpoint, never crosses the finish line of God's standard of perfection. We are among those who cannot even help themselves!

That God helps those who help themselves is pure "civil religion" and moralistic garbage for the believing Christian. In essence, the idea persuades us to believe that man is the measure of all things. In practice, we are led to conclude that we deserve some special blessing or advantage from God on account of all our self-motivated hard work. The very idea is built on the platform of human pride. It utterly opposes the Christian confession that we have within us a rebellious desire to live independent from God. It totally ignores our innate human limitations as creatures and replaces them with a philosophy of human dignity. In the end this idea amounts to nothing more than a "religious" pep-talk much like that of the preachers of the power of positive thinking: "You've got to prime the pump! You've got to reach down deep inside you to the source of your strength. Then work for your goals. Believe in yourself. And God will bless you!" If this is the "God" who helps those who help themselves, then he is nothing more than a god who rubber-stamps our decisions and picks up the slack after we have done the best that is in us—or so we think. He amounts to nothing more than a god for workaholics, the god of mind over matter, a god we can conveniently carry around in our hip pockets and make subservient to our own works and whims.

A god who helps those who help themselves is not the God of Biblical faith. Rather, the Bible testifies to a God who helps those who *cannot* help themselves. Oh sure, thousands of people around the world, believers and unbelievers alike, will "help themselves" to fame and fortune by writing great books, inventing new machines, curing dreaded diseases, and solving some pressing social or economic issue. But generally, the value of these works begins and ends in this world. The great work God is looking for is faith—belief in His mighty promises to help those who cannot help themselves. Yet no man, no woman, no child, no matter how hard and long they may have worked, can bring themselves into a believing relationship with God. They need help. We need help. We need the Christ who said that we come to the Father through Him....

We know and confess that Jesus Christ can help us because He went before us. As our pioneer in the faith He paved the way back to God in our place. He was the innocent Son of God who knew no sin, yet took our sin upon His shoulders—sins of pride, self-trust, and unbelief. Jesus is the Christ foretold in the Scriptures who took the form of a bondservant and came into the world in the likeness of our fleshly bodies. He became helpless in our behalf, even unto the helplessness of the cross of crucifixion, where in the darkness of Calvary's doom even His heavenly Father turned aside and did not help Him, the cursed One hanging upon the tree. Having cleared the way of our homecoming back to the Father, God resurrected His obedient Son back to new life and highly exalted Him, bestowing upon Him the name which is above every name, the name of Helper. It is to Christ that we now turn for help to conquer every sin, every temptation, and every foolish venture into worldly philosophies that glorify the creature and not the Creator of all men. It is to Jesus Christ that we now turn with our confession: "Help me, O God, for I cannot help myself!"...

Help in each daily context of need is as close as the Word of God and prayer, your pastor, and the body and blood of the Lord Jesus. Cling to Jesus, your Helper, through Word and Sacrament, for He clings to you through His Spirit in Word and Sacrament. Remember that those who seek help in themselves, apart from Jesus Christ, never see the Father and come to a hopeless end. But you who seek your help in Jesus Christ see the Father and live in the blessedness of an endless hope founded in the work of the Great Helper, even the Lord Jesus, who helps those who cannot help themselves.

Word Study

Technically, all sermon construction involves word study (exegesis). Careful, painstaking study of the language of a Biblical text, both in the original and in translation, is a normal and necessary step in the making of a sermon. What we have in mind, however, in this creative sermon format is the singling out of a word (or words) in a Biblical text and making of that selection a "motif," a point of reference, throughout the sermon. Or, as an alternative, the word (or words) singled out for such use may be *outside* the Biblical sermon text but obviously suggested by that text, associated with it and encapsulating its thrust or central meaning. As was the case in many of the creative formats already presented, the word study approach must be characterized by proper balance in order to be genuinely creative. On the one hand, the word (or words) selected should not serve merely as an introduction to or insert in the sermon; on the other hand, the word (or words) chosen dare not take over and dominate the sermon.

Study of a Word in the Text

To select a word (or words) from a Biblical text and to focus attention on this selection throughout the sermon does not guarantee creativity. Poorly done, the activity can end up as a pedantic exercise: abstract, dull, irrelevant, "scholarly" (in the bad sense of that word). The creativity of this approach depends upon the preacher's skill with words and his consideration for people. Despite this possible pitfall, this word study format enjoys the advantage of textualness. In the very nature of the case a sermon format that concentrates on the language of a Biblical text is likely to result in a textual rather than topical sermon.

In the parish sermon that follows note how the word "peculiar" from the sermon text serves as an introduction to the sermon, suggests its title or theme, and functions as a principle of division for its two-part outline (justification and sanctification).

> Titus 2:14—"[Christ] gave Himself for us that He might redeem us from all iniquity, and purify unto Himself a peculiar people, zealous of good works."

In many ways Christianity is a peculiar religion. For example, look at what it means to become a Christian. Jesus once told Nicodemus that it's something like being "born again," born a second time, a description so peculiar that it made Nicodemus scratch his head and ask, "How can a man be born when he is old? can he enter a second time into his mother's womb and be born?" Look at the means by which God makes us Christians: in connection with such ordinary things as marketplace words and table bread and tap water and in connection with such a shocking thing as an alcoholic beverage! Really, what could be more peculiar than the Gospel and the sacraments? Look at how the Son of God entered our world to carry out God's plan of salvation. A spirit to begin with, He changed into a creature of flesh and blood. He took on all the organs and appendages of a human

144

being, a process the peculiarity of which we can appreciate only if one of us, let us say, were suddenly to change into a bird and assume feathers, wings, claws, and beaks.

Look at what followed. He was born, of all things, of a virgin and, of all places, in a stable. Isn't it peculiar that He chose for His birthplace a little village in the hill country of Judea and overlooked a much more strategic locality a mere six miles away? Isn't it peculiar that some lowly shepherds were the first to know about this wonderful thing that had come to pass in Bethlehem?

Really, not only the event itself is peculiar, but also the whole idea behind it is strange, very strange. Why should the Son of God do this? Why should He leave the heavenly mansions for a 33-year sojourn on that infinitesimal speck in the universe called earth? Why should He show concern for that creature of clay called man, anymore than we should concern ourselves about the spiders that occupy our drains?

Our text today makes an interesting observation. It tells us what lies behind these peculiar aspects of our Christian religion. Their purpose, in the words of our text, is to "purify" unto God "a peculiar people." There you have it! These peculiar features are designed to make us a peculiar people.

As you well know, this play on words does not exist in the original Greek, although the English translation "peculiar," if understood correctly, is a correct translation. The word "peculiar" of course has various meanings. In everyday conversation we usually use the word "peculiar" in the sense of "odd," "queer," "eccentric," like "Isn't that a peculiar dress that Mrs. So-and-So is wearing?" That, however, is not the meaning of the word "peculiar" as used in our text. St. Paul does not mean to say that the purpose of the peculiar events of Christianity is to make us a peculiar, odd, queer, eccentric people. Now and then, to be sure, some people understand it this way. They feel that being a Christian requires being peculiar (odd, queer, eccentric). They bury themselves in caves or cloisters. They avoid marriage. They cut their hair a peculiar way. They wear peculiar clothing. They make peculiar sounds. They use peculiar words. They indulge in peculiar actions. They assume peculiar postures. They seem to go out of their way to make themselves ridiculous in the eyes of the world. But despite this point of view, that is not Paul's meaning in our text.

One of the meanings of the word "peculiar" listed in the dictionary is this: "exclusive, unique...belonging distinctively or especially to one person, group, or kind." For instance, we might say, even though it's not entirely true, that pineapples are peculiar to Hawaii, meaning that only Hawaii has them or grows them. Well, that is the meaning of the word "peculiar" in our text. Christ gave Himself for us that we might be God's peculiar people, that is, that we might belong exclusively to God, be His private property (and nobody else's). There is to be nothing common about us; we are intended to be unique, distinctive, extraordinary in the sight of God.

The specific thing that Christ did to make us God's exclusive, private, and unique property was to purchase the property, buy it back from the illegal ownership of Satan. As our text expresses it, He "redeemed us from all iniquity." You see, as we were, dilapidated and run-down with sin, we simply could not be the property of the pure and holy God. As we were we had no choice but to remain waste for all eternity—in hell. But Christ redeemed us from all iniquity. That means He bought us back, and bought us back in such a manner that we, in spite of our sins, appear to be an excellent piece of property in the sight of God because we've been credited with Christ's own righteousness. The price Christ paid? Blood! "The blood of Jesus Christ…cleanseth us from all sin," John tells us. The price Christ paid? Hell! Damnation! "My God, My God, why hast Thou forsaken Me?" Christ cried out on the cross.

But that isn't the end of the story. Christ not only buys the property; He also improves it. He clears it of litter and refuse. He repairs it and renovates it. He cultivates it and makes it bear fruit. As our text reminds us, He purifies "unto Himself a peculiar people, zealous of good works."

And here is where Christians, God's peculiar people, actually do become peculiar in the ordinary, conversational sense of the word. I don't mean to say that Christians are odd, queer, or eccentric, nor do I mean to recommend that they should be. But I do mean that they have a queer twist about them; something novel and refreshingly strange happens to them, something that some people might actually consider peculiar. If we were accustomed to nothing else than sand and desert, a sudden oasis might strike us as something odd; we might even think it was a mirage. If we had always lived in total darkness, a sudden burst of light might seem strange; we might even speak of light as something peculiar. If the natural man, as the Bible tells us, receives not the things of God but considers them foolishness, it is obvious that when he confronts someone who has received the things of God, he's going to consider him a fool. That person will seem peculiar to him. If all men are dead in trespasses and sins and a few of them come to spiritual life, those spiritual cadavers, accustomed as they are to death, are going to look askance at these living, moving creatures, for life is something abnormal to them. God's peculiar people are peculiar—in part, even in the ordinary sense of the word.

Let us be specific. Here is a person we know who contributes an unbelievable amount of money to church and to charity. "How does he do it?" we ask. "How can he afford it? Doesn't he have to live too?" You see, Christians are peculiar.

Here is another acquaintance of ours slandered, condemned, vilified. What does he do? He forgives. He turns the other cheek. He prays for those who despitefully use him. He loves his enemies. "Absurd!" we say.

"Why doesn't he stand up for his rights? If I were in his position, I surely wouldn't let people walk all over me like that." You see, Christians are peculiar.

Here is a church member living next to a family of another race, living on the best of terms with them, treating them as he would treat people of his own race, seemingly oblivious of anything out of the ordinary. "What's the matter?" we say. "Can't he see? Doesn't he know what kind of people they are, that if you give them an inch, they'll take a mile?" You see, Christians are peculiar.

Here is a woman putting up with a husband who scolds her, bosses her, drinks and gambles away his income, in short, does everything he can to make life miserable for her, and we begin wondering: "Why in the world doesn't she get a divorce? Certainly we can twist some Scripture passage somewhere to give her an out." You see, Christians are peculiar.

Here is a young lad with a strong right arm offered a fat contract and an opportunity for fame in the major leagues, and what does he do? He turns it down and instead goes off to a seminary to study for the ministry. You see, Christians are peculiar.

And we know of a time when they were most peculiar. They allowed themselves to be thrown to lions or burned at the stake rather than deny their Lord.

In summary, the peculiar events of Christianity have this purpose: to make us God's peculiar people. That means, to be sure, to make us God's exclusive, private, and unique property. But in a sense—in a sense!—it also means to make us people who are actually peculiar, pleasantly peculiar, peculiar as sugar would be in a bitter, brackish world; peculiar as light would be to a mole; peculiar as a living person would be on a battlefield covered with corpses. If society should ever become completely Christian-ized, such conduct will of course be the norm; it will lose its peculiar character. And in heaven for sure it will. There we shall recognize that what we did on earth, peculiar as it seemed at the time, was all along "the thing to do."

Study of a Word Suggested by the Text

Sometimes the central thought of a Biblical sermon text can be summed up with an expression outside that text. That extra-Biblical expression encapsulates the thrust of the text. It is that word or phrase, then, that functions as a refrain throughout the sermon. Although not as overtly textual as the preceding kind of word study format, this approach still results in a textual rather than topical sermon. Besides, this approach is uniquely designed to conform to the familiar homiletical saw that a sermon should hammer home one idea—and one idea only. The introduction should tell the listeners what the sermon is going to tell them, the body of the sermon then tells them, and the conclusion tells them what the sermon has told them. In summary, the word study format enjoys the advantage of "rifling" people with one point rather than "shotgunning" them with many points.

The sermon that follows, addressed to a college audience, uses a familiar Latin expression, "*carpe diem*," to capture and hammer home the central thought of the text.

> Matthew 11:12—"And from the days of John the Baptist until now the kingdom of heaven suffereth violence, and the violent take it by force."

At the risk of making it even more difficult than usual for you to make the necessary transition from the academic to the spiritual, I'm going to start out with a subject this morning that sounds more like classroom material than chapel material. That subject is the *carpe diem* poem. *Carpe diem* literally means "seize the day." To put it more elaborately, a *carpe diem* poem is the "eat, drink, and be merry" philosophy of life set to verse, a poetic version of the prosaic advice to "make the most of it" and to "get while the getting's good." For example, when Shakespeare wrote:

> What is love? 'Tis not hereafter.
> Present mirth hath present laughter;
> What's to come is still unsure.
> In delay there lies no plenty;
> Then come kiss me, sweet and twenty,
> Youth's a stuff will not endure.

that was a *carpe diem* poem.

But now let's get out of the classroom and into the chapel, where we belong. *Carpe diem* is descriptive not only of a kind of poem but also of a way of life. I need not go into detail. The *carpe diem* pattern of living may be obvious, as in the sentiments "You live only once" and "It's later than you think"; or it may be subtle, as in the advice "Make the most of your educational experience" and "Opportunity knocks but once." But whether they are obvious or subtle, all of us, I'm sure, can recognize a common denominator in these common sentiments: the conviction that life is short and the world passes away and we'd better lay hold on whatever is at hand and make the most of it while we can. *Carpe diem*! Seize the day!—the aggressive philosophy of the modern aggressive person, a kind of philosophy and a kind of person that conceivably could now and then even be on this campus, Satan being the master craftsman that he is.

For this *carpe diem* outlook on life our text suggests an antidote. And that is *carpe deum*—"seize God!" "And from the days of John the Baptist until now the kingdom of heaven suffereth violence, and the violent take it by force." In effect, our text urges us to redirect our aggressiveness, to rechannel our violence. Don't "devour widows' houses," but rather "take the kingdom of heaven by force." Don't "lay house unto house and field unto field," but rather "seek ye first the kingdom of God." Don't "lay up for yourselves treasures upon earth, where moth and rust doth corrupt, and where thieves break through and steal," but rather, "lay up for yourselves treasures in heaven." In short, don't *carpe diem* but rather *carpe deum;* don't seize the day but rather seize the deity, the Father of our Lord Jesus Christ.

"…the kingdom of heaven suffereth violence, and the violent take it by force." To ask a familiar catechetical question: What does this mean?

Well, suppose we define Scripture with Scripture. Think of Abraham insisting that God spare Sodom if only 50 righteous men could be found in the city and then trying God's patience all the way down to the number of 10. Think of Jacob wrestling until daybreak with the Angel of the Lord, refusing to release Him until he had extracted a blessing. Think of the men who literally tore up the roof in order to place a paralyzed man in front of Jesus. Think of blind Bartimaeus continuing to cry out, "Jesus, Thou Son of David, have mercy on me." even after the crowds ordered him to be quiet. Think of little Zacchaeus jostling his way through the throngs in order to gain a higher vantage point from which to see the Savior. Think of Mary monopolizing Jesus' time and presence when the Savior paid a visit to the home of Lazarus and his sisters. Think of the woman which was a sinner bursting into the home of Simon, the respectable Pharisee, in order to anoint Jesus' feet. Think of the woman of Canaan stubbornly crying after Jesus to heal her daughter even after the disciples suggested that Jesus dismiss her. Think of the woman who seized the hem of Jesus' garment. Think of the importunate widow who pestered the unjust judge until from nothing more noble than sheer annoyance at being bothered he gave her the justice she demanded. Think of the friend calling on another friend at midnight, asking him for bread even after the door to the house was locked and the occupants were in bed. Think of such passages as "Pray without ceasing," "Knock, and it shall be opened unto you," "Fight the good fight of faith," "Put on the whole armour of God," and "Work out your salvation with fear and trembling." Think of all this, and then think of our text," …the kingdom of heaven suffereth violence, and the violent take it by force." Suddenly it takes on meaning.

Really, the question posed by our text is this: Are we sufficiently aggressive in our dealings with God? Do we demand enough of this God who has placed Himself utterly at our disposal? Do we assault Him with prayer? Do we forsake all to follow Him? Do we sell everything that we have to buy the pearl of great price? Do we take the kingdom of heaven by force? You see, Jesus has made this bold relationship possible. His crucifixion and resurrection have made us the sons of God. Therefore, we can now approach God as dear children approach their dear father. "Perfect love casteth out fear." "Having, therefore, boldness, brethren, let us enter into the holiest by the blood of Jesus." *Carpe deum!* Seize God!

Grammar

Like the fairy tale format, the grammar format for preaching has always been a favorite of mine. There seem to be so many classifications in grammar conducive to communicating Christian truth. It was C. S. Lewis, I believe, who suggested in one of his books that God created us to be adjectives but that we decided to become nouns. What a striking yet economical way of describing God's purpose in creating us and at the same time of describing our fall into sin. Like an adjective we were intended by God to "modify" Him, that is to serve Him by describing His goodness and glory with our everyday behavior. But beginning with the fall of man into sin, we opted for nounhood; that is, we chose to be independent of God and attempted to stand by ourselves. I remember preaching a sermon on Isaiah 53:4-5, the title of which was "Christ, Our Blessed Pronoun." Even as a pronoun is a word that takes the place of a noun, so Christ, the Word, took the place of us nouns when on the cross He bore our sins and our punishment for sin. Here we see a grammatical classification facilitating our understanding of justification.

Grammatical classifications are useful also for our comprehension of sanctification. Human goodness, for example, is *dative*, not native. I mean "dative" in the old-fashioned Latin sense of the word. We don't inherit goodness. We don't earn it. We don't manufacture it. We don't stumble into it by accident. But God gives it—through Christ. *Deus dat.* Goodness is dative, not native; given, not attained. When it comes to goodness you and I are always in the dative case. God is the subject, the doer; goodness is the direct object, the thing given; we are the indirect object, the recipients. God does it all. How do we encourage one another in this God-given goodness? The best *imperative* is the *declarative.* That is, we foster goodness in one another, not by the imperatives of the Law, but by the simple declaration of the glorious facts of the Gospel.

Actually, there is Biblical precedent for this particular creative approach to communicating the Gospel. One of Christ's names is a grammatical classification, the "Word" (John 1:1-2, 14). Even as it is the function of a word to describe, explain, reveal, make clear, so the Second Person of the Trinity from eternity has had the function of describing, explaining, revealing, making clear the First Person of the Trinity. Given this awareness of Christ's function over against God His Father, the significance of His incarnation suddenly comes into sharper focus. As we have seen earlier, Christ, a spirit, an abstract Word, changes at Bethlehem into flesh, a concrete Word, so that He might even more clearly describe, explain, reveal His Father.

The brief homily that follows takes a grammar book concern, the proper use of an apostrophe, and exploits it for its Gospel potential.

1 Peter 3:18-19—"For Christ also hath once suffered for sins, the just for the unjust, that He might bring us to God, being put to death in

the flesh, but quickened by the Spirit: By which also He went and preached unto the spirits in prison."

Among their dubious diversions some homiletics teachers keep a list of humorous misspellings, malapropisms, and typographical errors contributed by students in their sermon work. But the humorous typographical error I want to bring to your attention today was one of my own. This time the joke was on me. In proofreading one of my own manuscripts, I discovered that I had omitted the apostrophe in the contraction for the words "he will," resulting in obscurity if not profanity. The word "hell" instead of "he'll" was there on my paper bold as you please. But if it is going too far in this case to be reminded of the Scriptural generalization that "all things work together for good to them that love God," it is at least true that this instance worked out for good. For my mistake suggested a profound Christian truth, namely, that Christ is the apostrophe that has invaded hell, split it apart in a sense, and totally altered its significance.

Our text speaks of a twofold descent of Christ into hell, the traditional literal one referred to by our Creed in the words "He descended into hell" and a prior descent into hell that can hardly be called metaphorical by way of distinction. I refer to what happened to Christ on the cross when He cried out, "My God, My God, why hast Thou forsaken Me?" That too was a descent into hell, so to speak, an immersion of the Son of God into the very alienation and desolation of the damned. This was the ultimate suffering for our sins in prospect for us, and Christ suffered it in our place so that He "might bring us to God." Listen to our text once again: "For Christ also hath once suffered for sins, the just for the unjust, that He might bring us to God, being put to death in the flesh, but quickened by the Spirit: By which also He went and preached unto the spirits in prison."

It is this double descent into hell that has interrupted its grip on our lives, split it apart, and changed it—at least for those who believe in Christ —into something much less than it was before. Even as the word "hell" disappears when invaded by an apostrophe (becoming "he'll"), so the threat of hell disappears for the Christian because of its twofold invasion by Christ: His suffering of hell on the cross and His triumphal entry into hell some time later. Christ is indeed a blessed apostrophe!

Logic

There are three different ways in which the preacher can use the discipline of logic to communicate Christian truth.

The first is simply to determine the logic that a given Biblical sermon text may contain. St. Paul particularly is a master at logic, and a careful study of his letters will often reward one with the discovery of some logical process that he employs. Take Galatians 2:20, for example. The King James translation especially highlights the logical process operative in that verse, a

151

process further highlighted by my insertion of slashes into the text: "I am crucified with Christ:/nevertheless I live;/yet not I, but Christ liveth in me:/and the life which I now live in the flesh I live by the faith of the Son of God, who loved me, and gave Himself for me." Be it reverently said, Paul can't seem to make up his mind in this passage. Every assertion he makes he immediately qualifies with another assertion—which he then qualifies with still another assertion. But there is a logical progression in these assertions. Each one builds on the one before it. Paul's thought snowballs as he confronts us with a series of exciting corrections about our relationship with Christ. The sequence of his thoughts is from good to better or from right to more right. "We are crucified with Christ" is his first assertion, a glorious truth indeed. But wait a minute! Correction! Even though it is true that we died with Christ, we're still alive. "Nevertheless I live" is his second assertion. But hold on! That claim may be misunderstood as ascribing too much to our self. All credit goes to Christ. His is the power and the glory. This leads to Paul's third assertion: "Yet not I, but Christ liveth in me." But how can such things be? How does this miracle of Christ dwelling in me and giving me His life occur? Faith is the answer. In the words of Paul's final assertion: "the life which I now live in the flesh I live by the faith of the Son of God."

A second way for the pastor to use logic in his preaching is to arrange Biblical texts in some logical sequence. An example cited earlier, in the subdivision dealing with multiple aspects of a given truth, will serve also as an instance of logical progression in the arrangement of texts. Note the progression from imperative to declarative, from Law to Gospel, from impossible to possible in the following sequence of passages:

1. "Be of the same mind one toward another" (Rom. 12:16).
2. "Let this mind be in you, which was also in Christ Jesus" (Phil. 2:5).
3. "We have the mind of Christ" (1 Cor. 2:16).

In the first passage Paul exhorts us to live in harmony with one another, as he says it, to "be of the same mind one toward another." One way to be of the same mind toward one another is to have the same mind, the mind of Christ, as Paul suggests in the second passage. If a Christian mother, for example, lets that mind be in her which was in Christ Jesus, and if her Christian son lets that mind be in him which was in Christ Jesus, it's going to be much easier for mother and son to be of the same mind toward each other. It is logical that things equal to the same thing (the mind of Christ in this instance) are going to be equal to each other. Then comes the ultimate surprise in the third passage: "We have the mind of Christ!" Our gracious God enables what He commands.

A third way for the preacher to tap the area of logic for creative purposes is simply to use something from the discipline of logic. W. E.

Sangster, for example, suggests the following syllogism as a three-part sermon outline:[10]

> Major premise: All men need a Savior.
> Minor premise: You are a man.
> Conclusion: Therefore, you need a Savior.

Or conceivably a sermon (at least the Law portion) could be built around some material fallacy. That is, a pastor in his homily could use one or the other of the designations logic texts apply to errors in human thinking (e.g., begging the question, hasty generalization) and apply it also to some related error in human behavior. Then in the Gospel portion of his homily the pastor could show how this sinful failing can be forgiven, even cured, by the *non sequitur,* the divine illogic, of God's grace, of Christ's dying for us while we were yet sinners.

The following excerpt from a sermon delivered to a college audience demonstrates the third way of using logic for preaching purposes. The sin it deals with is described in terms of the *post hoc ergo propter hoc* fallacy, a fallacy defined at the appropriate place in the excerpt.

> Romans 12:3—"For I say, through the grace given unto me, to every man that is among you, not to think of himself more highly than he ought to think; but to think soberly, according as God hath dealt to every man the measure of faith."

Among the better children's stories published in recent years is a masterpiece entitled *The Puppy Who Chased the Sun.* It's a story about a dog named Wilbur. At first he was quite a normal dog. He played with all the dogs in the neighborhood, and they were his friends.

But then it happened. One morning Wilbur woke up earlier than usual. He was hungry, so he barked. To his surprise the sun began to come up over the horizon. Scared, he barked again. Lo and behold, the sun came up some more. So Wilbur jumped to this conclusion: that his barking caused the sun to rise. Naturally, he felt very proud, so proud in fact that he no longer associated with his canine companions, Emma Jones and Fido and Toothy Perkins and No Tail Ryan. After all, he was the puppy who chased the sun up.

This coincidence, the sun rising when Wilbur barked, happened a few more times, confirming Wilbur in his mistaken opinion of himself. Then one morning Wilbur barked—and the sun didn't come up. He barked once, he barked twice, he barked three times. But still the sun didn't rise. All that happened was that Wilbur got wet because it began to rain. The next day the same thing happened. Wilbur felt very low.

The following morning Wilbur overslept. While he slept the rain stopped and the sun came up. By the time Wilbur woke up the sun was high in the sky. When Wilbur saw where the sun was, it suddenly dawned on him that he had not chased it up there. Thinking the whole thing over

153

carefully, Wilbur arrived at a revised conclusion: his barking did not cause the sun to rise; something else was responsible. Having finally returned to a proper estimate of himself, Wilbur goes back to his friends and of course lives happily ever after.

"Which things are a parable." "He that hath ears to hear let him hear." This is the interpretation thereof. To begin with, Wilbur committed what is called in logic the *post hoc ergo propter hoc* fallacy (literally translated, the "after this, therefore because of this" fallacy). You and I can easily commit this error in logic in our everyday thinking by mistaking a time sequence of events for a causal sequence. For example: Yesterday I walked under a ladder—today I had a car accident—therefore, walking under a ladder brings bad luck. That was the mistake Wilbur made. He barked one moment—the sun rose the next moment—therefore, he concluded, his barking caused the sun to rise.

Actually, Wilbur's trouble lay deeper than that. His thinking was not merely illogical—it was unethical. His real mistake was thinking of himself more highly than he ought to think. Undoubtedly, Wilbur had certain gifts. Perhaps he could speak for food, retrieve sticks, fetch the paper, jump through the hoop, and the like. For Wilbur to have modestly acknowledged these gifts would have been entirely in order. But Wilbur went too far: he assumed that he chased the sun up. Society today—and, I suppose, in all honesty we should include ourselves—society today is filled with Wilburs, people having certain gifts, perhaps, but claiming more. The way these people carry on, they act as if they chased the sun up—to put it in terms of our parable. Or to put it in terms of our text, they think of themselves more highly than they ought to think.

Every year a faculty screening committee meets to consider the spiritual fitness of our potential graduates for transfer to the seminary and eventually into the ministry. I suppose it is inevitable that those whose transfer is most seriously questioned are always those who get into the obvious trouble: wine, women, and crib sheets. To be sure, their fitness should be carefully weighed. But what is so often disturbing is the candidate who is guilty of nothing more than an arrogant attitude and a haughty disposition. Technically, his record is clean. His name is not in any of the proverbial files; he is respectable. It may be nothing more than his stony silence, his suave voice, his condescending chuckle, the precision of his enunciation, the casual lift of his eyebrow, or the slight shrug of his shoulder that betrays the putridness of pride within. But in one form or another he is a Wilbur; he conveys the impression that he chases the sun up. Everyone and everything are beneath him.

For the minister the sin of pride is an occupational hazard. People naturally look up to him. They accord him respect. They extend him professional courtesies. Frankly, it is so terribly easy to be successful in the ministry. Given the right location, a half-way decent personality, some degree of administrative ability, a knack for coaxing money out of people—and, lo and behold, you have it made; you are a man who gets things done. It is hard for even the humble not to be proud in the ministry, and if already in your period of preparation for the ministry you are plagued with the problem of pride, the damnable outcome is just that much more likely.

After all, that is why we're discussing the sin of pride this morning: because of its damnable outcome. Pride doesn't merely make a person a nuisance; pride can literally damn him. In fact, of all sins it is perhaps the most damning because it is the most difficult to detect. Pride by definition is the sin of not seeing sin. And how can one believe if he doesn't repent?

Now I hope that this sermon today does not cause those who are guilty of wrong in the wine, women, and crib sheet area to shout a "Hurrah!" over the fact that the so-called "nice" people have finally got their comeuppance and, further, does not cause them to begin a new orgy of living it up with the assurance that someone finally understands. What we have been discussing today has been C. S. Lewis' familiar classification of sin into sins of the flesh and sins of the disposition. While it is true that he calls the sins of the disposition the worse of the two because they are the harder to detect and therefore the more likely to damn, he points out also that it is better to be guilty of neither kind of sin. Furthermore, it would be a tragic misapplication of today's message to play that familiar guessing game: Whom did the speaker have in mind? All of us, I'm sure, have our moments of thinking that we chase the sun up. In varying degrees, to be sure, but to a degree, nonetheless, all of us need the cure.

And that, of course, is the important thing: the cure. If we diagnose a problem we do so in order to arrive at a cure. The cure for thinking of ourselves more highly than we ought to think lies in Him who, though He "thought it not robbery to be equal with God," nevertheless "made Himself of no reputation, and took upon Him the form of a servant, and was made in the likeness of men…and humbled Himself, and became obedient unto death, even the death of the cross." Because Christ did this we can, among many other blessings, share His humility. Faith in Christ is the key to this treasure. In faith we see ourselves as we really are, every bit as bad and as worthless as we are by nature but every bit as good and as valuable as we are through Christ. As our text points out, we "think soberly, according as God hath dealt to every man the measure of faith."…

Mathematics

In this creative format some mathematical element (from arithmetic, algebra, geometry, trigonometry, calculus, etc.) plays a prominent role in the development of a Biblical sermon text. One of my students wrote a two-part sermon on "Addition and Subtraction": the first part discussing on the basis of 2 Peter 1:5-7 the virtues the Christian should add to his everyday behavior; the second part discussing on the basis of Ephesians 4:22 the vices the Christian should subtract from his everyday behavior.[11] Another student sermon dealt with a paradoxical equation formulated from his analysis of Ephesians 2:8-10: "Faith minus works equals faith plus works." The first part of his equation captured the point Paul makes in verses 8 and 9 of the text: that saving faith is entirely the gift of God, to the exclusion of all human works. We go to heaven, not because of what we do, but because of what God has done through Jesus Christ. But once a person has been gifted with this faith that God does it all through Jesus Christ, the result will be a faith that does good works, God-manufactured good works—an assertion capturing the point Paul makes in verse 10 of the text. In other words, "Faith minus works equals faith plus works."[12] In my parish experience I once preached a wedding sermon on the familiar theorem "Things equal to the same thing are equal to each other." The point was that if the bridegroom was at one with God through Jesus and if the bride also was at one with God through Jesus, then both husband and wife would also be at one with each other. In a sermon preached to a college audience, I explored the idea, stated mathematically, that the spiritual denominator of a group is always lower than the spiritual denominator of any of the individuals composing that group. In other words, collective evil is normally worse than individual evil; the whole is greater than the sum of its parts.

The sermon below, also addressed to a college community, is concerned throughout with the significance of the number "seven" mentioned in the Biblical sermon text.

> Luke 11:24-26—"When the unclean spirit is gone out of a man, he walketh through dry places, seeking rest; and finding none, he saith, I will return unto my house when I came out. And when he cometh, he findeth it swept and garnished. Then goeth he, and taketh to him seven other spirits more wicked than himself; and they enter in, and dwell there: and the last state of that man is worse than the first."

The use of the number "seven" in this parable has always intrigued me. First, there is the irony that this number, customarily a holy number in Scriptural usage, should be employed to describe so unholy a situation as that detailed in our text. It would seem to buttress one theologian's view that evil is not, like goodness, a separate entity, a phenomenon existing in its own right, but rather that evil is goodness distorted, goodness twisted, goodness bent. Evil is merely holiness perverted.

Secondly, there is the size of the number. I used to regard it as hyperbole, as a legitimate exaggeration, to impress upon us the dire straits in which the man of our parable ultimately finds himself. After nearly a half century of struggle with sin, I no longer view the number as hyperbolic. If anything, it is conservative. In my youth I used to search out my pet sin. I tried to anticipate my tragic flaw. Maybe that's all I had then, a pet sin, a flaw. More likely, though, that's all I *saw* then. There was probably more if I had only had the vision. But having eyes, I saw not. However that may be, I know now that one does not have a pet sin—he has pet sins, plural. It is not a tragic flaw that threatens to destroy him—it is tragic flaws. While working tooth and nail to rid oneself of lust, one suddenly finds himself attacked on another flank by poor sportsmanship. Trying to overcome grumpiness, one suddenly finds himself assailed by a fondness for gossip. Then cynicism, materialism, and sloth invade with their legions. It seems that while plugging one leak in the dam, one is forever finding numerous other places where the water is gushing through. In a sense not exactly intended by medieval theologians, each of us may well have seven deadly sins, differing somewhat from, no doubt, but also overlapping somewhat with the seven deadly sins of the next person.

Thirdly, even the progress from one unclean spirit to the seven additional unclean spirits mentioned in our text may be more accurate than we realize. Maybe it isn't a failure of vision to begin with; perhaps we do deteriorate from pet sin to pet sins, from flaw to flaws, from one unclean spirit to seven additional spirits more wicked than the first. It is St. James who reminds us that lust conceives and brings forth sin. Sin proliferates, multiplies. It raises a family. One bad thing leads to another. In Shakespeare's *Othello* Emilia reacts to her husband's slander of Desdemona by crying out, "If he say so, may his pernicious soul/Rot half a grain a day!" Perhaps something like this actually happens to our soul: it rots half a grain a day, the situation getting progressively worse and worse until ultimately there is nothing but putrid rottenness in our soul and our last state is indeed worse than the first.

But the dismal picture I've painted so far today is predicated on the existence of a vacuum, an empty house "swept and garnished," to use the metaphor of our text. It is when the unclean spirit finds this state of affairs that he moves in with "seven other spirits more wicked than himself." Sin, like nature, abhors a vacuum and seeks to fill it. The logic of our text suggests, then, as a preventive that the vacuum be filled before sin and Satan get there, leaving them no place to settle down. If anything is clear from the Bible it is this: that God the Holy Spirit is willing and able to fill that vacuum called you or me. Our bodies can be quite literally the temples of God. He seeks to invade us and to fill every nook and cranny of our being. He promises to do this if we abide in His Word, regularly expose ourselves to the stupendous news of life in our crucified and risen Lord, and enthusiastically latch on to that good news. The result will be a blessed state of affairs. Consult the beatitudes, for example. And our last state of affairs? That will be even more blessed. The last state of such a man will be better than the first. Heaven is almost too trite a word for the blessed reality it describes.

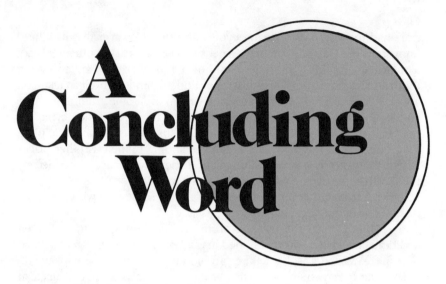

A Concluding Word

As the title of this book implies, the Gospel is itself creative. It creates saving faith in people. It creates goodness in people. The Gospel is *God's* power for salvation and sanctification. It is God's power because it literally contains God—Christ Himself, the Word. His is the power and the glory.

In His unsearchable wisdom and fathomless love the Word has chosen to transmit Himself through words, through human language. Maybe God could have chosen some other vehicle. We don't know. It is not our business to speculate over what God could have done or might have done. It is rather our task to recognize what God did. And what He in fact did is to tie together inextricably Word and words, Christ and language. In the introductory chapter I delineated the potential language has to do what God intends it and empowers it to do: its magic, its music, its rhythm, its beauty, its precision, its dynamite. We need not review that argument here. But what we need to do is encourage ourselves constantly to improve our skill in language and to tap its potential for our preaching. As the title of this book suggests, the creative Gospel deserves to be preached creatively—not with the false assumption that by our creativity we can help God do His job, but with the prayerful hope that through our creativity the Word of God, "as becometh it, may not be bound, but have free course and be preached to the joy and edifying of Christ's holy people."

Creativity in preaching need not be incompatible with responsibility in preaching. Loyalty to the Word is not necessarily compromised by skill in words. Sound doctrine does not have to sound unattractive to remain sound. On the contrary, responsible preaching can be fun, fun for the preacher and fun for the audience. The preceding chapters have provided some suggestions to guide you in your creative efforts to tap and unleash the joys of preaching. I hope these suggestions will jog your imagination and encourage you to be ever on the lookout for exciting ways to communicate to God's people that most exciting story ever told, the story of God's love for us in Jesus.

Endnotes

Introduction

1. S.I. Hayakawa, *Language in Thought and Action* (New York: Harcourt, 1972), p. 16.
2. R.E.O. White, *A Guide to Preaching: A Practical Primer of Homiletics* (Grand Rapids: Eerdmans, 1973), p. 77.
3. Dr. Martin Luther as quoted by Donald Deffner, *The Real Word for the Real World: Applying the Word to the Needs of People* (St. Louis: Concordia, 1977), p. 18.
4. See my article, "Echoes of the Gospel-event in Literature and Elsewhere," *Concordia Journal*, IX, 2 (March 1983), 50-58.
5. William J. Carl III, "As I See It Today," (Richmond, Virginia: Union Theological Seminary), VII, 9 (May 1977), 1.
6. White, p. 78.
7. Examples of homiletics texts that discuss this issue at length are: Fred B. Craddock, *As One without Authority* (Nashville: Abingdon, 1979); Fred B. Craddock, *Overhearing the Gospel* (Nashville, Abingdon, 1978); and Richard A. Jensen, *Telling the Story: Variety and Imagination in Preaching* (Minneapolis: Augsburg, 1980).
8. My representation of linguistic analysis and the semantic movement in the Introduction deals with only one area of their concern. Used technically, both of these terms refer to a wider and more legitimate sphere of concern.
9. Richard R. Caemmerer, *Preaching for the Church* (St. Louis: Concordia, 1959), p. 271.
10. William Shakespeare, *Twelfth Night or What You Will,* The Folger Library General Reader's Shakespeare, ed. Louis B. Wright and Virginia A. Lamar (New York: Pocket Books, 1960), III, i, 11-13.
11. Gustave Flaubert, *Madame Bovary,* trans. Merloyd Lawrence (Boston: Houghton Mifflin, 1969), p. 161.
12. Jonathan Swift, *Gulliver's Travels* (New York: New American Library, 1960), pp. 203-04.
13. Caemmerer, pp. 41-42.

Chapter One

1. I am not suggesting here that we can understand, admire, and believe in Christ's vicarious suffering and death apart from the work of the Holy Spirit through the Gospel. To be sure, in this aspect of the literal Gospel also "we cannot by our own reason or strength believe in Jesus Christ, our Lord, or come to Him, but the Holy Ghost must call us by the Gospel." I am suggesting, though, that from a purely human perspective there seem to be fewer impediments to the Holy Spirit's work on human hearts in the proclamation of a noble, innocent, and heroic death in behalf of others than, for example, in the proclamation of a more "difficult" miracle (like a virgin birth or a resurrection).
2. C.S. Lewis, *Mere Christianity* (New York: Macmillan, 1952), pp. 57-58.

3. Martin Scharlemann, "Lent Is for Life: Reflections on the Seven Words," *Concordia Journal,* III, 2 (March 1977), 55.
4. Note the simplicity of the language in which these two passages describe the profoundest of all Biblical truths. Nearly all the words in these two verses are monosyllables. Nowhere in my experience is there a better example of the magic of the Word in the magic of words. Here, if anywhere, is Scriptural precedent for creative preaching.
5. Richard Klann, "Righteousness and Holiness: A Study of Articles III-VI of the Formula of Concord," *Concordia Journal,* V, 2 (March 1979), 51.
6. Dr. Martin Luther as quoted by Robert Preus, "Perennial Problems in the Doctrine of Justification," *Concordia Theological Quarterly,* XLV, 3 (July 1981), 167.
7. Francis Pieper, *Christian Dogmatics,* II (St. Louis: Concordia, 1951), p. 311.
8. For a fuller treatment of this matter see my article, "Christ Has Abolished Death," *Concordia Journal,* VI, 2 (March 1980), 48-53.
9. Additional homiletical treatments of Christ's damnation will appear in a number of other sermons included in Chapter Four.

Chapter Two

1. C.S. Lewis, *Miracles: A Preliminary Study* (New York: Macmillan, 1947), p. 94.
2. Ibid., p. 88.
3. For additional significance of the water in Baptism see my article, "The Significance of the Visible Elements in the Sacraments," *Concordia Journal,* VIII, 4 (July 1982), 127-29.
4. Keeping the carefully chosen language of Luke 11:21-22 in mind will prevent the reader from slipping into the heresy of dualism in his consideration of the "classic" view of the atonement. Even though Satan and Jesus are indeed "two mighty opposites," Luke prevents the mistake of regarding the two as equals in power by calling Satan "a strong man" but Jesus "a stronger than he."
5. Jesus as "light" or "the light of the world," a Gospel-metaphor that plays a prominent role in the "classic" representation of the atonement, is so frequent that it deserves separate and individual treatment. For the sake of brevity, however, I have included this metaphor in my consideration of the "classic" approach.
6. The best homiletical use of the second Adam image I have ever encountered occurs in a non-homiletical book, C.S. Lewis' *Mere Christianity* (New York: Macmillan, 1952). For sheer delight and profound edification read the chapter entitled "The Obstinate Toy Soldiers," pp. 154-57. Although Lewis never uses the term "Second Adam," it is that concept that permeates the entire presentation.
7. This familiar citation from Shakespeare's *Romeo and Juliet* reminds me to point out, in passing, that the play is worth your reading not just for its portrayal of youthful love but also for its analysis of the full import of the word "name." The power in a name is a central concern of the play. Why should the mere family names Capulet and Montague keep two young people apart who love each other very much? Says Juliet: "That which we call a rose / By any other name would smell as sweet" (II, ii, 45-46). Later Romeo, drawing his dagger, asks Friar Laurence,
   O tell me, friar, tell me,
   In what vile part of this anatomy
   Doth my name lodge? Tell me, that I may sack
   The hateful mansion. (III, iii, 114-17)
8. This last example calls to mind another large field productive for Gospel preaching, Old Testament typology. The flood and its rainbow, the passover event in Egypt, the crossing of the Red Sea, the brazen serpent are familiar examples of Old Testament events rich in Gospel potential. The New Testament itself makes homiletical use of these historical incidents by pointing to spiritual counterparts to these literal events. In doing this the New Testament establishes Biblical precedent for us in our preaching practice. To be sure, there is a homiletical sin called "allegorizing" or "spiritualizing." But there is also the homiletical sin of unimaginativeness. So long as in our efforts to exploit Old Testament events for their Gospel potential, we do not eliminate the events themselves; so long as in our attempts to find symbolic significance in literal Old Testament happenings, we do not reduce those happenings to mere symbols; and so long as we do not allow meaning to nullify historicity, there is nothing irresponsible or "allegorical" about

161

our practice. Rather, we are conforming to our Lord's own hermeneutical directive in John 5:39: "Search the scriptures...they are they which testify of Me" (often in surprising ways!).

9. For more extensive illustrations of the homiletical potential of Gospel-metaphors, see the materials already alluded to in note six and in the sermon exemplifying the word study approach in Chapter Four, pp. 144-47. The former deals with the second Adam image, the latter with the redemption metaphor.

Chapter Three

1. Haddon W. Robinson, *Biblical Preaching: The Development and Delivery of Expository Messages* (Grand Rapids: Baker, 1980), p. 152.
2. Richard Lischer, *A Theology of Preaching: The Dynamics of the Gospel* (Nashville: Abingdon, 1981), pp. 18-19.
3. Ibid., p. 20.
4. I am indebted to Dennis Schiefelbein, one of my students, for the idea presented as well as for some of its development.
5. I am indebted to Joseph Bragg, one of my students, for the idea presented as well as for some of its development.
6. One of my students found still another approach to the Gospel in John 14:1-6. In a multiple text sermon he contrasted the warm welcome Jesus accords us when we arrive in heaven (described in John 14:2) with the cold and cruel reception we accorded Jesus when He came to earth to save us. There was no room for Him in the inn; He was born among animals. "He was in the world, and the world was made by Him, and the world knew Him not" (John 1:10). "He came unto His own, and His own received Him not" (John 1:11).
7. Still another approach to the Gospel in the Genesis 18:23-32 narrative is to contrast Genesis 18:23 with Luke 23:41. The answer expected to Abraham's question of God in verse 23, "Wilt Thou also destroy the righteous with the wicked?" is "Of course not! It's unthinkable! The righteous and holy God wouldn't do that." And yet on Calvary the unthinkable happened. There God did, in a sense, destroy the righteous with the wicked: the sinless Jesus was crucified with two criminals. As one of the thugs conceded, "We receive the due reward of our deeds: but this man [Jesus] hath done nothing amiss." This, of course, was not a capricious or whimsical action on the part of God. God "destroyed" His righteous Son on the cross because at the time, pure and righteous as He was by nature and by accomplishment, Jesus was in truth in that hour "made our sin." The Righteous One was made our wickedness.
8. I am indebted to Herbert Mueller, one of my students, for the idea presented as well as for some of its development.
9. I am not sure that this Gospel-handle is my own; if it isn't, I have ungratefully forgotten its source. At any rate, I assume responsibility for much of its development.
10. I am indebted to Randy Walquist, one of my students, for the idea presented as well as for some of its development.
11. I am indebted to a student for the idea presented. The development of the idea is a reconstruction of what I remember.
12. The idea presented, as well as much of its development, is a composite of materials contributed by a number of students.
13. These passages, it should be noted, discuss a literal fig tree. They are not alternate versions of the parable under consideration.
14. Clyde Kilby, quoted by Leland Ryken in "The Bible as Literature," in *The Christian Imagination: Essays on Literature and the Arts,* ed. Leland Ryken (Grand Rapids: Baker, 1981), p. 173.
15. Frank E. Gaebelein, "The Christian and Music," *The Christian Imagination,* p. 180.
16. Leland Ryken, "The Bible as Literature," *The Christian Imagination,* p. 445.
17. Sophocles, *Oedipus, King of Thebes* in *The Play's the Thing: An Anthology of Dramatic Types,* ed. Fred B. Millett and Gerald Eades Bentley (New York: D. Appleton-Century, 1936), p.8.
18. William Shakespeare, *Twelfth Night or What You Will,* The Folger Library General Reader's

Shakespeare, ed. Louis B. Wright and Virginia A. Lamar (New York: Pocket Books, 1960), I, iv, 31-36.

19. William Shakespeare, *Twelfth Night*, I, iv, 40-42.

20. Oscar Wilde, *The Picture of Dorian Gray* (New York: Penguin Books, 1980), p. 34.

21. In these Biblical instances there exists the distinct possibility that the dramatic irony is in the eye of the beholder rather than in the specific passages beheld. But if it is difficult in these examples to prove the presence of dramatic irony, it is equally difficult to disprove its presence.

22. *The Lutheran Hymnal* (St. Louis: Concordia, 1941), p. 14.

23. Without in any way meaning to negate the Biblical principle that what a man sows he reaps, let me, first of all, point out that just because the Jews of Christ's day wished a curse upon themselves (in the passage under consideration), it need not follow that God gave them their wish, that He took them at their word. Second, even assuming that He did—and I don't assume it—but for the sake of argument assuming that He did, it does not follow that we Christians are to participate in imposing the curse or to stand idly by while it's being imposed. Any discussion of Jewish history must always keep one thing crystal clear: God's Christ died and rose for them too, and His forgiveness is intended for them also. God is as dead serious about the eternal salvation and earthly welfare of any citizen of a Jewish nation or a Jewish community as He is about the eternal salvation and earthly welfare of you or me. No interpretation of Jewish history dare obliterate God's universal grace in Christ.

24. The only way this passage could qualify as dramatic irony is if our Lord imposed upon Himself, as a human being, the same momentary non-use of knowledge, or "emptying" of omniscience, that obtains in the well-known instance concerning the time of Judgment Day recorded in Mark 13:32. "But of that day and that hour knoweth no man, no, not the angels which are in heaven, *neither the Son,* but the Father" (emphasis added).

Chapter Four

1. George Heider is the author of this sermon.

2. Rolph Mayer is the author of this sermon.

3. For a fuller examination of this belief see my article, "Echoes of the Gospel-event in Literature and Elsewhere," *Concordia Journal*, IX, 2 (March 1983), 50-58.

4. Rolph Mayer is the author of this sermon. Ellipses indicate omissions.

5. One of the best, in my opinion, is *Voices of the Passion* by O.P. Kretzmann and A.C. Oldsen (New York: Ernst Kaufmann, 1944). A more recent publication is *They Were There: Two Series of Lenten Monologs,* by Roy Barlag and Richard Andersen (St. Louis: Concordia, 1977).

6. Rolph Mayer is the author of this sermon.

7. Christopher Dodge is the author of this sermon.

8. To achieve verisimilitude I would suggest—only in the instance of a letter format sermon —that the sermon be read rather than memorized.

9. William Yates is the author of this sermon. Ellipses indicate omissions.

10. W.E. Sangster, *The Craft of Sermon Construction* (Grand Rapids: Baker, 1951), p. 82.

11. Mark Smith is the author of the sermon referred to.

12. Leroy Pralle is the author of the sermon referred to.

Suggestions for Further Reading

Achtemeier, Elizabeth. *Creative Preaching: Finding the Words.* Nashville: Abingdon, 1980.

Adams, Jay E. *Communicating with Twentieth Century Man.* Phillipsburg, New Jersey: Presbyterian and Reformed, 1979.

Buechner, Frederick. *Peculiar Treasures: A Biblical Who's Who.* New York: Harper & Row, 1979.

. *Telling the Truth: The Gospel as Tragedy, Comedy & Fairy Tale.* New York: Harper & Row, 1977.

. *Wishful Thinking: A Theological ABC.* New York: Harper & Row, 1973.

Craddock, Fred B. *As One without Authority.* Nashville: Abingdon, 1979.

. *Overhearing the Gospel.* Nashville: Abingdon, 1978.

Daane, James. *Preaching with Confidence: A Theological Essay on the Power of the Pulpit.* Grand Rapids: Eerdmans, 1980.

Deffner, Don. *The Real Word for the Real World: Applying the Word to the Needs of People.* The Preacher's Workshop Series, ed. Richard Kapfer, Book 3. St. Louis: Concordia, 1977.

Fant, Clyde E. *Preaching for Today.* New York: Harper & Row, 1975.

Forsyth, P.T. *Positive Preaching and the Modern Mind.* Grand Rapids: Baker, 1980.

Halvorson, Arndt L. *Authentic Preaching.* Minneapolis: Augsburg, 1982.

Harms, Paul. *Power from the Pulpit: Delivering the Good News.* The Preacher's Workshop Series, ed. Richard Kapfer, Book 7. St. Louis: Concordia, 1977.

Jensen, Richard A. *Telling the Story: Variety and Imagination in Preaching.* Minneapolis: Augsburg, 1980.

Knoche, H. Gerard. *The Creative Task: Writing the Sermon.* The Preacher's Workshop Series, ed. Richard Kapfer, Book 5. St. Louis: Concordia, 1977.

Lewis, C.S. *The Chronicles of Narnia.* 7 vols. New York: Macmillan, 1965.

. *The Great Divorce.* New York: Macmillan, 1946.

. *Mere Christianity.* New York: Macmillan, 1952.

. *Out of the Silent Planet.* New York: Macmillan, 1947.

. *Perelandra.* New York: Macmillan, 1944.

. *The Screwtape Letters.* New York: Macmillan, 1946.

Lischer, Richard. *A Theology of Preaching: The Dynamics of the Gospel.* Nashville: Abingdon, 1981.

Rogahn, Kenneth W. and Walter M. Schoedel. *Parables from the Cross: Sermons for Lent and Easter with Matching Orders of Service.* St. Louis: Concordia, 1982.

Ryken, Leland, ed. *The Christian Imagination: Essays on Literature and the Arts.* Grand Rapids: Baker, 1981.

Stott, John R. W. *Between Two Worlds: The Art of Preaching in the Twentieth Century.* Grand Rapids: Eerdmans, 1982.

Swanson, Stephen O. *The Double Cross: Messages on the Seven Deadly Sins and the Seven Deadly Virtues.* Minneapolis: Augsburg, 1980.

Wedel, Alton. *The Mighty Word: Power and Purpose of Preaching.* The Preacher's Workshop Series, ed. Richard Kapfer, Book 1. St. Louis: Concordia, 1977.

Weisheit, Eldon. *A Sermon Is More than Words.* The Preacher's Workshop Series, ed. Richard Kapfer, Book 8. St. Louis: Concordia, 1977.

Index

SUBJECTS INDICES

SCRIPTURE PASSAGES

NAMES AND AUTHORS